This book would not have been possible without your collaboration. I us... ...c take this occasion to thank you again for your precious contribution. I also hope that there will be other occasions to collaborate.

With kind regards,

Eva Lein

Eva Lein

London, 11 June 2012

Dear Pippa,

The "Brussels I Review Proposal Uncovered" was published at the beginning of June.
Please find enclosed your author's copy.

British Institute of
International and
Comparative Law

Charles Clore House, 17 Russell Square
London WC1B 5JP, United Kingdom
Tel: 020 7862 5151 Fax: 020 7862 5152
email: info@biicl.org www.biicl.org

THE BRUSSELS I REVIEW PROPOSAL UNCOVERED

THE BRUSSELS I
REVIEW PROPOSAL
UNCOVERED

Edited by

Eva Lein

**British Institute of
International and
Comparative Law**

Published and Distributed by
The British Institute of International and Comparative Law
Charles Clore House, 17 Russell Square, London WC1B 5JP

© BIICL 2012

British Library Cataloguing in Publication Data
A Catalogue record of this book is available from the British Library

ISBN 978–1–905221–48–6

Typeset by Cambrian Typesetters
Camberley, Surrey
Printed in Great Britain by MPG Books Group Ltd

Contents

Contributors

Eva Lein is Herbert Smith Senior Research Fellow in Private International Law at the British Institute of International and Comparative Law in London. She previously held the position of Head of the Continental Law Section and Staff Legal Advisor at the Swiss Institute of Comparative Law in Lausanne, Switzerland. She is a qualified German lawyer and her fields of expertise are comparative, European and private international law. Her Dr Jur focused on European, international and comparative contract law, but she has also extensively published on European private international law. She has lectured comparative law, conflict of laws and international litigation in England, Italy, Spain and Switzerland. She is also an advisory board member of the *Yearbook of Private International Law*.

Pamela Kiesselbach is a Senior Professional Support Lawyer with Herbert Smith LLP, London, and a Senior Lecturer at the College of Law. Pamela is a dually qualified German lawyer and English solicitor specialising in dispute resolution and private international law. When practising she acted for clients from a wide range of industry sectors including energy, aviation and telecommunications, mostly in relation to cross-border disputes. More recently she has been involved in providing responses to the European Commission's Green Paper on the Review of the Brussels Regulation and the related Brussels I survey and has given presentations and published various contributions in relation to the Rome I, Rome II and Brussels I Regulations. She monitors and edits the firm's model forms and notes and advises across the firm in London and internationally in relation to choice of law and jurisdiction issues.

Jonathan Harris is a Professor of International Commercial Law at King's College London, Visiting Professorial Fellow at the University of New South Wales, Australia, and a barrister at Serle Court Chambers in London. He was previously Professor of International Commercial Law and Deputy Head of School at the University of Birmingham, and Reader in Law at the University of Nottingham. He holds an MA and BCL from Oxford University, and a PhD from the University of Birmingham. Professor Harris has written and edited numerous publications, including *Dicey, Morris and Collins: The Conflict of Laws* and *Benjamin's Sale of Goods*, and is a co-editor and co-founder of *The Journal of Private International Law*.

Alegría Borrás is Professor of Private International Law at the University of Barcelona. She has been Spain's representative at The Hague Conference on

Private International Law since 1987, and was the Spanish representative for Cooperation on Justice (Civil Matters) in the EU from 1993 – 2007. In 1994 and 2005 she was a Professor at the Academy of International Law in The Hague, and has also held positions at the University of Cordoba and the Autonomous University of Barcelona. Professor Borrás has written and published over 200 articles on private international and European community law, and has been Director of the *Revista Española de Derecho internacional* since 2009. She holds a Doctorate in Law from the University of Barcelona, and has been awarded the Spanish honours of the *Orden de San Raimundo de Peñafort* and *Encomienda de la Orden de Isabel La Católica*.

Alexander Layton QC is a barrister at 20 Essex Street Chambers in London, practicing in Commercial Law, Arbitration, and Private and Public International Law. He was called to the Bar in 1976, took silk in 1995, and is now a Recorder, sitting in both civil and criminal cases, a Deputy High Court Judge, and a Bencher of the Middle Temple. Alexander Layton studied at Oxford University, Ludwig-Maximilian University Munich, and the *Faculté Internationale pour l'Enseignement de Droit Comparé* in Strasbourg and Pescara. He is general editor of European Civil Practice, the leading practitioners' textbook on conflicts of law and jurisdiction in Europe, is recognised as an expert on the Brussels-Lugano jurisdictional regime, and frequently lectures on topics of commercial and private international law in the UK and abroad. He is a fellow of the Chartered Institute of Arbitrators, a member of the Commercial Bar Association, and former Chairman of the Board of Trustees of BIICL.

Ulrich Magnus is Professor emeritus of Civil Law, Private International Law and Comparative Law at the University of Hamburg and a former judge of the Civil Court of Appeal of Hamburg. He received his Dr Jur from the University of Heidelberg. Professor Magnus is a Director of the European Centre of Tort and Insurance Law and a Director of the International Max Planck Research School for Maritime Affairs. He was previously a Research Fellow at the Max-Planck-Institute for Foreign and International Private Law in Hamburg, and has acted as an advisor to the German Government and the European Commission. He has published extensively on European, comparative and international law of obligations and private international law and is co-editor of Magnus/Mankowski, *European Commentaries on Private International Law: Brussels I Regulation*.

Pippa Rogerson is a Senior Lecturer in the Faculty of Law, Cambridge University, and a Fellow and Director of Studies of Gonville and Caius College. She holds an MA and PhD from Cambridge, and prior to commencing her PhD she qualified as a solicitor with Clifford Chance LLP.

Dr Rogerson has published extensively on the subject of conflict of laws, and is an author of Magnus/Mankowski, *European Commentaries on Private International Law: Brussels I Regulation.* She has a particular academic interest in relation to intangible property and issues concerning corporations, and also teaches company law.

Michael Bogdan is Professor of Comparative and Private International Law at the University of Lund. He holds a BA, LLM and *juris doctor* from Lund, as well as JUDr from the University of Prague. Professor Bogdan is a member and former president of the Groupe Européen de Droit International Privé, member of the International Academy of Comparative Law and associated member of the Institut de Droit International. In 2010 he was invited to give the General Course on Private International Law at The Hague Academy of International Law. Professor Bogdan is the author of 12 books and more than 400 articles and reviews on various legal subjects.

Andrew Dickinson is Professor in Private International Law at the University of Sydney, a Visiting Fellow at BIICL, and a consultant at Clifford Chance LLP. He obtained an MA and BCL from the University of Oxford. Professor Dickinson is a specialist editor of *Dicey, Morris and Collins: The Conflict of Laws*, and the author of *The Rome II Regulation: The Law Applicable to Non-Contractual Obligations.* He is a member of the UK Ministry of Justice's Advisory Committee on Private International Law, of the editorial board of the Journal of Private International Law, and of the Hague Conference's expert working group on the law applicable to contractual obligations.

Andreas Furrer is Professor of Private, Comparative, Private International and European Law at the University of Lucerne, Switzerland, and a partner at Meyer Müller Eckert in Zurich. He is also Head of the Research Centre for International and European Private Law, Director of the Centre for Conflict Resolution, and Vice-Chancellor of the Research Committee at the University of Lucerne, as well as the Managing Director the Swiss Arbitration Academy. Professor Furrer studied at the Universities of Freiburg, Saarbrücken, St Gallen, Bremen and the European University Institute in Florence, gaining full professorial status in 2001.

Luboš Tichý is Professor of European, Private International and Comparative Law at Charles University Prague, where he is also Director of the Centre for Comparative Law. He studied in Prague, Heidelberg, and at the Max Planck Institute for Comparative and International Private Law in Hamburg, the Swiss Institute of Comparative Law in Lausanne and The Hague Academy of International Law. Professor Tichý is a board member of the Academic Society for Competition Law, a member of the European Centre of Tort and Insurance Law, and a member of the advisory board of three European journals including the European Review of Private Law. Professor Tichý has been a practicing lawyer in Prague since 1976, and was formerly a partner at Squire Sanders LLP and President of the Czech Bar Association. He has been a Legal Advisor to the Czech Federal Minister of Foreign Affairs and to the President of the Czech National Council.

Marta Pertegás is First Secretary at the Hague Conference of Private International Law and Professor of Private International Law at the University of Antwerp. She is a qualified advocate at the Barcelona Bar, and was an associate at Nauta Dutilh in Brussels practicing in the fields of international litigation and intellectual property. She was previously a lecturer at the Catholic University of Leuven, where she was also an Assistant at the Institute of International Trade Law. Professor Pertegás has published extensively on the subjects of conflict of laws and international litigation and regularly lectures throughout Europe on European and private international law.

Foreword

This book, originating in an all-day conference hosted by the British Institute of International and Comparative Law, appears at a useful moment. The process of revising the Brussels I Regulation 44/2001 on jurisdiction and the recognition and enforcement of judgments in civil and commercial matters is under way, and bound to continue well into 2012.

The United Kingdom took the decision to opt into that process in Spring 2011. The process can be viewed at two levels. The first, technical, concerns all who look for just, pragmatic and workable solutions to the procedural problems and tactical manoeuvring that can beset international disputes. The second, constitutional, arises from the interplay between decisions of the Court of Justice of the European Union, concerns about their effect, the Commission's willingness to respond to such concerns, the Parliament's reaction to the Commission's consequent proposals and the forthcoming negotiations involving the Council, the Parliament and the Commission.

At the technical level, the problems are well-known. The Court of Justice has insisted unremittingly on two themes: certainty and an obligation of mutual trust between Member States in each other's legal systems. Its decisions have led to concerns about the efficacy in a European context of choice of court clauses (Case C-116/02 – *Gasser v Misat*) and arbitration clauses (Case C-185/07 – *Allianz SpA v West Tankers*), as well as about a jurisprudence applying the existing Regulation in relation to third countries with regard to which litigants do not (apparently) enjoy any of the protections which exist where only Member States are involved (Case C-281/02 – *Owusu v Jackson* and the "Lugano" *Opinion* C-1/03 of 7 February 2006, para 153). Professor Jonathan Harris and Dr Eva Lein note that, far from promoting the internal market, some of the results may be positively detrimental to it.

The work addresses such concerns from the standpoint of both common and civilian lawyers, it outlines the Commission's proposals and the Parliament's present position, and it discusses the issues arising and makes positive suggestions as to how they may best be addressed.

It also addresses the Commission's other main aims. One is to harmonise and limit the grounds of jurisdiction in relation to defendants domiciled outside any Member State. The Parliament, rightly, regarded such attempt as inopportune. The Commission's reasoning for pressing this fails to convince. The limited grounds of jurisdiction which it contemplates (largely modelled on the internal European grounds) would, by superseding a well-tested English jurisdictional code developed over a long period to meet the needs of English civil and commercial litigation, inflict a gratuitous blow on English courts' ability to adjudicate comprehensively or at all in a significant number of cases currently coming before them. This would be detrimental to the over-all bundle of business, financial and legal services which London presently offers. Whether it would be within the EU's competence is, one hopes, an issue that can remain academic.

The Commission's other main aim is less radical. It is to simplify enforcement by abolishing wherever possible any requirement of *exequatur*, and so to permit automatic enforcement of judgments as between Member States without any prior procedure for their recognition or registration. The Commission wishes moreover to remove any public policy defence to enforcement. In relation to these proposed changes, Professor Andrew Dickinson rightly notes the need for greater protection for defendants against misuse and the poverty of the argument for removing any public policy defence.

At the constitutional level, the process must be seen as encouraging. Giving evidence to the House of Lords European Union Select Committee enquiry into the Lisbon Treaty (10th Report of Session 2007–08, HL Paper 62-I), Sir David Edward wondered whether the Brussels regime was really appropriate for the jurisdiction of the Court of Justice, and whether it might not have been better to create a tribunal consisting of civil judges of Member States who would sit every three or four months, with the necessary expertise, and would have a much clearer understanding of the practical problems of jurisdiction (S38, Q133). As he went on to recognise, the Lisbon Treaty was, however, concerned with very different issues. Maybe, one day, the idea will be pursued of a form of specialist chamber, to deal not only with jurisdictional issues, but also with the other civil law issues which are bound to arise with the EU's increasing activity in this field.

As matters stand, however, credit is due to the Commission for its energetic and positive reaction to perceived problems revealed or caused by the Court of Justice's jurisprudence, and highlighted by academic and practitioner comment. The Parliament's engagement is equally welcome. The negotiations between the representatives of Member States, the Commission and the Parliament will, one also trusts, prove Europe's ability to address such problems on a broad and sensible basis. A major concern for the United Kingdom will clearly have to be to ensure that there is no compulsory harmonisation and limitation of grounds of jurisdiction in relation to third country domiciliaries.

All these topics are discussed in the present book in wide-ranging and stimulating terms. The book will be a valuable guide to the issues, and a pointer to the way in which some might constructively be resolved. It is my pleasure to commend it to the many practising and academic lawyers, insurers, business people and others interested directly or indirectly in issues of jurisdiction or of recognition and enforcement of foreign judgments.

LORD MANCE

The Brussels I Review Proposal – An Overview

Pamela Kiesselbach[*]

I. INTRODUCTION

On 14 December 2010 the European Commission published its Proposal [1] for changes to the Regulation 44/2001 on jurisdiction and the recognition and enforcement of judgments in civil and commercial matters ('Brussels I Regulation'). This Proposal was preceded by detailed studies – the Heidelberg Report on the application of the Brussels I Regulation in the Member States[2] and the Nuyts Report on residual jurisdiction,[3] both published in September 2007, and the Commission's Report and Green Paper, published on 21 April 2009.[4] The Commission's Proposal is extensive and relates to a number of central topics within the Brussels I Regulation. Many of them are controversial.

This chapter will aim to provide an overview of the perceived shortcomings of the Brussels I Regulation in its current form, followed by a summary of the key proposals made by the Commission and of the reactions to these proposals, as expressed by the European Parliament and during the consultations initiated by the Ministry of Justice of the United Kingdom. This chapter will conclude with an outlook on what is likely to happen next.

II. THE BRUSSELS I REGULATION – PERCEIVED SHORTCOMINGS

Although the general perception is that the Brussels I Regulation has been

---

[*] Professional Support Lawyer at Herbert Smith LLP and Senior Lecturer at the College of Law.

[1] Proposal for a Regulation of the European Parliament and of the Council on jurisdiction and the recognition and enforcement of judgments in civil and commercial matters (Recast), COM(2010) 748 final.

[2] B Hess, T Pfeiffer and P Schlosser, *The Brussels I Regulation 44/2001 – Application and Enforcement in the EU* ('Heidelberg Report') (Beck, Hart, Nomos 2008).

[3] A Nuyts, *Study on Residual Jurisdiction* 2007.

[4] Green Paper on the Review of Council Regulation (EC) No 44/2001 on jurisdiction and the recognition and enforcement of judgments in civil and commercial matters, COM(2009) 175 final; Report from the Commission to the European Parliament, the Council and the European Economic and Social Committee on the application of Council Regulation (EC) No 44/2001 on jurisdiction and the recognition and enforcement of judgments in civil and commercial matters, COM(2009) 174 final.

a success and is working well, there are a number of key areas which are considered to require improvements.

A. *The free circulation of judgments*

Currently, judgments originating from the court of an EU Member State need to be either declared enforceable or registered by the enforcing court before enforcement measures can be taken in another Member State. Studies have shown that this process, which is known as *'exequatur'*, is potentially both costly and time-consuming. The studies have also shown that in more than 90% of cases the procedure is a pure administrative (and therefore, it is argued, unnecessary) formality, due to the absence of grounds for refusing the recognition or enforcement of the judgments. The cost and time factor inherent in the *exequatur* process is further exacerbated where a judgment creditor seeks to enforce a judgment across a number of Member States, as the judgment will need to be declared enforceable or registered in each Member State in which enforcement is sought. This is seen as an unnecessary burden on cross-border trade and contrary to the aim of the Brussels I Regulation of enabling the free circulation of judgments in the EU.

B. *The operation of the Brussels I Regulation in the international legal order*

Currently, the jurisdiction rules in the Brussels I Regulation only apply where the defendant is domiciled in an EU Member State (Articles 2, 5 and 6) or is deemed to be domiciled there (Articles 9(2), 15(2) and 18(2)), or at least one of the parties to a choice of court agreement is domiciled in a Member State (Article 23) or certain subject matters of the proceedings are located in a Member State (Article 22). Where these connecting factors do not exist, the national rules on jurisdiction continue to apply in order to determine whether a Member State court has jurisdiction to hear a dispute (Article 4).

These rules differ considerably from Member State to Member State and, the concern is, provide unequal access to justice for claimants across the EU, particularly where jurisdiction is based on the nationality of the claimant (as is the case in Luxembourg and France). There is a further concern that the different national rules result in non-EU defendants being treated 'less favourably' than EU domiciled defendants where the national rules are 'exorbitant' in nature.[5] Also, where the national rules do not

---

[5] See A Briggs and P Rees, *Civil Jurisdiction and Judgments* (5th edn, Informa Law 2009) para 7.04.

provide for the jurisdiction of a Member State court, this could result in a potential loss of protection afforded by mandatory EU legislation protecting weaker parties (eg consumers, employees and insured).

A separate category of issues has arisen as a result of *Owusu v Jackson*,[6] in which the Court of Justice of the European Union (CJEU) held that the jurisdiction rules in the Brussels I Regulation, in particular the basic rule in Article 2 based upon the defendant's domicile, are mandatory in nature and cannot be departed from in favour of another, in particular non-EU jurisdiction, even if the dispute is more closely connected to that jurisdiction and that jurisdiction is clearly the more appropriate forum. In other words, the common law concept of being able to stay proceedings on the basis of *forum non conveniens* grounds does not apply within the context of the Brussels I Regulation.

As a result of *Owusu* there is uncertainty whether a Member State court must also take jurisdiction in accordance with the Brussels I Regulation (ie may not stay or dismiss proceedings), even where the parties have entered into a(n) (exclusive) choice of court agreement in favour of a non-EU court, or the subject matter of the dispute as identified in Article 22 is located outside the EU, or earlier proceedings relating to the same cause of action and the same parties have been commenced in the courts of a non-EU country. These are questions which the CJEU expressly declined to answer in *Owusu*. There are voices in legal writings which advocate a 'reflexive'[7] application of the rules in Articles 22, 23, 27 and 28 in these cases which would allow (or even require) EU Member State courts to dismiss proceedings in favour of the relevant non-EU state court.[8] However, the matter remains uncertain in the absence of an express ruling by the CJEU (which according to its comments in Opinion 1/03 relating to the new Lugano Convention appears to suggest that it does not favour a reflexive effect[9]) or of (clarifying) changes to the Brussels I Regulation.

C. The efficacy of choice of court agreements

The ability of parties to determine the court that will decide disputes arising

---

[6] CJEU, C-281/02 *Owusu v Jackson* [2005] ECR I-1383.

[7] See also the contribution of A Layton, in this publication.

[8] See the discussions in GC Cheshire, P North and JJ Fawcett, *Private International Law* (14th edn, OUP 2008) 333; AV Dicey, JHC Morris and L Collins, *The Conflict of Laws*, vol. I (14th edn, Sweet & Maxwell 2006) paras 12-021–12-022; A Briggs and P Rees (n 5) paras 2.256–2.260; see also the remarks delivered by Alexander Layton QC to the Legal Affairs Committee of the European Parliament on 5 October 2009 in which he states that '...it is plainly unsustainable in today's conditions for Community law to require that choice of court agreements in favour of non-Member State courts be overridden in favour of the adjudicatory powers of the courts of Member States. Urgent reform is needed.'

[9] See para 153 of the CJEU Opinion 1/03 dated 7 February 2006, relating to the competence of the EU to conclude the New Lugano Convention.

between them is of considerable importance to the international commercial community.

However, the current interrelationship between Article 23, which gives effect to a parties' choice of court agreement, and Article 27, which contains the *lis pendens* rule, undermines the efficacy of choice of court agreements in an EU context. Article 27 requires a Member State court to stay its proceedings if another Member State court has been first seised of proceedings involving the same cause of action and between the same parties and to allow the court first seised to determine whether or not it has jurisdiction. The fact that this rule applies also where the first court has been seised in breach of a choice of court agreement and the second court is the chosen court was established by the CJEU in *Erich Gasser v MISAT*.[10] This allows a party to obstruct the bringing of proceedings in the chosen Member State court by bringing a 'torpedo' action in another Member State court (albeit in violation of the choice of court agreement). This problem is magnified where such violating proceedings are brought in a Member State court whose procedural rules do not provide for the determination of jurisdiction as a preliminary issue or in an otherwise speedy manner.

Further, the Commission has signed the 2005 Hague Convention on Choice of Court Agreements (Hague Convention) which allows the chosen court to continue proceedings regardless of whether parallel proceedings have been brought first in another court (Article 5), and which requires any court seised in breach of a choice of court agreement to suspend or dismiss its proceedings (Article 6). If ratified, the Hague Convention will apply where at least one of the parties to the agreement is a resident of a Contracting State other than an EU Member State, whereas the equivalent Brussels I rules will apply where at least one party is domiciled in an EU Member State and none of the parties to the agreement is domiciled in a Contracting State which is not also an EU Member State.

The concern is that different rules relating to the efficacy of choice of court agreements will give rise to confusion and complications and that the Brussels I regime should be brought in line with the Hague Convention in order to facilitate its ratification by the EU as soon as the Brussels I reforms have been finalised.

D. *'Torpedo' actions in patent claims*

Article 27 is considered to lead to particular difficulties in patent actions. The *lis pendens* rule allows a party which faces the prospect of an infringement action being brought in a 'quick' jurisdiction to bring a pre-emptive action (eg for a declaration of non-liability) in the courts of a 'slow' juris-

---

[10] CJEU, C-116/02 *Erich Gasser GmbH v MISAT Srl* [2005] QB 1.

diction (even though these courts may not have jurisdiction). Such pre-emptive proceedings would block any subsequent proceedings being brought in the competent courts pending a decision by the first seised court on its jurisdiction.

A further difficulty arises as a result of the interrelationship between Articles 27 and 22. The CJEU in *Overseas Union Insurance v New Hampshire Insurance*[11] left open the question whether the *lis pendens* rule also applied where the court second seised had exclusive jurisdiction under Article 16 of the 1968 Brussels Convention on Jurisdiction and the Enforcement of Judgments in Civil and Commercial Matters (Brussels Convention), the predecessor of Article 22 of the Brussels I Regulation. It was further decided in *GAT v Luk*[12] that where a party in a patent action raises the issue of validity of the patent by way of defence this will trigger the exclusive jurisdiction under Article 16 of the Brussels Convention (now Article 22(4) of the Brussels I Regulation). The combination of these two decisions raises the question of whether there is an exception to the *lis pendens* rule where the court seised second has exclusive jurisdiction under Article 22(4).[13] This would mean that a defendant in an infringement action could divert any proceedings to the courts of the Member State in which the patent was registered by simply raising the validity defence.

There is a sense that as a result of how the Brussels I Regulation rules operate in industrial property matters there is too much scope for the (prospective) defendant to manipulate and obstruct any infringement actions against him.

The latter problem can potentially also arise in the context of insurance or consumer contracts where the proceedings brought second can rely on the special jurisdiction rules set out in sections 3 (insurance contracts) and 4 (consumer contracts) of the Brussels I Regulation and a judgment of the court first seised made in breach of these protective rules would not be recognised in accordance with Article 35(1).

E. The interface between the Brussels I Regulation and arbitration

Although Article 1(2)(d) provides for the exclusion of arbitration from the scope of the Brussels I Regulation, the delineation of this exclusion has recently become blurred as a result of the CJEU decision in *Allianz SpA v*

---

[11] CJEU, C-351/89 *Overseas Union Insurance Ltd v New Hampshire Insurance Co* [1991] ECR I-3317.

[12] CJEU, C-4/03 *GAT v Luk* [2006] ECR I-6509.

[13] See AV Dicey, JHC Morris and L Collins (n 8) para 12-049 who are in favour of such an exception based on the argument that a judgment given by a court first seised in breach of art 22 would be unenforceable in accordance with art 35(1) and consequently 'there is no sensible purpose in deferring to a court whose judgment will be a nullity in England'.

West Tankers.[14] This decision has been widely criticised in the international arbitration community and has significantly undermined the efficacy of arbitration agreements which had until then been considered to be less vulnerable to 'torpedo' actions than choice of court agreements. The decision has raised uncertainty as to how far arbitration is, or should in fact, be excluded from the scope of the Brussels I Regulation.

West Tankers determined that a Member State court has jurisdiction to decide upon the existence, validity and scope of an arbitration agreement by way of an incidental or preliminary issue where, otherwise, the substance of the dispute falls within the scope of Brussels I. Consequently, the CJEU considered it to be incompatible with the principles of mutual trust and confidence underpinning the Brussels I Regime for the Member State court at the seat of the arbitration to grant an anti-suit injunction restraining a party from commencing or continuing court proceedings in breach of an arbitration agreement.

Following on from *West Tankers,* the English Court of Appeal in *National Navigation v Endesa Generacion,*[15] was compelled to decide that the judgment of a Member State court dealing with the incidental question of whether an arbitration clause had been validly incorporated into an agreement was covered by the Brussels I Regulation and was therefore binding on the Member State court at the seat of the arbitration dealing with the same issue in arbitration proceedings. This leads to the peculiar result that a judgment dealing with the efficacy of an arbitration agreement as an incidental issue in 'normal' court proceedings is binding on the court at the seat of the arbitration, whereas a similar judgment obtained from the court at the seat in the context of arbitration proceedings (which fall outside the scope of the Brussels I Regulation) would not need to be recognised by other Member State courts under the Brussels I Regulation. The Advocate General acknowledged in her Opinion in *West Tankers* that the approach recommended to and subsequently adopted by the CJEU gives rise to an increased risk of parallel court and arbitration proceedings and, consequently, of inconsistent judgments and arbitration awards. In a further twist in the struggle between arbitration and court proceedings in the context of the Brussels I Regulation, the English High Court has decided in *West Tankers v Allianz SpA*[16] that it was open to the victorious party in the arbitration to obtain a judgment in terms of the award under section 66 of the Arbitration Act 1996 even where the award was 'only' of a declaratory nature (ie contained a declaration of non-liability). The reason given was

---

[14] CJEU, C-185/07 *Allianz SpA v West Tankers* [2009] 3 WLR 696.
[15] *National Navigation Co v Endesa Generacion SA* [2009] EWCA Civ 1397.
[16] *West Tankers Inc v Allianz SpA and another* [2011] EWHC 829 (Comm), upheld by the Court of Appeal (2012) EWCA Civ 27.

that by going down this route there was a 'real prospect of establishing the primacy of the award over an inconsistent judgment'. A very similar judgment relating to the enforcement of an award declaring that an arbitral tribunal had jurisdiction to determine certain disputes was handed down in *African Fertilizers v BD Shipsnavo*.[17]

In support of this view, both judgments made reference to Article 34(3) of the Brussels I Regulation which provides that a judgment shall not be recognised where it is 'irreconcilable with a judgment given in a dispute between the same parties in the Member State in which recognition is sought...'. It was however also acknowledged that there was no determinative authority on whether Article 34(3) applied to judgments of a Member State court giving leave to enforce the award of an arbitral tribunal, or whether such a judgment fell outside the scope of the Brussels I Regulation.[18] Interestingly, the Commission in the Report accompanying its Green Paper mentions that 'judgments merging an arbitral award are frequently (though not always) recognised and enforced in accordance with the Regulation', presumably based upon the findings of the Heidelberg Report.[19]

F. Provisional measures

There are areas of doubt relating to the free circulation of provisional measures and the extent of the jurisdiction of Member State courts to grant provisional measures under Article 31 of the Brussels I Regulation. This Article allows a court to order provisional or protective measures even if it does not have jurisdiction as to the substance of the case.

In *Denilauler v SNC Couchet Frères*[20] the CJEU held that provisional and protective measures made *ex parte*, ie without giving prior notice to the defendant, were not enforceable in other Member States under the Brussels I Regulation, as they did not qualify as a 'judgment' in accordance with Article 32. It is however questionable whether this also applies where the defendant has (subsequently) had an opportunity to resist the claimant's application in *inter partes* proceedings and the order is confirmed or continued as a result of such proceedings.[21]

---

[17] *African Fertilizers and Chemicals NIG Ltd v BD Shipsnavo GmbH & Co Reederei KG* [2011] EWHC 2452 (Comm).

[18] See A Briggs and P Rees (n 5) para 7.22, who argue for the application of art 34 in this situation. The point was not considered by the Court of Appeal in *West Tankers Inc v Allianz SpA* [2012] EWCA Civ 27.

[19] See para 120 of the Heidelberg Report (however, without specific reference to national case law).

[20] CJEU, C-125/79 *Denilauler v SNC Couchet Frères* [1980] ECR 1553.

[21] For this approach see A Briggs and P Rees (n 5) para 7.06 who however also refer to a German judgment – *European Consulting Unternehmensberatung AG v Refco Overseas Ltd* (OLG Karlsruhe, 19 December 1994) which appears to have taken the opposite approach.

In *Van Uden Maritime v Kommanditgesellschaft in Firma Deco-Line*,[22] the CJEU made a number of points relating to the scope of Article 31 and introduced the requirement of a 'real connecting link between the subject matter of the measures sought and the territorial jurisdiction of the Contracting State of the court before which those measures are sought'.[23] There is some uncertainty as to what qualifies as such a 'real connecting link'. By way of an example of this uncertainty Professor Adrian Briggs refers to the English world-wide freezing injunction which may 'relate' to assets outside England, but which operates *in personam*.[24] The Heidelberg Report[25] points out difficulties of applying the 'real connecting link' requirement to interim payment orders.

Further, the Heidelberg Report has been particularly critical of the lack of any provision which allows the Member State court with substantive jurisdiction to vary or discharge a provisional or protective measure granted by another court under Article 31.[26]

III. THE COMMISSION'S PROPOSAL

The Commission's Proposal seeks to address most if not all of the concerns mentioned above although some suggestions aired in the Green Paper have not made it into the final version of the Proposal. Unless indicated otherwise, references to Articles below refer to the Articles in the Proposal.

A. *The free circulation of judgments*

The Commission's suggestion is to abolish *exequatur* and to treat a judgment as immediately enforceable across the EU (Article 38(2)). This proposal is premised upon the assumption of a high level of mutual trust and confidence in the maturity of judicial systems across the EU.[27] The proposed rules would allow judgment creditors to proceed with the immediate enforcement of a Brussels I judgment in accordance with national enforcement laws without the need for a prior declaration of enforceability. There is no requirement to serve the debtor with the judgment or otherwise warn him of imminent enforcement measures prior to enforcement

---

[22] CJEU, C-391/95 *Van Uden Maritime BV v Kommanditgesellschaft in Firma Deco-Line* [1999] QB1225.

[23] The judgment relates to art 24 of the Brussels Convention which is the predecessor of art 31 of the Brussels I Regulation.

[24] A Briggs and P Rees (n 5) para 6.10.

[25] Heidelberg Report, para 736.

[26] Heidelberg Report, paras 755–762 and 907.

[27] See para 3.1.1 of the Explanatory Memorandum accompanying the Commission's Proposal.

(save for any such requirements which may exist under national enforcement laws).

The Proposal contains some (limited) safeguards for the judgment debtor. The debtor may stop the enforcement of a judgment in another Member State by applying for a review of the judgment in the originating court if the judgment was entered in default and the debtor was not served in sufficient time (Article 45). This differs from the current rule which allows the debtor to challenge the enforcement of such a default judgment in the enforcing court (Article 34(2) of the Brussels I Regulation). Further (under the Proposal), the debtor may raise objections to the enforcement of a judgment in the enforcing court if there is an (earlier) conflicting judgment (Article 43) or fundamental principles underlying the right to a fair trial have been breached (Article 46). However, the onus will be firmly on the debtor to stop the enforcement of the judgment.

The Proposal will no longer allow the enforcement of a judgment to be challenged on the basis of public policy (of the enforcing Member State) or the fact that the judgment was obtained in breach of exclusive jurisdiction rules (in Article 22 of the Brussels I Regulation) or of the protective jurisdiction rules relating to insurance and consumer contracts.

The new rules shall not apply to judgments in defamation cases and compensatory collective redress proceedings which will continue to be subject to the 'old' *exequatur* process. Pending the introduction of more uniform rules relating to these types of proceedings, the Commission considers that there is currently a lack of sufficient mutual trust and confidence to merit an abolition of *exequatur*.

B. *The operation of the Brussels I Regulation in the international legal order*

The Commission is proposing to extend most of the jurisdiction rules in the Brussels I Regulation to defendants domiciled outside the EU. These rules would replace the national rules on jurisdiction which currently apply under Article 4 of the Brussels I Regulation, some of which are narrower and some of which provide jurisdiction on more liberal (some may say exorbitant) grounds. This extension of the jurisdiction rules is also to apply to the protective jurisdiction rules in sections 3, 4 and 5 which allow insured, consumers and employees domiciled within the EU to bring proceedings in their home jurisdictions.

To make up for the loss of national jurisdiction rules, and the fact that Article 2 of the Brussels I Regulation (which bases jurisdiction on the domicile of the defendant in the EU) will not be available in relation to non-EU defendants, the Proposal provides for two new grounds for jurisdiction over non-EU defendants. One applies where the defendant has assets in a

Member State and the value of those assets is not disproportionate to the value of the claim and the dispute has a sufficient connection to the relevant Member State (Article 25). The other provides for jurisdiction where there is no forum available (outside the EU) which would guarantee a fair trial, or if a judgment obtained in the (otherwise competent) third State court would not be enforceable or recognised in the Member State of the court seised (and such enforcement or recognition is necessary to ensure that the rights of the claimant are satisfied), and the dispute has a sufficient connection to the chosen Member State (*forum necessitatis*, Article 26).

The Proposal has dropped the suggestion of a third ground for 'subsidiary jurisdiction', which was included in the Green Paper based upon the carrying on of activities within a Member State, where the dispute relates to such activities.

The Green Paper acknowledged that the extension of the jurisdiction rules of the Brussels I Regulation to non-EU defendants was likely to result in an increase of competing parallel proceedings before Member State and third State courts. To address this issue, the Commission expressed a willingness to consider a reflexive effect of the *lis pendens* rules in Articles 27 and 28, as well as of the rules in Article 22 (relating to exclusive jurisdiction) and Article 23 (relating to choice of court agreements). However, the Proposal only provides for the application of the *lis pendens* rule in relation to proceedings involving the same cause of action and between the same parties (Article 34). The Commission's Proposal does not provide for a reflexive effect of the *lis pendens* rule in the case of related proceedings (Article 28) or of the provisions relating to exclusive jurisdiction (Article 22) or (exclusive) choice of court agreements (Article 23).

Also, the Green Paper indicated that it might be beneficial to include common rules in the Brussels I Regulation dealing with the effect of third State judgments across the EU, in particular where these are in breach of mandatory EU law or where EU law provides for the exclusive jurisdiction of a Member State's courts. Currently, the enforcement of third State judgments is governed by national rules which vary from Member State to Member State. However, the Proposal contains no such rules.[28]

C. The efficacy of choice of court agreements

The Commission's Proposal provides for a strengthening of exclusive choice of court agreements. It is suggested that in case of an exclusive jurisdiction clause in favour of a Member State court, 'the courts of other Member

---

[28] It is perhaps noteworthy in this context that the Hague Convention contains recognition and enforcement provisions relating to judgments given by a court of a Contracting State chosen in an exclusive choice of court agreement.

States shall have no jurisdiction over the dispute until such time as the court or courts designated in the agreement decline their jurisdiction' (Article 32(2)).

This presumably means that where proceedings are brought before a Member State court and a party pleads the (*prima facie*) existence of an exclusive jurisdiction clause in favour of another Member State court, the court seised in alleged violation of the choice of court agreement will need to stay its proceedings pending a decision on the existence, scope and validity of the alleged jurisdiction agreement by the named court. This is the same rule that already applies to choice of court agreements in favour of a Member State court where none of the parties are domiciled in the EU (Article 23(3) of the Brussels I Regulation). The Proposal also contains a new Recital (19) which explains the aim of the new rule: 'The effectiveness of choice of court agreements should be improved in order to give full effect to the will of the parties and avoid abusive litigation tactics. This Regulation should therefore grant priority to the court designated in the agreement to decide on its jurisdiction, regardless of whether it is first or second seized.'

In its Summary of the Impact Assessment which accompanied the Proposal, the Commission acknowledges the importance of ensuring the effectiveness of choice of court agreements beyond the EU's borders and refers to the Hague Convention which will improve 'legal certainty for forum-selection-clauses in B2B relationships', mentioning that the ratification process of this Convention is on-going.[29] The Commission's Proposal aims to bring the revised rule of the Brussels I Regulation in line with the rule provided for in Article 6 of the Hague Convention which provides that: 'A court of a Contracting State other than that of the chosen court shall suspend or dismiss proceedings to which an exclusive choice of court agreement applies…'. However, the Proposal does not contain any of the qualifications provided for in Article 6 of the Hague Convention which state that a court seised in breach of a jurisdiction clause is not obliged to stay its proceedings if:

1. the agreement is null and void under the law of the State of the chosen court;
2. a party lacked the capacity to conclude the agreement under the law of the State of the court seised;
3. giving effect to the agreement would lead to manifest injustice or would be manifestly contrary to the public policy of the State of the court seised;

---

[29] See para 2.3.1 second bullet.

4. for exceptional reasons beyond the control of the parties, the agreement cannot reasonably be performed; or
5. the chosen court has decided not to hear the case.

If both the Commission's Proposal and the Hague Convention are given effect this would mean that exclusive jurisdiction clauses will be given greater effect in many commercial situations. This priority rule will, however, not apply to consumer and employment contracts (both in the case of the Brussels I Regulation and of the Hague Convention) and insurance contracts (in the case of the Brussels I Regulation), nor in relation to exclusive choice of court agreements entered into between parties domiciled within different EU Member States providing for the jurisdiction of the courts of a third State, regardless of whether that third State has ratified the Hague Convention or not.

However, there is an important limitation to the scope of the Hague Convention which does not apply to asymmetric jurisdiction agreements which only provide for exclusivity of the chosen jurisdiction in favour of one party, a clause often found in financial agreements.[30] This limitation is likely to be a reflection of the fact that there are concerns in some countries that such 'one-sided' exclusive choice of court agreements should not be given effect on the grounds that they lack mutuality or are unconscionably one-sided. As such clauses are generally considered valid under the Brussels I Regulation,[31] it is perhaps unlikely that a similar limitation will apply to the proposed rule; however, this may merit a clarification.

Further, the Proposal includes a choice of law rule which provides that the validity of the choice of court agreement will be determined by the law of the country of the chosen court (Article 23(1)). This is in line with the choice of law rule provided for in the Hague Convention and departs from the current common law rule under English private international law according to which a jurisdiction clause will normally be governed by the same law governing the contract containing the clause[32] unless the reference in the Proposal to the chosen court's laws includes its private international law, in which case the law of the underlying contract may very well continue to apply as a result of *renvoi*.[33]

---

[30] See paras 105 and 106 of the Explanatory Report to the Hague Convention prepared by T Hartley and M Dogauchi according to which: 'It was agreed by the Diplomatic Session that, in order to be covered by the Convention, the agreement must be exclusive irrespective of the party bringing the proceedings.'

[31] Art 17 of both the Brussels Convention and the 'old' Lugano Convention expressly provided for such clauses.

[32] AV Dicey, JHC Morris and L Collins (n 4) para 12-090.

[33] That this may be the case is suggested by A Dickinson, 'The Revision of the Brussels I Regulation' (2010) 12 Yearbook of Private International Law 247, 301.

Suggestions in the Green Paper to (further) strengthen choice of court agreements by providing for damages in case of breach or by requiring the use of a standard form choice of court agreement have not found their way into the Proposal.

D. 'Torpedo' actions in patent claims

In the Green Paper, the Commission acknowledged that 'the possibility to effectively enforce or challenge industrial property rights in the Community is of fundamental importance for the good functioning of the internal market'. The Green Paper included a number of suggestions which would have addressed some of the concerns discussed earlier in this chapter. One was to exclude the application of the *lis pendens* rule in situations where the 'torpedo' action was for (negative) declaratory relief. The other was to provide for the consolidation of proceedings against several infringers (domiciled in different Member States) in the courts of the Member State 'where the defendant coordinating the activities or otherwise having the closest connection with the infringement is domiciled' (the 'spider-in-the-web' approach).[34]

However, the Proposal has not adopted any of these suggestions and there is little in the Proposal which is likely to assist in patent claims. The only rule that may assist is the new requirement that in the case of a *lis pendens* situation, the first seised court 'shall establish its jurisdiction within six months except where exceptional circumstances make this impossible' (Article 29(2)). There is however no indication of what happens where the first seised court fails to comply with the six-month deadline. It can only be assumed that in that case the second seised court may resume its proceedings which would, however, result in parallel proceedings (and possibly inconsistent judgments).

E. The interface between the Brussels I Regulation and arbitration

The Proposal introduces a rule on the relation between arbitration and court proceedings. This represents a departure from the total exclusion of arbitration from the Brussels I Regulation, as is illustrated by the amended wording of Article 1(2)(d): 'This Regulation shall not apply to: ... arbitration, save as provided for in Articles 29, paragraph 4 and 33, paragraph 3 ...'.

---

[34] Green Paper 5-7; see also the Heidelberg Report at paras 852 and 853 which suggest a re-draft of art 6(1) to provide for a 'spider-in-the-web' approach; such a rule would reverse the CJEU decision in C-539/03 *Roche v Primus* which held that such an approach was not possible under art 6(1) of the Brussels I Regulation.

The new rule requires a Member State court to stay its proceedings where there is an arbitration agreement and either the arbitral tribunal or the courts of the Member State at the 'agreed or designated' seat have been seised to determine the existence, validity or effects of an arbitration agreement (Article 29(4)). This rule neutralises the effects of the CJEU decision in *Allianz SpA v West Tankers* without re-instating the right of the court at the seat of the arbitration to issue anti-suit injunctions in relation to the offending proceedings (insofar as such a remedy is generally available in accordance with national procedural rules).

A new Recital provides that: 'The effectiveness of arbitration agreements should also be improved in order to give full effect to the will of the parties. This should be the case, in particular, where the agreed or designated seat of an arbitration is in a Member State. This Regulation should therefore contain special rules aimed at avoiding parallel proceedings and abusive litigation tactics in those circumstances. The seat of the arbitration should refer to the seat selected by the parties or the seat designated by an arbitral tribunal, by an arbitral institution or by any other authority directly or indirectly chosen by the parties'.

The rule does not assist where the arbitration agreement provides for a seat outside the EU regardless of whether the parties to the arbitration agreement are domiciled within or outside the EU.

The Proposal does not include any of the other rules on arbitration-related jurisdiction suggested in the Green Paper, such as a rule providing for the exclusive jurisdiction of the court at the seat of the arbitration in relation to proceedings in support of arbitration. Another suggestion was to provide for the recognition and enforceability under the Brussels I Regulation of judgments deciding on the validity of an arbitration agreement (where the judgment is made by the court at the seat of the arbitration in the context of arbitration proceedings) and/or of judgments merging an arbitration award. Instead, Recital (11) of the Proposal expressly provides that the Brussels I Regulation is not to cover 'the validity, annulment, and recognition and enforcement of arbitral awards'.

The Green Paper also suggested a choice of law rule similar to the rule provided for in the Proposal for choice of court agreements, ie that the law of the seat shall determine the validity of the arbitration agreement.[35] Finally, there was a suggestion to introduce a rule dealing with the potential conflict between an arbitral award and an inconsistent judgment along the lines of the current Article 34(4) of the Brussels I Regulation, allowing an enforcing court to refuse the recognition or enforcement of a judgment

---

[35] There is no such choice of law rule in the New York Convention which means that each Contracting State needs to apply its own private international law rules to determine the validity of an arbitration agreement.

which is inconsistent with an (earlier) award enforceable under the 1958 New York Convention on the Recognition and Enforcement of Foreign Arbitral Awards (New York Convention).

These suggestions are likely to have been dropped in light of strong criticism and concern from within the international arbitration community that such additional jurisdiction rules would constitute an unacceptable interference with the arbitration regime provided for in the New York Convention and the local arbitration laws which are considered to work well.

F. Provisional measures

The Proposal contains a number of clarifications in relation to provisional and protective measures.

Article 2(a) provides that the rules relating to the enforcement of 'judgments' (in chapter III of the Brussels I Regulation) are also to apply to 'measures ordered without the defendant being summoned to appear and which are intended to be enforced without prior service of the defendant if the defendant has the right to challenge the measure subsequently under the national law of the Member State of origin'. This clarifies the issue which currently arises under *Denilauler* in relation to protective or provisional orders made *ex parte*. In order to provide some protection to the defendant, Article 44(3) provides that the enforcement of an *ex parte* order in another Member State may be suspended pending the outcome of a challenge brought by the defendant in the Member State of origin.

Further, Article 2(b) confirms that the enforcement and recognition rules and the jurisdiction rule in Article 31 are also to cover '*protective* orders aimed at obtaining information and evidence' (emphasis added). Recital (22) seeks to clarify the difference between protective information orders (which fall within the Brussels I Regulation) and provisional information orders (which fall outside the Brussels I Regulation): 'The notion of provisional, including protective measures should be clarified. They should include, in particular, protective orders aimed at obtaining information or preserving evidence, thus covering search and seisure orders as referred to in Article 6 and 7 of Directive 2004/48/EC of the European Parliament and of the Council of 29 April 2004 on the enforcement of intellectual property rights. They should not include measures which are not of a protective nature, such as measures ordering the hearing of a witness for the purpose of enabling the applicant to decide whether to bring a case'.

This means that, for example, *Norwich Pharmacal* orders aimed at identifying a potential defendant[36] will fall outside the enforcement regime and

---

[36] The *Norwich Pharmacal* jurisdiction was established in the House of Lords' decision in *Norwich Pharmacal v Commissioners of Customs & Excise* [1974] UKHL 6 and is aimed at

Article 31, in so far as Article 31 provides for the jurisdiction of courts without substantive jurisdiction. It is assumed (but not entirely clear[37]) that the rule is not to affect the jurisdiction of the courts with substantive jurisdiction to make such orders (although they will not be enforceable in other Member State courts). On the other hand, search and seisure orders (formerly referred to as *Anton Piller* orders[38]) are classified as being 'protective' and will fall within chapter III and Article 31 of the Brussels I Regulation.

These changes clarify the situation in relation to provisional and protective information orders and are in line with the CJEU case law in this respect.[39] The exclusion of provisional information orders from the Brussels I Regulation (in so far as they are to be made by a Member State court without substantive jurisdiction) is explained by the fact that these are covered by a number of special evidence rules including those contained in the Regulation 1206/2001 on co-operation of the courts of the Member States in the taking of evidence in civil and commercial matters.[40]

Further, the Proposal takes all provisional (including protective) orders made by a court without substantive jurisdiction outside of the Brussels I Regulation enforcement regime (Recital (25) and Articles 2(a) and 42(2)(b)(i)). In other words, only provisional measures ordered by the court with substantive jurisdiction will retain their ability to be enforced across the EU. This is a significant departure from the current regime and is a proposal which was not included in the Green Paper and the ensuing consultation. It is however clear that this proposal is a direct consequence of the Commission's view (expressed in the Explanatory Memorandum accompanying the Proposal) that the diversity of the provisional measures available under different national laws makes their mutual recognition and enforcement particularly difficult.

---

obtaining information from a third party (often not party to the main proceedings) who has become involved or mixed up in a wrongdoing whether innocently or not.

[37] The opposite conclusion would appear to be suggested by the inclusion of a new rule in art 35 which expressly provides for the court with substantive jurisdiction to make 'provisional, including protective measures' and art 2(b) together with Recital 22, which aim to exclude provisional information orders from the scope of any rule referring to the terms 'provisional, including protective measures'. There is a question whether this is an unintended consequence resulting from a drafting error.

[38] Search and seisure orders which were formerly called *Anton Piller* orders (following the Court of Appeal judgment in *Anton Piller KG v Manufacturing Processes Ltd* [1976] Ch 55) are aimed at preserving evidence or preserving property which is subject of substantive proceedings. The High Court's power to grant search orders is derived from section 7(1) of the Civil Procedure Act 1997.

[39] CJEU, C-104/03 *St Paul Dairy Industries NV v Unibel Exser BVBA* [2005] ILPr 416.

[40] See also the Evidence (Proceedings in Other Jurisdictions) Act 1975 which gives effect to the Hague Convention on the Taking of Evidence Abroad in Civil and Commercial Matters.

The Proposal does not provide for a right by the substantive court to vary an order made by a court without substantive jurisdiction (as requested by the Heidelberg Report), which may, in any event, be considered less pressing now in light of the limited enforceability of such provisional orders. However, the Proposal introduces a rule which requires the court (without substantive jurisdiction) to cooperate with and seek information from the court with substantive jurisdiction (eg relating to the urgency of the measure sought or any refusal of a similar measure by the latter court) when making an order (Article 31). This requirement applies only where substantive proceedings have been brought, ie not in relation to pre-action orders.

It is not entirely clear whether the court making the order is required to contact the court dealing with the substantive proceedings before making a provisional order (which may defeat the object of obtaining an order urgently). Broadly, however, the Proposal is in line with the current practice of English courts which will take into account whether the provisional measure sought would have been available in the substantive jurisdiction and was or would be refused by the courts there, or would interfere with the case management of the substantive proceedings in some other way.[41]

Finally, the Proposal does not deal with and/or vary the requirement for a 'real connecting link' where provisional measures are granted under Article 31 by a court which does not have substantive jurisdiction.

IV. REACTIONS TO THE COMMISSION'S PROPOSAL

Following the publication of the Commission's Proposal in December 2010, the Ministry of Justice of the United Kingdom (MoJ) launched a public consultation between 22 December 2010 and 11 February 2011 which sought views on the Proposal to enable the MoJ to decide whether to opt into the changes to the Brussels I Regulation and any negotiations preceding those changes. Strong views were expressed in relation to the key proposals (both favourable and unfavourable) and as a result the MoJ decided (by letter dated 31 March 2011) to opt into the negotiations and the changes, and indicated that it would seek to influence the negotiations to give effect to the concerns raised by the stakeholders.

Further, the European Parliament has expressed strong views through its Committee of Legal Affairs both before and after the publication of the Commission's Proposal which run counter to many of the key proposals.

---

[41] Millett LJ and Cornhill LJ in *Credit Suisse Fides Trust SA v Cuoghi* [1998] QB 818 (CA); *Refco Inc v Eastern Trading Co* [1999] 1 Lloyd's Rep 159 (CA); AV Dicey, JHC Morris and L Collins (n 8) paras 8-028 to 8-031.

A. The free circulation of judgments

1. The Ministry of Justice's consultation

There appears to be general consensus that a simplification of the enforcement (and recognition) of judgments across the EU is welcomed.[42]

However, concerns have been raised about the fact that the simplified enforcement procedure does not provide for any form of notice to be given to the judgment debtor prior to the enforcement of a judgment in another Member State. This is of particular concern where the judgment to be enforced has been obtained in default of the defendant's appearance, as default judgments are those most likely to involve failure to follow due process, fraud or mistaken identity (although the majority will not be flawed in this way). This means that the first time a judgment debtor might learn of a default judgment entered against him in another Member State will be when the bailiff appears at his door or his property has been charged (depending upon the enforcing state's national enforcement rules).

It is noteworthy that existing EU rules which provide for immediate enforceability in relation to particular types of claims contained in, for example, the Regulation 805/2004 creating a European Enforcement Order for uncontested claims (EEO Regulation) include several limitations and safeguards which are not replicated in the Commission's Proposal. For example, the EEO Regulation lays down minimum requirements relating to the methods of service of the document instituting the proceedings (Articles 13 to 15) and the information to be included in that document (Articles 16 and 17) which need to be complied with for a resulting default judgment to be immediately enforceable without *exequatur*. Also, the EEO Regulation gives effect to the exclusive jurisdiction rules in Article 22 of the Brussels I Regulation and the protective jurisdiction rules relating to insured and consumers set out in sections 3 and 4 of the Brussels I Regulation by either providing that judgments obtained in breach of those rules will not be enforceable under the EEO regime (in relation to Article 22 and section 3) or any default judgment obtained against a consumer will only be enforceable under the EEO regime if obtained in the Member State of the consumer's domicile.

---

[42] See the transcript of the meeting of the House of Commons European Committee B (Recognition and Enforcement of Judgments) dated 28 March 2011 which provides a summary overview of the responses received to the MoJ's consultation on whether the UK should opt-in to the Brussels I Review Proposal and which refers to 94% of respondents supporting the 'principle of abolishing the intermediate procedure for the recognition and enforcement of judgments between member states'; and the letter of the Financial Law Committee of the City of London Law Society (CLLS) in response to the MoJ consultation dated 15 February 2011, at 2 available on the CLLS website http://www.citysolicitors. org.uk/Default.aspx?sID=924&lID=0.

There is concern that the Commission's Proposal undermines the rules relating to exclusive jurisdiction (Article 22) and the protective jurisdiction rules relating to insured and, in particular, consumers, as the enforcing courts would have no possibility to refuse the enforcement of judgments obtained in breach of these rules. Under the Proposal a consumer defendant will need to engage with proceedings brought in a Member State other than his Member State of domicile (despite the fact that such proceedings are brought in breach of section 4 of the Brussels I Regulation) to either stop a default judgment being entered against him or to have such a default judgment set aside.

This is, to a certain extent, an issue faced by all EU defendants sued outside the primary jurisdiction of their domicile, as, under the Proposal, they are forced to engage with foreign proceedings even if it is only to have a default judgment set aside, rather than being able to challenge the enforcement of the default judgment in the enforcing court (which is more likely to be at their place of domicile). This is particularly inequitable in extreme cases such as where the default judgment was obtained as a result of fraud (eg identity theft) or mistaken identity.

More generally (not only in relation to default judgments), there are concerns that the Proposal does not allow the enforcing court to refuse the enforcement of a judgment on the basis that the judgment was obtained by fraud, unless the judgment debtor can show that this has had an affect on 'the fundamental principles underlying the right to a fair trial' (Article 46(1)).

However, the greatest and most serious criticism has been reserved for the Proposal to drop the right of the enforcing Member State court to refuse the enforcement (or recognition) of a judgment on grounds of substantive public policy. The MoJ has indicated that it has particularly strong reservations in this regard and that these reservations are shared by 'many member states', and that it is confident that an acceptable outcome will be reached in the negotiations which will precede a definitive version of the Proposal.[43]

2. *The European Parliament's views*

The European Parliament's Committee on Legal Affairs (the 'Committee') prepared a Report relating to the reform of the Brussels I Regulation which was adopted on 29 June 2010, before the publication of the Commission's Proposal in December 2010 (the 'Initial Report'). In its Initial Report, the Committee set out its suggestions in relation to the key areas of concern

---

[43] See the transcript of the meeting of the House of Commons European Committee B (Recognition and Enforcement of Judgments) dated 28 March 2011 recording the statements made by the Under-Secretary of State of Justice (Jonathan Djanogly) in this respect.

identified in the Heidelberg Report and its views relating to suggestions made in the Commission's Green Paper. After the publication of the Commission's Proposal, the Committee's rapporteur, Tadeusz Zwiefka, published a Draft Report on 28 June 2011 suggesting numerous amendments (numbered 1 to 58) to the Proposal ('Draft Report'). Further Amendments (numbered 59 to 120) where published on 19 October 2011 including further or other amendments requested by amongst others Diana Wallis, MEP for Yorkshire and the Humber, whose views are perhaps likely to mirror the MoJ's views ('Further Amendments'). The Parliament's views are of particular importance in light of its role in the co-decision procedure which requires both the Parliament and the Council to agree on the text of the Proposal before it can become law.

In its Initial Report, the Committee advocates the retention of an 'exceptional procedure' which allows the judgment debtor to challenge the enforcement of a judgment 'before any steps are taken by way of enforcement' and, in any event, that the creditor should not be able to take any 'irreversible' enforcement steps before the time limit for initiating this procedure has expired or an application made by the judgment debtor has been decided upon by the relevant court in the Member State of enforcement.

More importantly, the Initial Report requests that the grounds on which the judgment debtor should be able to challenge the enforcement of a judgment in the enforcing courts (listed in Annex III of the Brussels I Regulation) should continue to include public policy and the fact that the judgment debtor was not served in sufficient time to enable him to arrange for his defence, the grounds currently provided for in Articles (34(1) and (2) of the Brussels I Regulation).

The Draft Report which responds to the Proposal reiterates the requirement for a right of the judgment debtor to 'apply for a refusal of recognition or enforcement of a judgment' (in the Member State of enforcement) on grounds of public policy, insufficient service in the case of a default judgment, the existence of an irreconcilable judgment, and the breach of the consumer jurisdiction rules in section 4 of the Brussels I Regulation. The rapporteur emphasises in his Explanatory Statement annexed to the Draft Report that: 'Excluding substantive public policy is incompatible with Member States' international obligations and indeed at odds with the fact that both the Rome I and Rome II Regulations contain exceptions for public policy and overriding mandatory provisions. A Member State before which proceedings are brought is entitled to preserve its fundamental values; therefore, equally, it must be the case for a Member State in which the enforcement of a judgment is sought.'

A 'Further Amendment' tabled by Tadeusz Zwiefka proposes that recognition and enforcement of a judgment should also be denied in the case of a breach of the exclusive jurisdiction rules or the rules relating to insurance and employment contracts.[44] The Draft Report and Further Amendments are therefore not only seeking to retain the grounds for challenging the enforcement of an EU Member State judgment currently provided for in Articles 34 and 35(1) of the Brussels I Regulation but are suggesting the inclusion of an additional ground (breach of the jurisdiction rules relating to employment contracts) currently not provided for. Another 'Further Amendment' tabled by Diana Wallis MEP requires that the judgment debtor is informed about the intended enforcement before enforcement measures may be taken.[45]

Also, the Draft Report does not agree with the special treatment of defamation claims and compensatory collective redress proceedings (or any other types of proceedings),[46] and consequently does not provide for an exemption of these types of proceedings from the new simplified enforcement rules.

B. The operation of the Brussels I Regulation in the international legal order

1. The Ministry of Justice's consultation

There is fundamental and widespread concern about the extension of the jurisdiction rules in the Brussels I Regulation to non-EU defendants.[47] The view, which is (or at least was) shared by the MoJ,[48] is that in order to ensure reciprocity and in the interest of international comity, the harmonisation of jurisdiction rules beyond the EU is more suitably dealt with on a multilateral basis, preferably within the ambit of the Hague Conference on Private International Law.

There is serious concern that the extension of the Brussels I Regulation rules will result in a loss of the (wider) set of English grounds of jurisdiction set out in the Civil Procedure Rules (PD 6B 3.1) and, if *Owusu* is applied consistently, a complete loss of the English courts' ability to stay proceedings on *forum non conveniens* grounds.

Examples of frequently used English jurisdiction rules which would be lost are, in relation to contract claims, the right to bring a claim in the English courts where the contract was made or breached in the jurisdiction, or contains a choice of English law clause (PD 6B 3.1(6)). Article 5 of the

---

[44] Amendment 117.

[45] Amendment 114.

[46] See the Explanatory Statement to the Draft Report under the heading 'Abolition of Exequatur'.

[47] The transcript of the meeting of the House of Commons European Committee mentions that 100% of the responses expressed concerns.

[48] As expressed in the MoJ's preliminary assessment in its Consultation Paper (CP 18/10) para 29.

Brussels I Regulation simply allows for the jurisdiction of the courts at the place of performance of the contract. Another commonly used English ground is the right to join a defendant as a 'necessary and proper' party to a claim (PD 6B 3.1(3)). Puzzlingly, the Proposal does not extend the equivalent rule in Article 6(1) to non-EU defendants. Article 6(2) only allows for non-EU defendants to be joined to Member State court proceedings within the context of 'third party proceedings' such as 'an action on a warranty or guarantee', and these requirements are likely to be much narrower than the 'necessary and proper party' basis.

Although the extension of the *lis pendens* rule to allow for a stay in the case of earlier non-EU proceedings is welcomed, concern has been expressed about the fact that Articles 22 (exclusive jurisdiction) and 23 (exclusive choice of court agreements) have not also been given reflexive effect.[49] This means a continuation of the unsatisfactory uncertainty as to whether Member State courts which have jurisdiction under the Brussels I Regulation (eg because the defendant is domiciled in a Member State) may or may not stay proceedings if there is an exclusive choice of court agreement in favour of a third State court.

The MoJ has also highlighted the fact that the extension of the protective jurisdiction rules is not justified in relation to insured acting in a commercial capacity.[50] Such an extension would result in a further (unwelcome and unnecessary) restriction of parties' ability to enter into choice of court agreements and is not mirrored in the Hague Convention which applies to choice of court agreements in insurance contracts entered into between commercial parties (Article 2 of the Hague Convention).

The MoJ has indicated that the approach it intends to adopt in the negotiations is to aim for an extension of the jurisdiction rules in the Brussels I Regulation as a minimum set of rules only and that the national rules should continue to apply in parallel. This suggests that the MoJ may be dropping its opposition in principle against an extension of the jurisdiction rules in the Brussels I Regulation beyond the EU. As a fall-back position the aim will be to introduce further jurisdiction rules into the Brussels I Regulation, in addition to those already suggested by the Commission, to replicate some of the key English (and other EU Member States') rules, in order to compensate for the loss of those national rules.[51]

---

[49] See the letter of the CLLS Financial Law Committee para 7. Consistent with this concern Diana Wallis MEP has suggested Further Amendments which provide for reflexive effect of art 28 (Amendment 106), art 22 (Amendment 112) and art 23 (Amendment 113).

[50] See the MoJ's preliminary assessment in its Consultation Paper (CP 18/10) paras 33 and 34.

[51] It is interesting in this context that Further Amendments tabled by Diana Wallis MEP provide both for the extension of the Brussels I rules to non-EU defendants in parallel to the continued application of national rules (Amendments 67 to 69) and the introduction of additional grounds of jurisdiction based upon the directing of contractual or non-contractual activ-

2. *The European Parliament's views*

In its Initial Report, the Committee takes a similarly critical view of the Commission's attempt to extend the Brussels I Regulation to non-EU defendants and considers that the issue 'has not been sufficiently considered and that it would be premature to take this step without much study, wide-ranging consultations and political debate, in which the Parliament should play a leading role...'.[52] The Initial Report also refers to the fact that there are a large number of bilateral agreements in place between Member States and third countries which contain jurisdiction rules and that a solution is better sought 'in parallel in the Hague Conference through the resumption of negotiations on an international judgments convention ...'.[53]

The Draft Report is even more scathing in that it points out that the Commission has no mandate from the Parliament in this respect and that the Commission 'cannot simply ignore the sentiments of the democratically elected Parliament, which took the view that it would be premature to take this step without wide-ranging consultations and political debate'.[54] Consequently, the Draft Report objects to all the changes proposed by the Commission which bring about such an extension of the Brussels I Regulation rules. However, Diana Wallis MEP has tabled Further Amendments which would allow for the extension of the Brussels I rules to non-EU domiciled defendants in addition to existing national jurisdiction rules and also provides for the inclusion of additional jurisdiction rules in relation both to EU and non-EU domiciled defendants (eg based upon contractual or non-contractual activities directed to a particular Member State or the inclusion of a choice of law in a contract).[55]

Perhaps surprisingly, the Initial Report also advocated the complete reversal of *Owusu* and the introduction of a general right of Member State courts to stay proceedings if they consider that the courts of another Member State court or a third State are better placed to hear the case. The Initial Report refers to the fact that such discretion has already been introduced (allowing a stay in favour of another Member State court) into the Regulation 2201/2003 concerning jurisdiction and the recognition and enforcement of judgments in matrimonial matters and matters of parental responsibility (Article 15). It is unclear whether the Parliament will pursue this point further in the course of the co-decision procedure, as it does not feature in the Draft Report.

---

ities to a certain Member State or the inclusion of a choice of law clause in a contract (Amendment 89). On the other hand she opposes the proposed additional jurisdiction ground based upon the location of property (Amendments 84 and 85).

[52] At para 15 of the Initial Report.
[53] ibid.
[54] See the Justification to Amendment 3.
[55] See (n 52).

C. The efficacy of choice of court agreements

1. The Ministry of Justice's consultation

The Commission's Proposal which seeks to strengthen the efficacy of choice of court agreements (made in favour of Member State courts) has been widely welcomed. Most criticisms are aimed at tightening up drafting, and clarifying how the rule is to work in practice.

For example, there is an argument for the introduction of a requirement that the party wishing to achieve a stay of proceedings must show some form of *prima facie* case that a valid choice of court agreement in favour of another Member State court exists; otherwise there is a risk that the existence of a choice of court clause may be too easily raised in bad faith to stop unwelcome proceedings. However, such a *prima facie* test must be very easy to meet, eg where there is at least some plausible argument for the existence of a relevant choice of court agreement. It must be left to the allegedly chosen court to rule on whether the agreement is valid and applies to the dispute; otherwise there will be no improvement to the current situation.

There is, however, a further question as to the commencement of proceedings before the allegedly chosen court. The current Proposal raises the question whether a Member State court must decline jurisdiction as soon as a choice of court agreement is raised without deciding upon the issue, even if there are no proceedings pending before the allegedly chosen court. In particular, there appears to be no obligation on the defendant to commence proceedings in the allegedly chosen court within a particular time frame after raising the jurisdiction agreement in the allegedly offending proceedings. Does this mean that the claimant who wishes to progress the proceedings needs to commence proceedings in the 'chosen' court to prove the invalidity of the agreement before being able to recommence his original proceedings, even though he does not believe in the existence or application of a jurisdiction agreement?

To avoid these questions it may be more sensible to require a Member State court to stay its proceedings only as and when an allegedly chosen Member State court has been seised with the question of the validity and application of the choice of court agreement, either as a main object or an incidental issue. There could be a rule that requires the first seised court to allow the parties (most likely the defendant) a certain period of time within which to bring proceedings in the allegedly chosen court, before carrying on to decide the jurisdiction issue itself should no such proceedings be brought. This would bring the Proposal more in line with the similar rule suggested in relation to arbitration agreements (discussed below).[56]

---

[56] A similar approach is suggested by A Dickinson (n 33) 247, 297 and has been included in Further Amendments tabled by Diana Wallis MEP (Amendment 97) and Tadeusz Zwiefka (Amendment 103).

In any event, there should be a rule that ensures that the apparently chosen court (whether first or second seised) must rule on its jurisdiction swiftly and as a preliminary point (the six months rule provided for in Article 29(2) could be extended to this situation), to enable proceedings to recommence in the unnamed Member State court if it is found that the agreement is invalid or inapplicable. Otherwise the new rules would provide for the possibility of bringing a new type of 'torpedo' action against legitimate proceedings which are not in fact in breach of an alleged choice of court agreement.

Further, there should perhaps be a clarification within the drafting of Article 32(2) according to which the rule that any Member State court other than the court chosen in the exclusive choice of court agreement will have jurisdiction may be displaced if the defendant submits to the jurisdiction of another Member State court in accordance with Article 24.[57]

2. The European Parliament's views

The Initial Report suggested that there should be a requirement that the chosen court deal with the question of its jurisdiction 'expeditiously as a preliminary issue' (paragraph 12). There was also a suggestion for a new rule setting out the circumstances in which a third party may be held to an exclusive choice of court agreement to which it is not a party (paragraph 13).

Although the Draft Report does not appear to pick up on the points aired in the Initial Report, it includes a very detailed rule dealing with the law applicable to the question of the validity of a choice of court agreement which differs from the Commission's Proposal which refers simply to the law of the Member State of the chosen court. The Committee's rule considers a choice of court agreement to be valid if it is valid in accordance with the law of the chosen Member State court, or the law chosen by the parties, or (in the absence of such a choice) the law otherwise applicable to the underlying contract, or (in all other cases) the law otherwise applicable to the parties' relationship (Article 23(a)(1)). The Committee's suggested rule expressly excludes the concept of *renvoi* from the choice of law provision (Article 23(a)(3)).

There is also a suggestion for a rule incorporating the principle of severability of choice of court agreements from the underlying agreement, clarifying that the choice of court agreement 'shall not be affected by the nullity, the non-existence, the lapsing, the termination or determination or any other cause of ineffectiveness of the contract' (Article 23(b)).

---

[57] Such a clarification has been suggested in Further Amendment 103 tabled by Tadeusz Zwiefka.

D. 'Torpedo' actions in patent claims

1. The Ministry of Justice's consultation

The MoJ consulted on the suggestions initially aired in the Green Paper. It is likely that none of these suggestions were in fact incorporated into the Commission's Proposal as there appeared to be some consensus that such rules were best left to the special regimes which were either already in force or were under consideration in relation to patent proceedings (eg within the context of the planned European Patent Litigation System).[58]

Although not in response to the MoJ consultation, there was, however, evidence of support for a rule that disapplied the *lis pendens* mechanism in relation to negative declaratory relief proceedings where infringement proceedings are subsequently brought by the patent owner. There was also support for the reinstatement of the 'spider-in-the web' approach to cross-border injunctions.[59] Neither of these suggestions was, however, adopted in the Proposal.

2. The European Parliament's views

Although the Committee floated the idea in its Initial Report that there might be merit in relieving the second seised court from its obligation to stay proceedings where the first seised court 'evidently' has no jurisdiction, it took the view, on balance, that 'issues concerning jurisdiction would be best resolved in the context of proposals to create a Unified Patent Litigation System.'[60] Consequently, the Draft Report does not contain any patent related suggestions either.

E. The interface between the Brussels I Regulation and arbitration

1. The Ministry of Justice's consultation

The question whether and to what extent there should be a modification of the current (complete) exclusion of arbitration from the Brussels I Regulation is a hotly debated topic, and different views are being expressed from within the international arbitration community.

One side of the argument welcomes the rule suggested by the Commission and the resulting limited inclusion of arbitration, whereas the other side of the argument is fiercely defending the complete exclusion of arbitration and is requesting a rule cementing such a complete exclusion and reversing the *West Tankers* decision.

---

[58] See for example the comments made in the report published by the House of Lords on 27 July 2009 in relation to the Green Paper at para 77.

[59] In relation to both suggestions, see the response to the Green Paper submitted by the European Patent Lawyers Association on 29 June 2009.

[60] At para 22 of the Initial Report.

The argument in favour of the Commission's rule recognises that the proposed rule is likely to reduce the risk of conflicting court and arbitration proceedings within the EU and the ensuing conflict of having to decide between the enforcement of an arbitral award under the New York Convention and the enforcement of an inconsistent judgment under the Brussels I Regulation. The rule would also dispense with the race for a judgment on the validity of an arbitration agreement as illustrated both in the *National Navigation v Endesa* and *African Fertilizers* litigation.[61]

It is suggested that the Commission's Proposal complements the New York Convention by providing additional options to parties seeking to enforce arbitration agreements in the face of court actions brought in a Member State in an attempt to frustrate an arbitration agreement. Article II(3) of the New York Convention envisages parties requesting the court of a Contracting State seised of a matter which is subject to an arbitration agreement to refer the parties to arbitration. The Commission's Proposal provides the parties with the alternative option of commencing arbitration or seeking a declaration as to the existence or scope of the arbitration agreement from the courts of the seat of arbitration, in order to bring about a stay of the offending proceedings.

Further, there are views that the proposed rule should be extended to arbitration agreements which designate an arbitration seat outside the EU, at least where the seat is in a country which is party to the New York Convention.[62]

The opposing argument which is being pursued by the MoJ takes the view that the New York Convention and the national arbitration laws applicable in the Contracting States provide a complete and independent regime which works well and should not be interfered with by the Brussels I Regulation in any way. In its response to the Green Paper the MoJ argues that: 'As long as there is no obligation under the Regulation to give priority to other Member States' courts that may be seised first, or to recognise or enforce their decisions on arbitration matters, then difficulties such as parallel proceedings are resolved by the New York Convention and national laws. In other words, the arbitration regime within the EU would simply be brought back into line with that outside the EU, where the problems identified in the Green Paper are regularly resolved by a combination of the international and the relevant national arbitration regime.'[63]

The MoJ has indicated that it proposes to continue to negotiate for a fully comprehensive exclusion of arbitration from the scope of the Brussels

---

[61] See references in (n 15) and (n 17).
[62] See the letter of the CLLS Financial Law Committee para 12.
[63] See the MoJ's response to the Green Paper dated 3 September 2009 para 36.

I Regulation and that the negotiability of that approach 'should be strengthened by the support of other member states.'[64]

2. The European Parliament's views

The Committee's Initial Report expressed strong opposition to the (even partial) abolition of the exclusion of arbitration from the scope of the Brussels I Regulation and took pretty much the same view expressed by the MoJ.

This approach is upheld in the Draft Report which suggests the inclusion of the following wording into Recital (11): 'The whole matter of arbitration should be excluded from the scope of this Regulation. Consequently, this Regulation does not apply to any dispute, litigation or application which the parties have subjected to an arbitration agreement or settlement or which relates to arbitration by virtue of an international treaty. Likewise this Regulation does not apply to any dispute or decision concerning the existence or validity of an arbitration agreement or settlement, or to any provisional or preventive measure[65] adopted in the context of a dispute, litigation or application which the parties have subjected to an arbitration agreement or settlement, or which relates to arbitration by virtue of an international treaty.'[66]

However, the suggestion (made in the Initial Report) that a rule be included into the Brussels I Regulation which provides for the non-recognition and non-enforceability of a judgment obtained in breach of an arbitration agreement does not appear to have found its way into the Draft Report.

F. Provisional measures

1. The Ministry of Justice's consultation

The proposals relating to provisional measures have been less in the limelight than the other areas which are clearly considered more key. However, the proposal clarifying the approach in relation to *ex parte* orders by expressly bringing them within the scope of the Brussels I Regulation, provided the defendant 'has the right to challenge the measure subsequently

---

[64] This is mentioned in the transcript of the meeting of the House of Commons European Committee dated 28 March 2011.

[65] This presumably means that the Parliament should also be objecting to the arbitration wording in art 36 of the Proposal which does not appear to have been picked up by the Draft Report.

[66] An (alternative) Further Amendment (numbered 62 and 65) proposed by Tadeusz Zwiefka no longer contains this clarifying wording and simply suggests to retain the wording currently contained in the Brussels I Regulation. It is not quite clear where that leaves the CJEU's decision in *West Tankers*.

under the national law of the Member State of origin', appears to be widely welcomed as clarifying the uncertainty arising from the *Denilauler* decision.

There is perhaps less enthusiasm for the proposal which limits the enforceability of provisional (including protective) measures across the EU where such measures are made by a Member State court which does not have substantive jurisdiction.[67]

Although the author has not seen any recent indications of the MoJ's views on the various proposals relating to provisional measures, comments in the Report published by the House of Lords in relation to the Green Paper on 27 July 2009[68] suggest that the Government is content to retain the 'real connecting link' requirement if this means that there is no power of the Member State court with substantive jurisdiction to vary or discharge provisional (including protective) measures made by other Member State courts.

Also, in its response to the Green Paper, the MoJ takes a favourable approach to bringing protective information orders within the scope of Article 31 and, presumably, leaving provisional information orders outside of its scope.

2. The European Parliament's views

The Committee does not seem to have any particular issues with the Commission's Proposal in this regard and, consequently, neither the Draft Report nor the Further Amendments provide for any relevant amendments.

V. WHAT NEXT?

According to the co-decision procedure, the Commission's Proposal will need to be adopted by the European Parliament jointly with the Council of the European Union. The procedure may comprise one, two or even three readings aimed at achieving a consensus between the two institutions.

The Council, through a working party for the relevant policy area, will be considering the Commission's Proposal and it is here where the MoJ and indeed other Member States' governments will be articulating their concerns in an attempt to modify the Proposal.

The rapporteur of the Parliament's Committee on Legal Affairs has prepared his Draft Report which was considered in a workshop held in October 2011, following which the Further Amendments referred to above were tabled. According to current timing the Draft Report is due to be adopted by the Committee on 31 May 2012 and is to be voted upon by the Parliament on 11 September 2012.

---

[67] See the letter of the CLLS Financial law Committee para 17.
[68] In paras 79 to 85.

In light of the significant opposition and differing views expressed by the Parliament in relation to a number of key areas of the Commission's Proposal and the importance of the Proposal to the international community, it is safe to assume that the co-decision procedure is likely to be drawn out and that changes to the Brussels I Regulation are unlikely to take effect any earlier than towards the end of 2013.

A Neverending Story?
Arbitration and Brussels I:
The Recast

Jonathan Harris & Eva Lein[*]

I. INTRODUCTION

The interface between arbitration and the Brussels I Regulation is a continuing source of controversy. As court litigation and arbitration are often perceived as alternatives for dispute resolution, subject to different legal frameworks,[1] it seems an understandable objective to keep arbitration separated from the Brussels I regime and equally appropriate that the Brussels I Regulation should contain an exclusion for arbitration. Yet the reality is somewhat different, and prevents a complete separation of arbitration from the court processes and national regulation: arbitration proceedings might need support from the courts with respect to certain tasks – for example, to appoint an arbitrator, to grant supportive provisional relief, to seize assets, or to levy execution. As Andrew Dickinson puts it, '[...] arbitration processes cannot be said to be small islands in the sea of dispute resolution that enjoy total independence from national legal systems – at best they are semi-autonomous.'[2] In particular, the fact that courts can be seised in parallel to arbitral proceedings where the validity of the arbitration agreement is challenged by one party as a principal or preliminary issue clearly shows an interface between litigation and arbitration. Article II(3) New York Convention allows courts to examine the validity of an arbitration agreement while arbitral proceedings are already pending.[3] The intersections between arbitration and cross-border litigation therefore need to be carefully

---

[*] Jonathan Harris is Professor at King's College, London, and Barrister at Serle Court, London; Eva Lein is Herbert Smith Senior Research Fellow in Private International Law, British Institute of International and Comparative Law, London.
[1] The New York Convention on Recognition and Enforcement of Foreign Arbitral Awards of 1958 and the European Convention on International Commercial Arbitration were the origins of the arbitration exclusion.
[2] See A Dickinson, *Brussels I Review – Interface with Arbitration*, conflictoflaws.net, June 17, 2009.
[3] It provides that '[t]he court of a Contracting State, when seized of an action in a matter in respect of which the parties have made an agreement within the meaning of this article, shall, at the request of one of the parties, refer the parties to arbitration, unless it finds that the said agreement is null and void, inoperative or incapable of being performed.'

outlined and coordinated, and their respective legal frameworks need to be reconciled. A transparent, predictable coordination of court and arbitral proceedings that regulates the interplay in a satisfactory way seems more sensible than the current blank exclusion of arbitration from the scope of the Brussels I Regulation without any explanation of how the Regulation interacts with the arbitration process.

The Brussels I Review Proposal tries to establish such a system of coordination, contrary to the current Article 1(2)(d) Brussels I Regulation and its predecessor provision in the Brussels Convention.[4] But does the Proposal give the necessary clear and appropriate guidance as to how the intersections between arbitration and the Regulation are to be dealt with?

II. BACKGROUND

The complete exclusion of arbitration from the Brussels I regime at first seemed a logical step, in order to keep arbitration apart from the court system and its legal framework, but the exclusion in Article 1(4) Brussels Convention/ Article 1(2)(d) Brussels I Regulation led to considerable difficulties. It turned out that the 'simple' exclusion was in fact not at all simple, and interpretation of the arbitration exception troubled parties, practitioners and courts alike.[5]

Uncertainty as to the interpretation of the arbitration exception was latent from the outset. It was alluded to in the Schlosser Report[6] which demonstrated the difficulties of understanding Article 1(4) Brussels Convention. The Report revealed divergent views of the Contracting States. According to some, only proceedings before national courts referring to arbitration proceedings, whether concluded, in progress or to be started, were regarded as part of arbitration.[7] According to others, the provision covered all disputes which the parties had effectively agreed to settle by arbitration, including any connected secondary disputes.[8] No attempt, however, was made to determine which of these views was correct.

Despite this initial uncertainty, things ticked along fairly well for many years – perhaps because the Member States were content with their own

---

[4] Art 1(2), sub-para (4), Brussels Convention.

[5] See eg B Hess, T Pfeiffer and P Schlosser, *The Brussels I-Regulation 44/2001, The Heidelberg Report Application and Enforcement in the EU* ('Heidelberg Report') (Beck, Hart, Nomos 2008).

[6] See P Schlosser, *Report on the Convention on the Association of the Kingdom of Denmark, Ireland and the United Kingdom of Great Britain and Northern Ireland to the Convention on jurisdiction and the enforcement of judgments in civil and commercial matters and to the protocol on its interpretation by the Court of Justice* ('Schlosser Report') [1979] OJ C 59/5, para 61.

[7] This view was expressed by the original Member States of the EEC.

[8] The view was principally expressed on behalf of the United Kingdom.

understanding of the arbitration exception and of the CJEU statement in *Marc Rich*[9] that the Brussels regime excludes 'arbitration in its entirety', and does not cover ancillary proceedings such as the appointment of arbitrators. The decision has, however, been difficult to read and to interpret and all it really made clear is that if the subject matter of the proceedings is related to arbitration, they are excluded from the Convention regardless of whether a preliminary issue falls under the Convention or not.[10]

The controversy was fuelled by subsequent CJEU case law, starting with *Van Uden*,[11] according to which the courts of a Member State have jurisdiction under the Regulation[12] to grant provisional measures regarding the claim on the merits in support of arbitration; and reaching its climax in *West Tankers*,[13] where an issue of parallel proceedings was at stake. Here, the CJEU made it clear that, if a party attacks an arbitration clause in the courts of a Member State as a preliminary issue, the resulting judgment is enforceable under the Regulation if the subject matter of the substantive dispute falls within the scope of the Brussels I Regulation, even if this court has been seised in a 'torpedo' action. As a consequence of this, anti-suit injunctions preventing the continuation of court litigation by the plaintiff were excluded due to the 'mutual trust' principle the Regulation establishes; meaning that the courts of another EU Member State were equally competent to decide if they had jurisdiction notwithstanding the existence of an English arbitration clause and that decision could not be second-guessed by the English courts. The fact that the court had no power over the arbitrator

---

[9] CJEU, Case C-190/89 *Marc Rich & Co AG v. Società Italiana Impianti* [1991] ECR I-3855. The case concerned English proceedings between a Swiss claimant and an Italian defendant on the appointment of an arbitrator. The Italian defendant, who had already commenced proceedings in Italy, disputed the validity of the arbitration agreement as a preliminary issue in the English proceedings, while the claimants challenged the jurisdiction of the Italian courts because of the allegedly valid arbitration agreement. The question referred to the ECJ by the English Court of Appeal was whether the proceedings in England fell within the scope of the Brussels Convention.

[10] See *Marc Rich* (n 9) at 26–28:
'26 In order to determine whether a dispute falls within the scope of the Convention, reference must be made solely to the subject-matter of the dispute. If, by virtue of its subject-matter, such as the appointment of an arbitrator, a dispute falls outside the scope of the Convention, the existence of a preliminary issue which the court must resolve in order to determine the dispute cannot, whatever that issue may be, justify application of the Convention.
27 It would also be contrary to the principle of legal certainty [...] to vary according to the existence or otherwise of a preliminary issue, which might be raised at any time by the parties. 28 It follows that, in the case before the Court, the fact that a preliminary issue relates to the existence or validity of the arbitration agreement does not affect the exclusion from the scope of the Convention of a dispute concerning the appointment of an arbitrator.'

[11] CJEU, Case C-391/95 *Van Uden Maritime BV (t/a Van Uden Africa Line v Kommanditgesellschaft in Firma Deco-Line* [1998] ECR I-7091.

[12] The case was decided in respect of the Brussels Convention but the same principle applies to the Brussels I Regulation.

[13] CJEU, Case C-185/07 *Allianz SpA (formerly Riunione Adriatica di Sicurtà SpA) and Generali Assicurazioni Generali SpA v West Tankers Inc* [2009] ECR I-663.

whatsoever, and no mechanism to address conflicting arbitration awards and judgments, appeared to be irrelevant to the decision. The result is commercially unattractive, since it seems that now court decisions on the merits in which the validity of an arbitration clause was, or should have been, determined as a preliminary question can freely circulate within the EU under the Regulation. This obviously jeopardizes arbitral proceedings on the same issue and the recognition and enforcement of an arbitral award;[14] not to mention that this has the potential to undermine the application of the New York Convention. The situation encourages a party seeking to escape from an arbitration agreement to allege (possibly in bad faith) its invalidity and bring proceedings on the merits in a Member State where it is likely to obtain a favourable decision.[15] The *lis pendens* rules of Brussels I block the court at the seat of the arbitration from ruling on the validity of an arbitration agreement. The seat court further has to recognise the decision of the court first seised under the mutual trust system of Brussels I. *West Tankers* therefore promptly added to a litany of decisions[16] which, far from promoting the internal market, smacked of the EU shooting the internal market in the foot. Even worse, whereas decisions such as *Gasser, Turner* and *Owusu* could, at least, be blamed on the wording of the Regulation and the CJEU's literal construction thereof, the CJEU decision to interpret the ambiguous arbitration exception so narrowly seemed to many not so much a result of the wording of the Regulation as a product of its own choice. The thin nature of the CJEU's reasoning in *West Tankers* and cursory reference to its prior case law doubtlessly added to the frostiness of the reception that the judgment received, although, as one must admit, it did not actually contradict the *Marc Rich* reasoning.

---

[14] European Commission, Impact Assessment to the Proposal, Accompanying document to the Proposal for a Regulation of the European Parliament and of the Council on jurisdiction and the recognition and enforcement of judgments in civil and commercial matters (Recast) (SEC(2010) 1547 final) para 2.4.1.1.

[15] UK Ministry of Justice, Impact Assessment on the Repeal and Replacement of Regulation (EC) 44/2001 (Brussels I) at 3.51. The MOJ Consultation on the Commission Proposal also criticised the result of the *West Tankers* ruling as excessively reducing the scope of the exclusion of arbitration from the Regulation: 'In particular, whenever a court characterises the subject matter of a claim brought before it as a matter within the scope of the Regulation, any issue as to the existence, scope or validity of an arbitration clause is a preliminary or incidental issue. Consequently the courts of an arbitral seat are powerless to protect the arbitration or take any action themselves [...]. Further, once a court, other than the one where the seat of the arbitration is located has rendered a judgment on any issue concerning the arbitration, it would appear that courts in every other Member State will have to recognise and enforce this decision, thereby undermining the role of the courts of the arbitral seat and the operation of the New York Convention more generally.' See also UK Ministry of Justice, 'Revision of the Brussels I Regulation - How should the UK approach Negotiations? Response to Consultation CP(R) 18/10' at 5, 79 and 81 f.

[16] See, in particular, CJEU, Case C-116/02 *Erich Gasser GmbH v MISAT srl* [2003] ECR I-14693; Case C-281/02 *Owusu v Jackson (t/a Villa Holidays Bal Inn Villas)* [2005] ECR I-1383; Case C-159/02 *Turner v Grovit* [2005] ECR I-3565.

Therefore, under the present legal framework, court proceedings dealing with the validity of arbitration agreements as a preliminary issue in proceedings which are civil and commercial are subject to Brussels I, even if the acting court has been seised in a torpedo action, with the risk of abusive circumvention of the agreed arbitration, and expensive and long parallel court and arbitration proceedings with potentially conflicting results. The courts at the arbitral seat are unable to determine the jurisdiction of the arbitrators as this determination is in the hands of the court first seised. They are prevented from taking any action. Neither the effectiveness of an arbitration agreement nor a transparent and predictable coordination of court and arbitral proceedings is guaranteed.[17]

Meanwhile, none of this is likely to have any effect on the arbitration process itself. Indeed, in *West Tankers*, West Tankers obtained negative declaratory relief in the arbitral proceedings and the Court of Appeal ruled[18] that it had the power under the Arbitration Act 1996 to order judgment to be entered in the terms of the arbitral award. That measure, designed at least in part to produce an English judgment that might trigger a defence to the recognition of any irreconcilable Italian court judgment pursuant to Article 34(3) of the Regulation, would, if successfully relied upon, prevent the recognition of the Italian judgment in England but not, apparently, in other EU Member States. In the meantime, the arbitral award itself would appear to qualify for recognition and enforcement under the New York Convention, notwithstanding the Italian judgment.

Against such a background, the need for clarification and reform of the arbitration exception is essential and urgent. However, while future legislative action is widely supported, fears have been expressed as regards the impact of any legislative action on the EU as a competitive place for arbitration and on the effectiveness of the New York Convention. Therefore, views diverge on the best way forward – either to coordinate better and 'actively promote arbitration agreements by avoiding parallel proceedings and abusive litigation tactics' or to 'exclude arbitration more broadly from the scope of the Regulation.'[19]

---

[17] See also the UK Consultation Paper CP 18/10 'Revision of the Brussels I Regulation – How should the UK approach the negotiations' at 20 ff.

[18] [2012] EWCA Civ 27.

[19] Proposal for a Regulation of the European Parliament and of the Council on jurisdiction and the recognition and enforcement of judgments in civil and commercial matters (Recast) (COM(2010) 748 final) at 5, point 2.

III. OPTIONS FOR AND STEPS TOWARDS A NEW SOLUTION

The Heidelberg Report[20] proposed a deletion of the arbitration exception,[21] combined with an exclusive head of jurisdiction for ancillary proceedings in favour of the courts of the seat of arbitration and a *lis pendens* mechanism favouring the seat courts to decide on the validity of arbitration clauses. Subsequently, the Commission's Green Paper suggested that the way forward might rather lie in a reduction of the scope of the arbitration exclusion by a partial deletion thereof.[22]

Indeed, in the Green Paper, several suggestions were made, in particular to include proceedings in support of arbitration within the scope of the Brussels regime, potentially in combination with a special jurisdictional rule granting exclusive jurisdiction to the courts of the Member State of the seat of arbitration, either directly or via agreement of the parties.[23] Further, as court imposed provisional measures ensure the effectiveness of arbitration, particularly until the arbitral tribunal is established, it was suggested that these should also be included. A partial deletion of the arbitration exception was also seen as a way of ensuring the recognition of judgments deciding on the validity of an arbitration agreement or setting aside an arbitral award. Further, it was perceived as a means of securing the recognition and enforcement of judgments merging an arbitration award, and preventing parallel proceedings between courts and arbitral tribunals drawing different conclusions as to the validity of an arbitration agreement. Further suggestions were made for: closer cooperation between the courts seised; the coordination of proceedings before a court and an arbitral tribunal by giving priority to the courts of the Member State of the seat of arbitration for questions regarding the existence, validity, and scope of an arbitration agreement; and a uniform conflict rule regarding the validity of arbitration agreements. It was also acknowledged that the recognition and enforcement of arbitral awards under the New York Convention,[24] which requires the courts of the Contracting States to give effect to a private agreement to arbitrate and to recognize and enforce an arbitral award made in another Contracting State, should be fostered, for example by a rule declaring judgments unenforceable if incompatible with the arbitral award. All Member

---

[20] B Hess, T Pfeiffer and P Schlosser, *Heidelberg Report* (n 5).

[21] B Hess, T Pfeiffer and P Schlosser, *Heidelberg Report* (n 5) 106 ff.

[22] European Commission, Green Paper on the Review of Council Regulation (EC) No 44/2001 on Jurisdiction and the Recognition and Enforcement of Judgments in Civil and Commercial Matters, COM(2009) 175 final.

[23] Green Paper (n 22) 8-9.

[24] New York Convention on the Recognition and Enforcement of Foreign Arbitral Awards 1958.

States are party to the New York Convention and it is also widely ratified throughout the rest of the world.[25]

However, a notably different approach has been taken in the Commission Proposal. The impact assessment accompanying the Proposal[26] presented three options for legislative reform, of which the status quo (Policy Option 1) was clearly acknowledged as unsatisfactory and capable of facilitating abusive litigation tactics.[27] The remaining options were:

First, an extension of the arbitration exception (Policy Option 2) to 'any court proceedings related to arbitration proceedings', particularly those in which the validity of an arbitration agreement is contested. The potential side-effects of Option 2 were, however, not encouraging: no protection from parallel court and arbitration proceedings or 'sabotage' tactics; inefficiency; uncertainty for businesses; and imposing an obstacle to the creation of a genuine area of justice through 're-nationalisation' of recognition and enforcement.[28] A total exclusion of arbitration with no mechanism for coordination between courts and arbitration at all could therefore lead to uncertainty and unpredictability – particularly if it is not accompanied by any provisions explaining whether, for instance, a judgment from the courts of a Member State ostensibly in violation of an arbitration agreement is entitled to enforcement in other Member States.

Second, an inclusion of EU-wide uniform rules for selected aspects of arbitration (Policy Option 3), to 'enhance the effectiveness of arbitration agreements'. The inclusion of a specific *lis pendens* mechanism (stay of proceedings in favour of a court at the seat of the arbitration or an arbitral tribunal dealing with issues of existence, validity or effects of an arbitration

---

[25] See http://www.uncitral.org/uncitral/en/uncitral_texts/arbitration/NYConvention_status.html.

[26] Impact Assessment (n 14).

[27] Proposal (n 19) at 4: 'The interface between arbitration and litigation needs to be improved. Arbitration is excluded from the scope of the Regulation. However, by challenging an arbitration agreement before a court, a party may effectively undermine the arbitration agreement and create a situation of inefficient parallel court proceedings which may lead to irreconcilable resolutions of the dispute. This leads to additional costs and delays, undermines the predictability of dispute resolution and creates incentives for abusive litigation tactics.'

[28] Impact Assessment (n 14) at 38: '[...] However, the general problem of parallel court and arbitration proceedings and risk of conflicting decisions would remain. Moreover, the total exclusion of all judgments in cases involving an arbitration agreement from the scope of the Regulation would enable cynical litigants to 'torpedo' the recognition and enforcement of a judgment simply by claiming that the parties have concluded an arbitration agreement. Furthermore, option 2 would go against the overall objective of creating a genuine area of justice in the European Union because it would re-nationalise part of the rules which are today harmonised on the European level. Judgments which currently circulate under Regulation Brussels I would cease to do so; their recognition and enforcement in another Member State would again be governed by the national laws of the 27 Member States. This would constitute a step backwards in the creation of a European area of civil justice which should be avoided.'

agreement) to prevent parallel proceedings and abusive litigation tactics has ultimately been favoured by the Commission.[29]

In its Proposal, the Commission opted for a partial deletion of the arbitration exception in Article 1(2)(d)[30] and to introduce in Article 29(4) a special *lis pendens* provision[31] to solve the issue of parallel proceedings, especially in light of potential 'torpedo' actions but also more generally to prevent parallel arbitration and court proceedings. A further specific rule was introduced in Article 33(3) to establish an EU wide concept of 'seisure' of an arbitral tribunal, an essential condition on which the application of Article 29(4) can be based.[32] Article 36 of the Proposal[33] on provisional measures responds to the *Van Uden*[34] decision of the CJEU and grants jurisdiction for such measures to Member State courts even though an arbitral tribunal decides on the substance of the matter. Recital (11)[35] is meant to clarify that the deletion of the arbitration exception is very narrow and

[29] Impact Assessment (n 14) at 40: 'Arbitration agreements would also be made more effective. Any other court whose jurisdiction is contested on the basis of the existence of an arbitration agreement would have to suspend proceedings on the matter insofar as the question of the existence, validity, or effects of the agreement is brought before the courts of the seat of the arbitration in the Union or before an arbitral tribunal. This will reduce the risk of parallel proceedings and abusive litigation tactics by parties seeking to evade an arbitration clause.'

[30] Art 1(2)(d) of the Proposal:
'The Regulation does not apply to [...]
(d) arbitration, save as provided for in Articles 29, paragraph 4 and 33, paragraph 3.'

[31] Art 29(4) of the Proposal: 'Where the agreed or designated seat of an arbitration is in a Member State, the courts of another Member State whose jurisdiction is contested on the basis of an arbitration agreement shall stay proceedings once the courts of the Member State where the seat of the arbitration is located or the arbitral tribunal have been seised of proceedings to determine, as their main object or as an incidental question, the existence, validity or effects of that arbitration agreement.

This paragraph does not prevent the court whose jurisdiction is contested from declining jurisdiction in the situation referred to above if its national law so prescribes.

Where the existence, validity or effects of the arbitration agreement are established, the court seised shall decline jurisdiction.

This paragraph does not apply in disputes concerning matters referred to in Sections 3, 4, and 5 of Chapter II.'

[32] Art 33(3) of the Proposal:
'For the purposes of this Section, an arbitral tribunal is deemed to be seised when a party has nominated an arbitrator or when a party has requested the support of an institution, authority or a court for the tribunal's constitution.'

[33] Art 36:
'Application may be made to the courts of a Member State for such provisional, including protective, measures as may be available under the law of that State, even if, under this Regulation, the courts of another Member State or an arbitral tribunal have jurisdiction as to the substance of the matter.'

[34] See (n 11).

[35] Recital (11) of the Proposal:
'(11) This Regulation does not apply to arbitration, save in the limited case provided for therein. In particular, it does not apply to the form, existence, validity or effects of arbitration agreements, the powers of the arbitrators, the procedure before arbitral tribunals, and the validity, annulment, and recognition and enforcement of arbitral awards.'

limited to the circumstances described in Articles 29(4), 33(3) and 36 of the Proposal; and, indeed, appears to suggest that, otherwise, issues relating to the validity and effects of an arbitration clause fall outside the ambit of the Regulation. Recital (20)[36] contains further explanations of the mechanism of Article 29(4) and the determination of the seat of arbitration.

IV. ISSUES ARISING FROM THE COMMISSION PROPOSAL

First and foremost, the Commission's attempt to clarify the interface between arbitration and the Brussels I regime deserves credit. The Commission Proposal reveals little support for *West Tankers* and its commercially unattractive outcome. Between the options of an extension of the arbitration exception and the inclusion of limited specific provisions to coordinate the interface between arbitration and parallel court proceedings, it chooses the latter – coordination. The Commission claims that the proposed rules will enhance the effectiveness of arbitration agreements and guarantee the attractiveness of the EU as a place for arbitration. Although this approach seems the right one, the question remains whether the suggested provisions in their current wording achieve this goal. Indeed, the closer one looks at the proposed provisions, examined below, the less sure one can be as to what is and what is not excluded from the Regulation.[37]

---

[36] Recital (20) of the Proposal:
'The effectiveness of arbitration agreements should also be improved in order to give full effect to the will of the parties. This should be the case, in particular, where the agreed or designated seat of an arbitration is in a Member State. This Regulation should therefore contain special rules aimed at avoiding parallel proceedings and abusive litigation tactics in those circumstances. The seat of the arbitration should refer to the seat selected by the parties or the seat designated by an arbitral tribunal, by an arbitral institution or by any other authority directly or indirectly chosen by the parties.'

[37] For instance, the UK Ministry of Justice had read the Commission Proposal as failing to reinforce the protection for arbitration clauses and failing to meet its desire to widen the scope of the arbitration exclusion: 'The Government notes that the Commission has not adopted the approach advocated by the UK in response to the Commission's consultation, namely a reinforcement of the current exclusion of arbitration from the scope of the Brussels I Regulation in order to remove the entirety of the arbitral process from the scope of the Regulation. [...] The Government reserves its position on the viability of the Commission's proposals until it has consulted extensively with the arbitration community. One factor which the Government will weigh carefully is the extent to which the Commission's proposals could potentially create problems by because they are based on the extended scope of EU competence in this area which has resulted from the West Tankers decision'. UK Ministry of Justice, 'Revision of the Brussels I Regulation – How should the UK approach the negotiations, CP 18/10' at 22, point 48, 49.

A. The mechanism of Article 29(4)

1. The lis pendens rule

Article 29(4) of the Proposal coordinates parallel proceedings between a court, which may, in many cases, be a 'torpedo court', and the arbitral tribunal or the courts at the seat of the arbitration. It provides for a special *lis pendens* rule in cases in which a Member State court has been seised with proceedings dealing with the validity of arbitration clauses, either as a preliminary or main issue. If one party contests jurisdiction on the basis of an arbitration agreement, the court seised has to stay proceedings once the courts at the seat of arbitration or the arbitral tribunal are seised.[38] The jurisdiction of the 'torpedo' court needs to be actively challenged and the arbitral tribunal or courts of the seat must be seised, otherwise proceedings are not stayed pursuant to Article 29(4),[39] even if they contravene an arbitration agreement. The provision tries to avoid a free-for-all between courts and arbitrators, which would occur if it was left to the discretion of national courts to determine the relationship between proceedings before them and arbitration. The proposal strengthens the competence of arbitrators and of courts of the seat of arbitration to determine the validity of arbitration clauses. Article 29(4) should therefore help to prevent parallel court and arbitral proceedings and inconsistent decisions from the outset.

The solution to include a *lis pendens* provision has important advantages compared to a norm granting exclusive jurisdiction in favour of the courts of the seat of the arbitration: it does not block supportive state court proceedings, in particular the obtaining of evidence. If assistance of the arbitral tribunal in the taking of evidence would be within the exclusive competence of the courts at the seat of the arbitration 'the parties would not be able to directly request judicial assistance in the state where the evidence is located', as Illmer and Steinbrück have remarked,[40] but would have to make an official request for cross-border judicial assistance. At the same time, jurisdiction for judging the validity of the arbitral agreement is incidentally conferred on the courts of the seat of the arbitration, as, once seised, they have the power to exclusively determine this validity, albeit in the limited circumstances of Article 29(4).[41] This reflects the fact that the

---

[38] This is different from art II(3) New York Convention.

[39] Neither would the court refer to arbitration pursuant to art II(3) New York Convention as this referral also presupposes a request by one party.

[40] M Illmer/ B Steinbrück, *Submission to the European Commission regarding the Green Paper COM(2009) 175* http://ec.europa.eu/justice/news/consulting_public/0002/contributions/civil_society_ngo_academics_others/max_planck_institut_fur_auslandisches_und_internationales _ privatrecht_en.pdf.

[41] See also M Illmer, 'Brussels I and Arbitration Revisited – The European Commission's Proposal COM(2010) 748 final' (2011) 75 RabelsZ 645 (658).

New York Convention also gives the court at the seat special powers.[42] The granting of an exclusive power to intervene at an early stage and to render a decision on the validity of an arbitration agreement potentially even before arbitral proceedings begin can be beneficial in light of legal certainty and procedural economy.

2. The prioritisation of the seat of the arbitration

Article 29(4) refers to the Member State courts at the 'agreed or designated seat of an arbitration.' According to Recital (20), the seat of the arbitration should refer to the seat selected by the parties or the seat designated either by an arbitral tribunal, an arbitral institution or by any other authority directly or indirectly chosen by the parties.

One might ask if the grounding of Article 29(4) in the seat is justified as it is seemingly attempting to localise, or confer too much significance on a territorial connection in an internationalised and, some would argue, delocalised process. However, this localisation seems the only sensible choice. The proximity of the seat court to the arbitration proceedings justifies its prominent role. Its intervention at an early stage fosters procedural economy, given the fact that the seat court is also the forum to set aside or suspend an arbitral award.[43] It is a form of 'home country control'.[44] Unlike domestic arbitration, the determination of the seat of an international arbitration is one of the core issues, as this will be the place whose laws give a framework to the proceedings and where the award will be issued.[45] Moreover, the seat court is predictable for the parties and can be determined by them in their arbitration agreement. They can thus avoid unhappy surprises due to the interference of a state court that is hostile to arbitration by choosing the 'right' seat country.

It is not clear though, if a seat can be implicitly agreed upon for the purposes of Article 29(4) (eg by a choice of law clause, previous course of dealings or trade practice). It is also unclear which law decides if the seat has been agreed upon or whether the latter determination should follow an autonomous, 'factual' concept.

It is further questionable whether the mechanism of Article 29(4) can be triggered if a seat of the arbitration was not agreed upon by the parties and yet has not been determined in accordance with Recital (20), but where the

---

[42] See art V(1)(e) New York Convention.

[43] See art V(1)(e) New York Convention: '(e) The award has not yet become binding on the parties, or has been set aside or suspended by a competent authority of the country in which, or under the law of which, that award was made.'

[44] See also L Radicati di Brozolo, 'Arbitration and the Draft Revised Brussels I Regulation: Seeds of Home Country Control and of Harmonisation?' (2011) 7 JPIL 423 (425).

[45] G Born, *International Arbitration and Forum Selection Agreements: Drafting and Enforcing* (2nd edn, Kluwer 2006) 61.

arbitral tribunal has nonetheless already been seised.[46] Pursuant to Article 33(3) of the Proposal, seisure occurs with the nomination of an arbitrator by a party or when a party has requested the support of an institution, authority or a court for the tribunal's constitution. Such nomination of an arbitrator does not necessarily require the determination of the seat, as several national laws show.[47] However the first condition of Article 29(4) suggests that the provision does not yet apply under these particular circumstances, as it requires establishment of the seat (it reads 'where the agreed or designated seat of an arbitration is in a Member State").

Article 29(4) applies only if the seat court is located in a Member State. Otherwise a third State court's determination of the validity of an arbitration clause would have priority over the decisions of Member States' courts. Nevertheless, if the designated seat is in a non-Member State that is party to the New York Convention, an arbitral award rendered in that non-Member State would, in principle, qualify for recognition and enforcement in other Contracting States to the New York Convention; and arguably, a mechanism should exist to prevent the delivery of a potentially conflicting judgment of the courts of a Member State.

It must also be noted that there is no uniform assessment as to the validity of arbitration agreements. As the validity test for arbitration agreements is rudimentary in the New York Convention, and no common choice of law rule exists, there is no harmonised approach for the control of the seat courts.[48]

3. The concept of seisure

Article 29(4) applies only where jurisdiction of a Member State court is contested and if either the court at the seat of arbitration is seised (see Article 33(1)) or arbitral proceedings are already underway. The determination of the point in time when an arbitral tribunal is seised is subject to divergent tests in national legal systems, but Article 33(3) gives uniform guidance here, stating that an arbitral tribunal is 'deemed to be seised, when a party has nominated an arbitrator or when a party has requested the support of an institution, authority or a court for the tribunal's constitution.'

The wording of Article 29(4) is not equivalent to Article 32(2), [49] which

[46] As suggested by M Illmer (n 41) 645 (661).

[47] See eg sec. 2(4), 18 of the English Arbitration Act 1996 or § 1025(3), 1035 of the German Code of Civil Procedure.

[48] L Radicati di Brozolo (n 44) 425.

[49] Art 32(2): 'With the exception of agreements governed by Sections 3, 4 and 5 of this Chapter, where an agreement referred to in Article 23 confers exclusive jurisdiction to a court or the courts of a Member State, the courts of other Member States shall have no jurisdiction over the dispute until such time as the court or courts designated in the agreement decline their jurisdiction.' Hence, this rule applies irrespective of whether the court putatively chosen by the clause was first seised or not. To compare with art 29(4) see (n 31).

deals with *lis pendens* in the case of exclusive choice of court agreements. It is indeed questionable whether Article 29(4) establishes a parallel system of priority to Article 32(2), or whether it applies a 'first seised' approach.[50] The wording of Article 29(4) seems unclear in this respect, as it is drafted in a somewhat more complicated manner than Article 32(2).

It is conceivable that Article 29(4) could be understood as suggesting that the mechanism provided is triggered only when a court has been, chronologically, seised 'first'. This means that the seat court is only then called into action and given 'exclusive competence' under the Regulation to determine the validity of an arbitration agreement. So any time the seat court is called 'first', this would not be a 29(4) case and would therefore be outside the scope of the Regulation even if a torpedo action were to be initiated 'subsequently'. Such an approach would, at least, render it clearer from the outset whether the courts of a Member State were competent to conclusively determine the validity and effectiveness of an arbitration clause.

A different, and apparently more natural reading would be to interpret Article 29(4) as establishing a system of priority of the court at the seat of arbitration or the arbitral tribunal 'once' one of the latter has been seised, regardless of whether the non-seat/'torpedo' court has been seised 'first' or 'second', as long as the defendant in these proceedings challenges the jurisdiction of the courts of another Member State.

Any non-seat court would then have to stay proceedings whether the seat court or arbitral tribunal has been seised before or after it. Under this interpretation, the situation would also be covered in which, for instance, an arbitral tribunal has been seised first, e.g. by the nomination of an arbitrator by party A pursuant to Article 33(3) of the Proposal without a dispute as to the validity of the arbitration clause and in which party B subsequently seised a court outside the seat (e.g. intending a torpedo action) the jurisdiction of which is then contested by party A. This interpretation makes more sense, as under the 'first seised' idea, a torpedo action in the non-seat forum after the seisure of an arbitral tribunal could not be prevented and many cases of parallel litigation would persist. The idea of Article 29(4) rather seems to be to a general prevention of a court (other than the seat court) from taking a decision on the validity of an arbitration clause where either the seat court or the arbitral tribunal have been seised, regardless of the order.

4. *To stay or to decline jurisdiction*

According to the first sentence of Article 29(4) of the Proposal, courts have to stay proceedings pending a decision at the seat of the arbitration or before the arbitral tribunal as to the validity of the arbitration clause; and

---

[50] See also M Illmer (n 41) 645 (661).

then to decline jurisdiction once an arbitration clause is upheld (Article 29(4)3). While one can see the sense in this mechanism, it is less obvious why, as the second sentence of Article 29(4) envisages, national courts should be given, at the outset, the choice to stay or to decline jurisdiction depending upon their national law. This seemingly reflects the approach of countries such as France, which will decline jurisdiction once the arbitral tribunal is seised.[51] This rule will, however, encourage a non-uniform approach due to the divergences between national laws. On the other hand, it may be that the procedural differences between national laws regarding their approach to the seisure of foreign arbitral tribunals or the courts of the seat are irreconcilable, so Article 29(4) goes as far as it possibly could, given that the Proposal needs the support of the Member States in the Council.

5. Time limits

In contrast to Article 29(2) of the Proposal, according to which a court first seised shall, in cases falling under Article 29(1),[52] establish its jurisdiction within six months except where exceptional circumstances make this impossible, no time limits are provided for under Article 29(4).[53] Although the party challenging the jurisdiction of a 'torpedo' court will usually have an interest in quickly triggering the mechanism of Article 29(4), the seat court or arbitral tribunal's priority in taking a decision is not limited by any time bar. The same is true under Article 32(2) of the Proposal in the case of an exclusive choice of court agreement.

It is hard to imagine that more time is needed to verify the validity of a choice of court or arbitration agreement than to verify jurisdiction based on another head of jurisdiction. Also, the fact that Article 29(4) explicitly states that the seat court or arbitral tribunal is not limited to deciding on 'jurisdiction' or 'competence' only, but that the latter can be verified as a preliminary issue in potentially time consuming proceedings on the merits or other issues[54] does not justify the omission of a time limit, as the same is true under Article 29(1). By alleging that there is a valid arbitration clause, a party can effectively deploy a torpedo of its own by bringing proceedings in the courts of another Member State to a grinding halt.

---

[51] Art 1448(1) Code de Procédure Civile.

[52] ie where proceedings involving the same cause of action and between the same parties are brought in the courts of different Member States.

[53] Art 29(2) does not indicate any sanctions or consequences for failure to meet this six month deadline. Given the idea behind art 29(1) and (2), the natural consequence should be that the court that did not have priority is reattributed the power to decide upon jurisdiction itself.

[54] Art 29(4) applies where the courts of the seat or the arbitral tribunal have been seised of proceedings 'to determine *as their main object or as an incidental question*, the existence, validity or effects of that arbitration agreement.'

6. Consumer, employment and insurance contracts

Article 29(4)4 of the Proposal makes it clear that the *lis pendens* mechanism of Article 29 does not apply to consumer, employment and insurance contracts. One can, of course, see the protectionist desire behind the provision, which allows a consumer suing in its home courts to subject the validity of an arbitration agreement to the scrutiny of those courts and not the arbitral tribunal or courts of the seat allegedly chosen. Arguably however, a consumer may be less protected if Article 29(4) does not apply to him than if it does. Although the competent court will normally be the consumer's home court, the exclusion from the application of the first sentence of Article 29(4) leaves consumers to the vagaries of national law and exposes them to the risks of parallel court and arbitration proceedings, as by virtue of Article 1(2)(d) and Recital (11), arbitration is otherwise outside the terms of the Regulation.

Moreover, if a business sues a consumer in the courts of a Member State in ostensible breach of an arbitration agreement, the consumer is apparently deprived of the mechanism in Article 29(4) to challenge the jurisdiction of the court on this basis and to subject the determination of the validity of the clause to the scrutiny of the arbitral tribunal or courts of the seat putatively chosen. One might expect that any provision in favour of weaker parties should be worded so as to prevent a party acting in the course of business reaping the benefit of bringing torpedo proceedings in the courts of a Member State without being subject to the coordination mechanism in Article 29(4).

B. Consequences of the application of Article 29(4)

Article 29(4) is clearly tailored to be an exception from the arbitration exception for the sake of coordinating parallel proceedings. It seeks to prevent and quickly solve problems arising from court actions bypassing the efficacy of arbitration agreements. While there are some uncertainties as to its meaning and application, there are further doubts as to the consequences once Article 29(4) has been triggered.

1. Binding effect upon the 'torpedo' court

If the arbitration clause is upheld by either the seat court or the arbitral tribunal, Article 29(4)3 states that this decision is binding upon the 'torpedo' court, obliging it to decline jurisdiction. According to Article 29(4)1 and 3 a torpedo action is effectively stopped and the situation in *West Tankers* is avoided insofar as it leads to a lack of protection due to the seat courts' inability to issue anti-suit injunctions, which were held incompatible with the Brussels regime.

If the invalidity of the arbitration clause has been established by either the seat court or the arbitral tribunal, the 'torpedo' court's jurisdiction suspension will, presumably, be lifted, although this is not clearly mentioned in Article 29(4). Otherwise, although the 'torpedo' court is competent under the jurisdiction rules of Brussels I, and the invalidity of the arbitration clause is established, the plaintiff of the 'torpedo' court proceedings would be left without judicial protection and no proceedings on the merits would take place.

It is not clear though, what would happen if the clause is considered invalid by the seat court but not by the arbitral tribunal and arbitral proceedings continue in parallel. It might be that the arbitration is at some point challenged, again in the seat courts, which have already ruled on the invalidity of the agreement, but meanwhile, it seems that the 'torpedo' court still has to stay pursuant to Article 29(4). Although the invalidity of the agreement has been established by the seat court, court proceedings on the merits before the 'torpedo' court would still be blocked.

Also, the decision of the arbitral tribunal on the validity of an arbitration agreement is binding on the 'torpedo' or non-seat court, as Article 29(4)3 of the Proposal makes clear. Much weight is therefore given to the arbitrators' determination of the validity of an arbitration agreement.[55] For the first time, the relationship between a national and an arbitral court is directly addressed in the Brussels I Regulation.

2. Mutual trust for the decision of the seat court in all Member States

There is, however, a measure of uncertainty as to whether a decision of the seat court confirming the validity of an arbitration agreement is recognised under the mutual trust principle of the Brussels I regime in Member States other than the one whose courts have been seised in a 'torpedo' action. Although Article 29(4) appears expressly to recognise the competence of the courts of the seat, Recital (11) suggests that the decision of the courts of the seat on arbitration matters is wholly outside the scope of the Regulation, which, if taken literally, would appear to mean that the resulting ruling as to the validity of the arbitration agreement does *not* have *res judicata* status.

Aside from the fact that Recital (11), second sentence, excludes the question of the validity of arbitration clauses from the scope of the Regulation, it would be a radical step forwards if a decision of the seat court could qualify as a Brussels I judgment in which it decides upon the validity of the arbitration clause as the *main* issue of the proceedings. The prior CJEU jurisprudence has made it clear that a decision which does, as a main issue,

---

[55] This binding effect does not extend to the seat courts, eg in proceedings setting aside an arbitral award or regarding recognition and enforcement.

deal with an arbitration related matter, cannot circulate under the mutual trust system of Brussels I.[56] Furthermore, it seems perfectly possible to confer the power to stay on the courts of a Member State in the face of proceedings in the seat, *without* giving judgments from the seat the benefit of mutual trust and free circulation around the EU. By analogy, the new power in the Proposal to stay proceedings where the courts of a non-Member State are first seised patently does not make the judgments of the courts of the non-Member State subject to enforcement under the Regulation.[57]

The ruling of the seat-court will usually, it would seem, concern a subject matter that is outside the ambit of the Regulation even if the question of the validity of an arbitration clause is dealt with as a *preliminary* question. Usually, the actions of the seat court are limited to typical arbitration related issues, such as the nomination of an arbitrator. The validity of an arbitration agreement could then well be a 'preliminary issue', but not in the sense that the term is used after *West Tankers*. It is a preliminary question, but arises prior to an action where the subject matter is still arbitration related. It seems unlikely that the seat court will have jurisdiction to decide on the merits of the dispute between the parties (eg a damages claim) and that the validity of an arbitration agreement would be dealt with as an incidental question thereof. The mere fact that the seat of the arbitration is located in a certain country does not mean that the courts at the seat would have jurisdiction to decide on the merits. Indeed, to interpret Article 29(4) as conferring the power to the seat court to also decide on the merits of the lawsuit (without any other jurisdictional base under the Regulation) would go too far. There can be no intention for the Regulation generally to allow the enforcement of the decisions of the courts of the seat of the arbitration in support of the arbitration process. So whether the judgment is as to the validity of an arbitration agreement only or about the appointment of an arbitrator and, as a preliminary question, the validity of the agreement, one might think that the determination of the binding effect of an arbitration award lies outside the ambit of the Regulation for enforcement purposes.

On the other hand, it seems strange that a decision on a matter in respect of which Article 29(4) clearly confers exclusive jurisdiction on an EU court would not be subject to recognition under Brussels I. What, it may be asked, is the value in the courts of another Member State staying their proceedings if the ruling of the courts of the seat on the validity of the arbitration clause is not binding and conclusive? If the decision of the seat court is not subject to the Brussels I mutual trust regime, only the already seised 'torpedo' court is directly bound by this judgment pursuant to Article 29(4)3 and has to

---

[56] See the CJEU case law quoted above.
[57] See art 34 of the Proposal.

decline jurisdiction. Once this has happened however, it seems that a (new) torpedo action would no longer be blocked, if the seat court decision has no EU wide *res iudicata* effect. This maintains the unsatisfactory situation that an arbitration clause that is considered to be valid by the court at the seat can be considered invalid by a court of another Member State, with the attendant consequence of parallel proceedings and irreconcilable judgments. Only on-going arbitration proceedings could still block a new 'torpedo' action, provided that Article 29(4)1 is to be understood in the sense mentioned above,[58] ie as a rule giving priority to the seat court and arbitral tribunal over any other EU court, regardless of whether a 'torpedo' court is first or subsequently seised.

3. Mutual trust for the decision of the arbitral tribunal

It should also be noted though that there is no mutual trust in the arbitral tribunal's decision in subsequent court proceedings setting aside an arbitral award or regarding recognition and enforcement. Its effects are limited to the suspension of the 'torpedo' court's jurisdiction. It would appear that the arbitral tribunal's findings on the validity of an arbitration clause can be tested again in annulment proceedings before the court at the seat or enforcement proceedings before any court

4. Relationship between Article 29(4), Article 1(2)(d) and Recital (11)

The above discussion indicates that the interaction between Article 1(2)(d) and Recital (11), second sentence, and Article 29(4) is not terribly clear. Recital (11) suggests that the exclusion of arbitration in Article 1(2)(d) is very broad, stating that 'the Regulation does not apply to arbitration, save in the limited case provided for therein', and continues '[i]n particular, it does not apply to the form, existence, validity or effects of arbitration agreements, the powers of the arbitrators, the procedure before arbitral tribunals, and the validity, annulment, and recognition and enforcement of arbitral awards.' Article 29(4) describes one of the 'limited cases provided for' in the Regulation, where arbitration comes at least partially within its ambit.

For most arbitrators, and many commentators,[59] the second sentence of Recital (11) seems promising as it would appear to reverse *West Tankers*, insofar as it purports to exclude *in its entirety* questions as to the validity and effects of an arbitration clause, even though they are examined as a

---

[58] See supra IV A 3.

[59] See eg G Carducci, 'Arbitration, Anti-Suit Injunctions and Lis Pendens Under the European Jurisdiction Regulation and the New York Convention – Notes on West Tankers, the Revision of the Regulation and Perhaps of the Convention' (2011) 27(2) Arb. Int'l 179 ff.; A R Markus/ S Giroud, 'A Swiss Perspective on West Tankers and its Aftermath – What about the Lugano Convention?' (2010) 2 ASA Bulletin 28; P Pohjankoski, 'Can International Arbitration Remain Unaffected by EU Law?' (2010) 2 Helsinki Law Review 81 ff.

preliminary issue. This can, however, either mean that a judgment of the seat court is not a Regulation judgment or that in cases in which Article 29(4) applies, the judgment of a seat court is a Regulation judgment, since the exclusion in Article 1(2)(d) is stated to be subject to Article 29(4).

More generally, Recital (11) creates something of a paradox. First, if issues relating to the validity and effects of arbitration clauses are excluded from the Regulation, then how can civil and commercial proceedings in which the validity of an arbitration clause is at issue fall under the Brussels I Regulation at all? The answer, of course, is that the first sentence of Recital (11) uses the words 'save in the limited case provided for herein', but if issues as to the validity of arbitration clauses are excluded from the Regulation, one would expect it to be up to each Member State to determine what to do when confronted with an arbitration clause, and not to the Regulation.

5. *Relationship between Article 29(4) of the Proposal and Article II(3) New York Convention*

According to Article II(3) of the New York Convention 1958, the court of a Contracting State shall at the request of one party, when it is seised of an action in a matter in respect of which the parties have made an arbitration agreement,[60] refer the parties to arbitration, unless it finds that the said agreement is null and void, inoperative or incapable of being performed.[61] The New York Convention tries to ensure a priority of a transferral of the case to the arbitral tribunal if a party so requests, while giving the courts the option to verify the validity of an arbitration clause themselves. As the EU Member States are also Contracting States of the New York Convention, it is worth examining how the approach in Article 29(4) of the Proposal fits with the underlying ideas of Article II(3) New York Convention.

While in both cases, a State court is involved that has been seised by one of the parties and the jurisdiction of which has been contested by the other, the mechanism in Article II(3) 1958 New York Convention engages two fora, a court and the arbitral tribunal; Article 29(4) of the Commission Proposal potentially involves three: a ('torpedo') court, the seat court and the arbitral tribunal.

Under the New York Convention, if so requested by one party, a court 'shall' refer the parties to arbitration, but it is recognised that there is no discretion of the court if there is no doubt about the validity of the arbitration agreement. In case of doubt regarding the validity of an arbitration

---

[60] Within the meaning of art III(1) New York Convention 1958.
[61] In light of the 'pro-enforcement' attitude of the Convention, the provision is to be interpreted narrowly, and arbitration agreement should only be considered invalid in 'manifest cases'.

agreement, the New York Convention leaves it to the courts to decide upon the validity of an arbitration clause (whilst they may still refer the parties directly to arbitration). Article 29(4) of the Proposal obliges any non-seat Member State court to stay proceedings and deprives this court of the option to test the validity of an arbitration clause itself. Also, it confers, within the specific circumstances of Article 29(4), exclusive powers on the seat court which that court would not have under the New York Convention. The question therefore is whether Article 29(4) establishes a mechanism that is compatible with, or complementary to, the New York Convention.

It can be argued that the protection of arbitral proceedings, which is the underlying objective of the New York Convention, is further strengthened by the Commission initiative. Indeed, given that the 'torpedo' court has to stay its proceedings under Article 29(4) of the Proposal, if and when arbitral proceedings have been initiated, the result goes even beyond the protection that the New York Convention provides, as the latter allows for a verification of the arbitration agreement by the court itself. Similarly, the fact that the 'torpedo' court has to stay its proceedings under Article 29(4) if and when the seat court is seised to determine the validity of an arbitration clause, does not undermine the New York Convention. It can be argued that this approach supports arbitration, given that the seat court is unlikely to decide on the merits and is closer to the case in its decision making process.

On the other hand, if Article II of the New York Convention requires the courts of the signatory state to make *their own decision* as to whether an arbitration agreement is null and void, inoperative or incapable of being performed, the proposed Article 29(4) could thwart this rule.[62] For if a court of a Member State before which a dispute with regard to the merits has been brought considers the arbitration agreement to be valid, operative and capable of being performed, it would still have to bow to the decision of the seat court in this regard if the validity of the agreement is contested there. In other words, the decision on the validity is taken out of the hands of the court before which the arbitration agreement is invoked. This could lead to a situation in which the court has to violate its international obligations under the New York Convention because the Brussels I Regulation forces it to do so. This is notwithstanding the fact that Article 71 of the Regulation[63] currently defers to international conventions governing jurisdiction and the recognition and enforcement of foreign judgments. It is

---

[62] The following has already been remarked by M Lehmann, 'Anti-suit injunctions zum Schutz internationaler Schiedsverfahren und EuGVVO, Anmerkung EuGH, Urt. vom 10. Februar 2009 – Rs. C-185/07, *Allianz SpA und Generali Assicurazioni Generali SpA gegen West Tankers Inc.*' (2009) NJW 1645 ff.

[63] Art 82 of the Proposal, which is substantively unchanged as compared to the existing art 71 of the Regulation.

particularly unfortunate when seen from the perspective of a non-Member State that is a party to the New York Convention.

C. Relationship between judgments and arbitral awards

Within its sphere of application, Article 29(4) seemingly prevents irreconcilable decisions of an arbitral tribunal considering an arbitration agreement to be valid and of a 'torpedo' court holding it to be invalid. If any court decision other than from the seat court (which is unlikely to extend to the merits) is prevented, as long as either the seat court proceedings are pending or the arbitral proceedings are ongoing, the risk of conflicting decisions on the merits between an arbitral tribunal and a court is unlikely.

However, some questions remain. Although now likely to arise less frequently, it is uncertain whether a court judgment delivered in ostensible violation of an arbitration clause (perhaps because the court delivered judgment before the arbitral proceedings or courts of the seat were seised, or because the court failed to give effect to its obligations under Article 29(4)) could be refused enforcement in other Member States. This is somewhat unclear under the present version of the Regulation. The *Marc Rich* decision suggested that if the principal subject of a dispute is arbitration, it falls outside the Regulation entirely. The *Hoffmann* decision rather suggests that if an 'incidental' or 'preliminary' issue arises that for determination that would have fallen outside the scope of the Regulation, this brings the whole judgment outside Regulation.[64] However, the Court of Appeal's judgment in *The Wadi Sudr*[65] suggests that *Hoffmann* does not justify withholding recognition of a foreign court judgment ruling on the validity of an arbitration agreement, even where it is in ostensible breach of an arbitration agreement in the eyes of English law. This seems to follow, correctly, from the extremely narrow conception of the arbitration exception in *West Tankers*, but it can lead to a something of a mess if there is an irreconcilable arbitral award; and could conflict with a Member State's obligations under the New York Convention.

The new provisions in Recital (11) and Article 29(4) of the Proposal make the position even less apparent. Again, the question arises of whether the validity of an arbitration clause is a matter that is outside the scope of the Regulation lock, stock and barrel under the Proposal, or partially outside and partially inside.

One obvious way of addressing the problem would have been to include a provision stating that where an arbitral award was entitled to enforcement

---

[64] CJEU, Case C-145/86 *Hoffmann v Krieg* [1988] ECR 645.
[65] *National Navigation Co v Endesa Generacion SA (The Wadi Sudr)* [2009] EWCA Civ 1397; [2010] 1 Lloyd's Rep. 193.

under the New York Convention, a court could refuse to recognise and enforce a court judgment from a Member State that was irreconcilable with that award. The provision might be drafted along similar lines to Article 34(4) of the Brussels I Regulation.[66]

An alternative would be to grant the Member State where the arbitral award was issued exclusive jurisdiction to certify its enforceability as a precondition to free circulation within the EU. This, however, is somewhat radical as it would, in substance, convert arbitral awards into freely enforceable EU orders. Certainly, it seems somewhat difficult to reconcile with the exclusion of arbitration, and arbitral awards, from the Regulation.

Alternatively, if the intention is that the validity of arbitration agreements should be entirely excluded from the Regulation's scope (as the second sentence of Recital (11) suggests) then it could be argued that it is not inconsistent with that exclusion to have an express provision in Article 35 to the effect that a judgment of the courts of a Member State need not be recognised/ enforced in other Member States if it is in violation of an arbitration agreement – just as judgments from non-Member States fall outside the Regulation but there is a provision in Article 34(4) concerning their irreconcilability with judgments from Member States. After all, mutual trust would not operate in respect of a court judgment in violation of the arbitration agreement. The integrity of the arbitration process would be strengthened by such a provision and the current uncertainty as to the status of court judgments in violation of arbitral awards would be alleviated.

D. Arbitration in a non-Member State

Lord Hoffmann's request in the House of Lords for a preliminary ruling in *West Tankers* had noted that 'the European Community is engaged not only with regulating commerce between Member States but also in competing with the rest of the world.'[67] Yet, the Commission is effectively powerless to prevent the courts of a non-Member State from exercising parallel jurisdiction, refusing to enforce judgments from the courts of Member States exercising jurisdiction under the Brussels I Regulation and issuing anti-suit injunctions directed at the pursuit of proceedings in the courts of Member States.

At least there is a limited mechanism to deal with *lis pendens* in the courts of a non-Member State in Article 34 of the Commission Proposal,

---

[66] Which provides that a judgment shall not be recognised 'if it is irreconcilable with an earlier judgment given in another Member State or in a third State involving the same cause of action and between the same parties, provided that the earlier judgment fulfills the conditions necessary for its recognition in the Member State addressed'.

[67] [2007] UKHL 4; [2007] 1 Lloyd's Rep. 391, n 21.

but in the arbitration context, no provision is made for the courts of a Member State to stay their proceedings in favour of arbitration in a non-Member State. The first question, therefore, is whether the courts of a Member State have power to stay proceedings in favour of arbitration in a non-Member State at all. If not (and no such power is expressly provided in the Proposal) then does this mean that the courts of a Member State are competent, within the sphere of the Regulation, to assert jurisdiction notwithstanding the arbitration clause; that, arguably, they must accept jurisdiction conferred on them by the Regulation and, if so, is their resulting judgment entitled to enforcement in the courts of EU Member States? How is this to be reconciled with the New York Convention obligations of Member States in Article II(3)? Or, is it correct to say that, by virtue of the second sentence of Recital (11), there is no mutual trust between Member States in the interpretation of arbitration clauses; and, instead, each Member State is left to its own devices in determining whether to stay its proceedings in the face of an arbitration clause for a non-Member State; and there is no obligation to enforce judgments from the courts of Member States interpreting such clauses?[68] This latter view is probably correct, but it still means that there is no EU mechanism to address arbitration clauses in a non-Member State, prevent parallel proceedings and ensure uniform solutions across the EU for the treatment of such clauses. Moreover, it is in stark contrast to the fact that the jurisdiction to decide on the validity of arbitration agreements is concentrated at the seat court where the seat is in an EU Member State. Arguably, if the seat is outside of the EU, it would be impossible to confer exclusive competence on the non-Member State seat courts, there being no 'mutual trust' in the decisions of non-Member States. It would however not be beyond the imagination to enact a more limited mechanism to smooth out differences between the Member State courts with regard to the validity of arbitration agreements where the seat is in a non-Member State, for instance by setting out the terms under which a stay may be granted, by analogy to the proposal in Article 34 for stays in favour of the courts of non-Member States. A *lis pendens* rule might play a significant role in this regard.

E. Interim relief

The catalyst for the *West Tankers* decision, which, in turn, led to the Commission's Proposal for reform, was the ECJ's decision in *Van Uden* that the courts of a Member State could exercise jurisdiction under Article 31 to grant interim relief in support of arbitration in civil and commercial

---

[68] Compare, in respect of jurisdiction clauses for the courts of non-Member States, CJEU, Case C-387/98 *Coreck Maritime GmbH v Handelsveem BV* [2000] ECR I-9337.

matters, subject to the 'real connecting link' requirement.[69] Although arbitration itself is now outside the Regulation by virtue of Recital (11) it seems debatable whether interim measures in support of that arbitration still fall within the ambit of the Regulation.

Article 36 is the answer to that question and again one of the exceptions from the arbitration exception mentioned in Article 1(2)(d) of the Proposal. It is arguably further complicated by the revised proposals for interim relief, which include, inter alia, coordination between the courts seised as to the substance and the courts granting interim relief; and which strip interim orders from courts without jurisdiction on the substance of the right to enforcement around the EU, effectively 'downgrading' the competence of states other than that with jurisdiction on the substance in respect of such measures. If Article 31 does not apply to interim relief in support of arbitral awards, the courts of Member States would apply their national rules to determine whether they can, and should, grant such relief; but, again, it would be hard to see how harmonisation in the EU had not taken a backwards step.

V. AMENDMENTS SUGGESTED BY OTHER EU INSTITUTIONS

The European Economic and Social Committee's Opinion on the Commission Proposal[70] highlights that the Proposal's provisions on arbitration do not sufficiently deal with the interface between court proceedings and arbitration.

The European Parliament Rapporteur Zwiefka, in his Draft Report of 28 June 2011,[71] does not agree with the Commission Proposal. He seemingly dislikes the coordination approach of the Commission and advocates a total exclusion of arbitration in a new Recital (11) and Article 1(2)(d) and a deletion of the suggested Articles 29(4) and 33(3). As already suggested in the Parliament's Resolution of 7 September 2010 on the implementation and review of the Brussels I Regulation, the Rapporteur proposed that 'all aspects of arbitration must be clearly and unambiguously excluded' from the scope of the Brussels I Regulation. He therefore suggested a new Recital (11) that reads as follows:

---

[69] CJEU, Case C-391/95 *Van Uden* (n 11).

[70] Opinion of the European Economic and Social Committee on the Proposal for a Regulation of the European Parliament and of the Council on jurisdiction and the recognition and enforcement of judgments in civil and commercial matters, COM(20100) 748 final (2011/C 218/14) point 4.5.

[71] Draft Report of 28 June 2011 on the Proposal for a Regulation of the European Parliament and of the Council on jurisdiction and the recognition and enforcement of judgments in civil and commercial matters (Recast) (COM(2010) 748), PE467.046v01-00.

(11) This Regulation does not apply to arbitration. In particular, it does not apply to the form, existence, validity or effects of arbitration agreements, the powers of the arbitrators, the procedure before arbitral tribunals, and the validity, annulment, and recognition and enforcement of arbitral awards. The whole matter of arbitration should be excluded from the scope of this Regulation. Consequently, this Regulation does not apply to any dispute, litigation or application, which the parties have subjected to an arbitration agreement or settlement or which relates to arbitration by virtue of an international treaty. Likewise, this Regulation does not apply to any dispute or decision concerning the existence or validity of an arbitration agreement or settlement, or to any provisional or preventive measure adopted in the context of a dispute, litigation or application which the parties have subjected to an arbitration agreement or settlement or which relates to arbitration by virtue of an international treaty.

Article 1(2)(d) of the Rapporteur's proposal reads:

This Regulation shall not apply to [...] arbitration, including judicial procedures ruling on the validity or extent of arbitral competence as a principal issue or as an incidental or preliminary question.

However, the position of the European Parliament still seems unclear, as the clarifications that the Rapporteur originally suggested have been taken out in the amendments of 19 October 2011 by the Rapporteur himself. The version presented there, is the original, current Brussels I text. Instead of the coordination approach of the Commission or the attempt of a clear and unambiguous exclusion of arbitration, the European Parliament currently seemingly prefers the status quo. This solution, however, does not solve the extensive problems to which the present arbitration exception has given rise.

VI. CONCLUSION

To reiterate, it would be churlish not to give the Commission considerable credit for its efforts to address the problems created by the *West Tankers* decision. There appears to be a widespread view that the law is not currently in a satisfactory state, although some argue that the status quo should be maintained.

As the Schlosser Report showed, the uncertainties as to what the arbitration exception was intended to achieve, and how broadly it was to operate, were evident at the outset. To some extent, the issue was swept under the carpet at the time; or at least left unresolved. If there is one lesson to be learnt from the intervening years, it is that if a rule in EU private international law is not clear at the outset, then the CJEU will have to determine exactly what it means and its answer may well not be broadly appreciated.

Yet, although the approach of coordination which the Commission adopts seems a helpful strategy, the extent of the arbitration exception is not clear under the Commission Proposal and there are at least as many questions as answers. On one view, articulated in the second sentence of Recital (11), issues concerning the validity and effectiveness of arbitration agreements are entirely outside the Regulation and no regime of mutual trust operates in respect of them. This, however, is not how the UK Ministry of Justice reads the Proposal; and one can understand why, given that Article 29(4) does purport to regulate the relationship between the seat of the arbitration and the courts of other Member States to a limited extent. These uncertainties need to be worked through since, it would seem, the answers to a number of the questions posed above are unclear.

Hence, more work is needed, especially to determine what exactly is excluded by the arbitration exception; and whether it is excluded only when the conditions in Article 29(4) are met, or in all cases. More thought is also needed as to whether, and how, to address the effects on the Regulation of arbitration in non-Member States. The problems of conflicting court and arbitration judgments still need to be resolved and additional provisions on recognition and enforcement would be highly desirable.

Whatever solution is adopted, however, needs to be a comprehensive one that clearly answers the questions posed above. The EU cannot afford to swap one regime that ill serves the needs of the arbitration community for another; or to store up problems for another day by failing to clearly determine the ambit of the revised arbitration exception from the outset.

The Application of the Brussels I Regulation to Defendants Domiciled in Third States: From the EGPIL to the Commission Proposal

*Alegría Borrás**

I. INTRODUCTION

The application of the Brussels I Regulation to defendants domiciled in third States constitutes an interesting issue from the perspective of the revision of Regulation 44/2001 ('Brussels I Regulation'), in particular in the Proposal made by the European Commission on 14 December 2010 ('Proposal').[1] For reasons which will be examined in due course, this extension of the Regulation to third State defendants constitutes one of the essential points of the reform, together with the abolition of *exequatur*, choice of court agreements, and the Regulation's interrelation with arbitration. The Commission closely followed the European Parliament Resolution of 7 September 2010,[2] which makes reference to the 'Operation of the Regulation in the international legal order' and emphasises three particular points:

First, the Resolution stresses the inclusion of reflexive-effect rules, particularly with regard to exclusive jurisdiction and exclusive choice of court clauses in favour of third State courts. This is a matter on which the European Parliament urges a consultation process and the opening of a

---

* Chaired Professor of Private International Law, University of Barcelona. This contribution follows closely the publication 'Application of the Brussels I Regulation to External Situations: from Studies Carried out by the European Group for Private International Law (EGPIL/GEDIP) to the Proposal for the Revision of the Regulation' (2010) 12 Yearbook of Private International Law 333-350.

[1] European Commission, Proposal for a Regulation of the European Parliament and of the Council on jurisdiction and the recognition and enforcement of judgments in civil and commercial matters (Recast), COM(2010) 748 final. See also the Stockholm Programme, adopted in the Council of 10–11 December 2009: An Open and Safe Europe which Serves and Protects the Citizen ([2010] OJ C 115/1) and the Communication from the Commission to the European Parliament, the Council, the European Economic and Social Committee and the Committee of the Regions: Delivering an Area of Freedom, Security and Justice for Europe's Citizens, Action Plan Implementing the Stockholm Programme (COM(2010) 171 final).

[2] European Parliament Resolution of 7 September 2010 on the Implementation and Review of the Brussels I Regulation (2009/2140(INI)).

political debate, pointing out that it would be premature to take this step without studying the matter in depth.

Second, the Resolution stresses the pertinence of the matter in light of the numerous bilateral agreements existing on this point, and highlights the need to work in parallel with the Hague Conference by way of resumption of negotiations on an international judgments convention.[3] This latter point is not convincing, but this issue will not be dealt with here.[4]

Thirdly and finally, the Resolution states that 'the question of a rule overturning *Owens Bank v Bracco* should be the subject of a separate review', being a question of *lis pendens* and related actions in a procedure of *exequatur* of a judgment given in a third State.[5]

The question of the application of the Brussels I Regulation to external situations has been the main subject of study over the last few years of the European Group for Private International Law ('EGPIL'),[6] whose mission is to work on the interface of Private International Law and EU Law in the broad sense. This topic was the subject of the Hamburg Session (2007) and the Bergen meeting (2008), where a specific proposal on the necessary modification of the Brussels I Regulation in relation to international jurisdiction was advanced. Afterwards, considering that the issue has to be addressed separately, recognition and enforcement of judgments given in third States were the object of the Padua (2009) and Copenhagen meetings (2010). In addition, the sub-group on external relations[7] met several times during this period in Paris, Barcelona and Hamburg.

---

[3] Which, using language not normally associated with the European Parliament, is described as 'the Holy Grail of Private International Law'. This coincides, in terms of content, with the Joint Statement issued by the Commission and the Council included in an act relating to the adoption of the Brussels I Regulation, which, unfortunately, was not published.

[4] The failure of this project after many years of work and effort, together with the fact that the Hague Convention of 2005 was concluded on choice of court agreements means that, at least, the idea of working on this matter must be considered as premature. See in particular A Borrás, 'Una nueva etapa en la Conferencia de La Haya de Derecho internacional privado: la elaboración de un Convenio sobre competencia judicial y ejecución de sentencias en materia civil y mercantil', in *Responsa Iurisperitorum Digesta*, vol III (Ediciones Universidad de Salamanca 2002) 45; A Borrás, 'Consejo sobre los Asuntos Generales y la Política de la Conferencia de La Haya de Derecho internacional privado (7–9 de abril de 2010)' (2010) 62(1) Revista Española de Derecho Internacional 323; A Borrás, 'Consejo sobre los Asuntos Generales y la Política de la Conferencia de La Haya de Derecho internacional privado (5–7 de abril de 2011)' (2011) 63(2) Revista Española de Derecho Internacional 309–314.

[5] CJEU, Case C-129/92 *Owens Bank Ltd v Fulvio Bracco SpA* [1994] ECR I-00117; comments by A Borrás, (1995) Revista Jurídica de Catalunya 278; H Gaudemet-Tallon, (1994) Revue critique de droit international privé 382; H Tagaras, (1995) Cahiers de droit européen 195; H Huet, (1994) Journal de droit international 546.

[6] On the studies carried out by EGPIL, see <http://www.gedip-egpil.eu/>. See also M Fallon, P Kinsch and Ch Kohler (eds), *Le droit international privé européen en construction. Vingt ans de travaux du GEDIP. Building European Private International Law. Twenty years' Work by GEDIP* (Intersentia, Antwerp 2011) 662–663 and 702–715.

[7] The sub-group on external relations was made up of J Basedow, A Borrás, M Fallon,

II. REASONS FOR THE EXTENSION OF THE REGULATION'S JURISDICTION RULES

Before an examination of the suggested modification of the Brussels I Regulation is undertaken, it is essential to contextualise the approach to third State defendants. It deals with the external implications of the communitarisation of Private International Law,[8] also known as the 'ERTA effect' (1971), a consequence of the first judgment of the Court of Justice of the European Union ('CJEU') in which this theory was applied.[9] This judgment stated that once the Community has exercised an *ad intra* competence, then it also acquires an *ad extra* competence. In the area of civil justice, the main example is the conclusion of the revised Lugano Convention of 30 October 2007.[10] This important case has its origin in the request made by the Council to the CJEU for an opinion on the exclusive or shared competence of the Community and its Member States for the conclusion of the revised Lugano Convention, which is, like its predecessor of 1988, a 'parallel' Convention to the regime laid out in the Brussels Convention of 1968 (now in the Brussels I Regulation). It is precisely this 'parallel' character, which gave rise to the belief that the Community and its Member States could maintain shared competence. However, in its Opinion C-1/03, delivered on 7 February 2006, the CJEU, on the grounds of the existence of the Brussels I Regulation, stated that competence for the conclusion of the revised Lugano Convention 'falls entirely in the sphere of the exclusive competence of the European Community'. The Court's determination of the matter was conclusive, stating that 'the main provisions of the agreement envisaged are capable of affecting the unified and coherent

C Kessedjian, P Lagarde, F Pocar and HD Tebbens, but also received contributions of other members such as H Gaudemet-Tallon.

[8] Among the abundant bibliography on this matter, see A Borrás, 'Diritto internazionale privato comunitario e rapporti con Stati terzi' in R Baratta et al, *Diritto internazionale privato e diritto comunitario: a cura di P. Picone* (CEDAM 2004) 449; A Borrás, 'Le droit international privé communautaire: réalités, problèmes et perspectives d'avenir' (2005) 317 Recueil des Cours 467; B Hess, 'Les compétences externes de la Communauté européenne dans le cadre de l'Article 65 CE' in A Fuchs, H Muir Watt, E Pataut (eds), *Les conflits de lois et le système juridique communautaire* (Dalloz 2004) 81; M Wilderspin and AM Rouchaud-Joët, 'La compétence externe de la Communauté européenne en droit international privé' (2004) Revue critique de droit international privé 1; B Audit, and GA Bermann, 'The Application of Private International Norms to 'Third Countries': The Jurisdiction and Judgments Example' in A Nuyts and N Watté (ed), *International Civil Litigation in Europe and Relations with Third States* (Bruylant 2005) 55; A Borrás, 'The Frontiers and the Institutional Constitutional Question', in A Nuyts and N Watté (ed), *International Civil Litigation in Europe and Relations with Third States* (Bruylant 2005) 27.

[9] CJEU, Case C-22/70 *Commission of the EC v Council of the EC (ERTA)* [1971] ECR I-00263, in particular para 17.

[10] The conclusion of the revised Lugano Convention by the EU was authorised by the Decision of the Council of 27 November 2008, being jointly published with the Convention in [2009] OJ L 147/1. For more details, see A Borrás, 'La firma del Convenio de Lugano revisado' (2007) 59(2) Revista Española de Derecho internacional 851.

nature of the rules of jurisdiction laid down by Regulation No 44/2001' and, as a consequence, 'affect the uniform and consistent application of the Community rules on jurisdiction and the proper functioning of the system established by those rules'.[11]

It is understood, therefore, that the Brussels I Regulation constitutes a uniform and complete system of rules, even taking into account that the common rules do not cover the entire array of international disputes; ie, on the matter of jurisdiction it affects only those disputes in which a defendant is domiciled in a Member State, with the exception of exclusive jurisdiction, whereas on the matter of *exequatur*, it refers to any judgment given in a Member State.

Without exploring other aspects of this Opinion,[12] it is important to highlight that the Opinion C-1/03 states that 'the proper functioning of the internal market' shall not affect the conclusion of the revised Lugano Convention, but shall solely affect the adoption of the internal act.

The progress of EU rules, however, is not limited to the conclusion of bilateral or multilateral conventions by Member States, but also affects the possibility for Member States to establish autonomous rules on Private International Law. For example, in the field of jurisdiction, EU competence implies that in the event that the national courts have no competence according to the Brussels I Regulation, if Article 4 of the Regulation is deleted, some rules on jurisdiction are modified and a subsidiary rule on jurisdiction of a European nature is included for those cases in which the defendants' domicile is outside of a Member State, and internal rules of the Member State no longer apply. They would be superseded by an EU provision and the national rule of the relevant State would only be applied to the execution proceedings. This issue arises in relation to all EU instruments, but in this contribution, the scope of consideration will be limited to the Brussels I Regulation.

What is clear is that the Brussels I Regulation is unsatisfactory in disputes involving defendants from outside the EU and that one of the objectives of the revision is the extension of the jurisdiction rules to disputes

---

[11] Paras 160 and 161 of the Opinion.

[12] On this important opinion, see A Borrás, 'Competence of the Community to conclude the revised Lugano Convention on jurisdiction and the recognition and enforcement of judgments in civil and commercial matters. Opinion C-1/03 of 7 February 2006: Comments and immediate consequences' (2006) 8 Yearbook of Private International Law 37 and also in (2006) Revista Jurídica de Catalunya 879 and in (2006) Revista General de Derecho Europeo, available at <http://www.iustel.com/revistas/>. See also the comments made by T Baumé, 'Competence of the Community to conclude the New Lugano Convention: Opinion 1/03 of 7 February 2006' (2006) 7(8) German Law Journal 681; RA Brand, 'The Lugano Case in the European Court of Justice: Evolving European Union Competence in Private International Law', (2004–05) 11 ILSA Journal International and Comparative Law 297. For broader comments on this matter, see A Borrás, 'Le droit international privé communautaire: réalités, problèmes et perspectives d'avenir' (2005) 317 Recueil des Cours 467.

involving third country defendants. Therefore, first, the relevant international jurisdiction rules shall be considered; second the possibilities for recognition and enforcement of judgments rendered in third States; and, finally, the possibilities to conclude conventions regarding matters included in the Brussels I Regulation. It has to be noted from the outset that the approach of the Commission's Proposal is much more limited than the EGPIL Proposal.

III. INTERNATIONAL JURISDICTION – THE COMMISSION AND THE
GEDIP PROPOSALS COMPARED

It is important to point out that unlike the current Brussels I Regulation in which an allocation of competences is made among the jurisdictions of the Member States, the Proposal does not allocate competences among the jurisdictions of the Member States and third States, but unilaterally regulates international jurisdiction. This is the essence of the proposed modifications.

In the current text of the Brussels I Regulation, the basic rule on jurisdiction is included in Article 2[13] which provides that 'subject to this Regulation, persons domiciled in a Member State shall, whatever their nationality, be sued in the courts of that Member State'. In this way, the classic rule of civil procedure is accepted – *actor sequitur forum rei* – without considering the (EU or non-EU) nationality of the defendant. Thus, Article 2 represents the basic principle for the application of the Regulation: it is only applied if the defendant has his domicile in a Member State, leaving aside the cases of exclusive jurisdiction as provided in Article 22.

As the Commission states, the diversity of national laws leads to unequal access to justice for EU companies in transactions with partners from third countries: some can easily litigate in the EU, while others cannot, even in situations where no other court guaranteeing a fair trial is competent. In addition, where national legislation does not grant access to court in disputes with parties outside the EU, the enforcement of mandatory EU law protecting consumers, employees or commercial agents, for example, is not guaranteed.

The reform which was proposed by EGPIL on this matter aimed to establish a set of rules applicable if the defendant does not have his domicile in a Member State, such that the 'uniform and consistent' nature, which

---

[13] On this provision, see J Kropholler, *Europäisches Zivilprozessrecht* (8th edn, Recht und Wirtschaft 2005); U Magnus and P Mankowski (ed), *Brussels I Regulation: European Commentaries on Private International Law* (Sellier 2007); H Gaudemet-Tallon, *Compétence et exécution des jugements en Europe. Règlement 44/2001, Conventions de Bruxelles (1968) et de Lugano (1988 et 2007)* (4th edn, LGDJ 2010) at 79.

is attributed by the Opinion C-1/03 to the system laid out in the Brussels I Regulation, comes into effect. EGPIL adopted the first document in its Hamburg Session (2007),[14] in which it modestly put forward the need to delete Article 4 of the Brussels I Regulation, which currently sets out that 'If the defendant is not domiciled in a Member State, the jurisdiction of the courts of each Member State shall, subject to Articles 22 and 23, be determined by the law of that Member State'.[15] Several ideas proposed in the document have been subsequently developed and approved in the Bergen Session (2008),[16] including a proposal which was sent to the EU institutions and which includes an overall regulation of international jurisdiction, replacing entirely the relevant national rules.

Even though the text of the current Article 2 of the Brussels I Regulation is maintained in the Commission's Proposal (as a new Article 3), this objective is completed by two rules in a new Article 4:

1. Persons domiciled in a Member State may be sued in the courts of another Member State only by virtue of the rules set out in Sections 2 to 7.
2. Persons not domiciled in any Member States may be sued in the courts of a Member State only by virtue of the rules set out in Sections 2 to 8, which implies adding subsidiary jurisdiction (Article 25 of the Proposal) and *forum necessitatis* (Article 26 of the Proposal).

The result is that the revised Regulation will apply whenever the question of determining jurisdiction in an international dispute arises, where the defendants are domiciled either in the EU or in a third country. This implies that amendments might be brought to a series of Articles so that their application extends to any defendant, whether domiciled or not, in the territory of a Member State. In particular, this is the case in Articles 5 and 6 as to special jurisdiction, or in relation to protective jurisdiction as regards insurance (Articles 8 and 9), consumers (Article 15) and individual contracts of

---

[14] European Group of Private International Law, 'L'application des règles de l'Union européenne sur la compétence judiciaire aux situations externes (17e Session, Hambourg, 16 septembre 2007)'. See A Borrás, 'La XVII Sesión del Grupo Europeo de Derecho internacional privado (Hamburgo, 14–16 de septiembre de 2007)' (2007) 59(2) Revista Española de Derecho Internacional 869; E Jayme, 'Das Europäische IPR löst sich vom Binnenmarkt – Tagung der Europäischen Gruppe für Internationales Privatrecht in Hamburg' (2008) 1 IPRax 72.

[15] Art 22 and 23 of the Brussels I Regulation refer to exclusive jurisdiction and, respectively, express prorogation of jurisdiction.

[16] A Borrás, 'La XVIII Sesión del Grupo Europeo de Derecho internacional privado (Bergen, 19–20 de septiembre de 2008)' (2008) 60(2) Revista Española de Derecho Internacional 716; Ch Kohler, 'Erstreckung der Europäischen Zuständigkeitsordnung auf drittstaatsverknüpfte Streitigkeiten – Tagung der Europäischen Gruppe für Internationales Privatrecht in Bergen' (2009) 3 IPRax 285.

employment (Articles 18 and 19) or, finally, in the drafting of the rules on examination as to jurisdiction and admissibility (Articles 27 and 28 of the Proposal) and in Article 31, in relation to provisional and protective measures.[17]

In the EGPIL Proposal, a new Article 24 *bis* includes a rule of jurisdiction based on the technique of *forum necessitatis*, which also exists in some recent national Private International Law provisions. This mechanism fulfils a different function to that of the previous rules. This jurisdiction is subject to two types of conditions:

1. The first condition serves to identify the jurisdiction criteria by referring to a 'sufficient connection'. Reference was not made to a *forum patrimonii* or to a 'doing business' jurisdiction, but instead it was sought to include other connections, even nationality, although the rule gives precedence to the presence of property in the territory of the State;
2. The second condition refers to the necessity for the court to deal with the case, which directly or indirectly affects the conditions of access to justice in a third State (when it is impossible to act in the third State) or the impossibility of enforcing the judgment given in the non-Member State.

The solution proposed by the Commission differs to some extent to that proposed by EGPIL notwithstanding that the two proposals have the same objective. In the proposal of the Commission, there are two different Articles: Article 25, including a subsidiary jurisdiction, and Article 26, including a *forum necessitatis*. These harmonised rules compensate the removal of the existing national rules.

With regard to Article 25, the Proposal of the Commission provides that a non-EU defendant can be sued at the place where moveable assets belonging to him are located, provided their value is not disproportionate to the value of the claim, and that the dispute has a sufficient connection with the Member State of the court seised. Although not unanimously agreed upon, the Commission considers this ground of jurisdiction necessary in addition to *forum necessitatis,* since this forum based on the location of assets outbalances the absence of the defendant in the EU, and has the advantage of ensuring that a judgment can be enforced in the State where it was issued.

---

[17] Of particular relevance on these points is the report prepared by Prof. A Nuyts, *Study on Residual Jurisdiction, General Report* (2007). See also B Hess, T Pfeiffer and P Schlosser, *Report on the Application of Regulation Brussels I in the Member States* (2007), available at <http://ec.europa.eu/justice/civil/document/index_en.htm>.

Article 26 includes a *forum necessitatis,* affecting the conditions of access to justice in a third State (when it is impossible to act in the third State) or the impossibility of enforcing the judgment given in the non-Member State, in a similar sense to the EGPIL Proposal. As the Commission states, Article 26 aims to guarantee the right of the EU claimants to a fair trial, which is of particular relevance for EU companies investing in countries with 'immature' legal systems.

The final amendment proposed by EGPIL to be highlighted refers to the introduction of a new Article, which, on the grounds of the definitions provided in Articles 27 and 28, establishes a mechanism of *lis pendens* and related actions in the case of a plurality of proceedings which affect the courts of a third State, with the objective of avoiding parallel proceedings inside and outside the EU. In such a case, it is established that the judge of the EU court seised second may exceptionally stay the proceedings until the court seised first gives its judgment, if it appears that the judgment is to be given within a reasonable time and it will be recognised under the law of that Member State. The court will only decline jurisdiction if the court of the third State first seised gives a judgment recognisable under the law of that Member State. A similar, but more detailed rule is included in Article 34 of the Commission's Proposal, to which another paragraph is added, allowing the court to discharge the stay at any time if the proceedings in the court of the third State are stayed or are discontinued, and if it appears that the proceedings will not conclude within a reasonable time or, alternatively, if the discharge of the stay is required for the proper administration of justice.

However, as stated above, the EGPIL Proposal was more ambitious than the Proposal of the Commission. In fact, the essential amendment proposed by EGPIL affected Articles 22 and 23, by introducing 'mirror rules', both on the matter of exclusive jurisdiction, through a new Article 22 *bis,* and on the matter of choice of court, through a new Article 23 *bis.* The Commission's Proposal does not include such rules and in this regard follows the aforementioned Parliament Resolution. The European Parliament has stressed that the inclusion of reflexive-effect rules, especially in regard to exclusive jurisdiction and exclusive choice of court clauses in favour of third State courts, is a matter on which it recommends the initiation of a consultation process and the opening of a political debate, considering that it would be premature to take this step without studying the matter in depth. One could agree with this assertion; nevertheless, the proposals of EGPIL could be borne in mind and taken into account if and when the appropriate moment for reform of this particular issue arrives.

From the perspective of EGPIL, in the case of exclusive jurisdiction, the issue of proximity does not disappear simply because the pertinent location element (location of a property, company headquarters or public registry) is situated in a third State. Notwithstanding that a court in a Member State would have jurisdiction under another provision of the Regulation, it can decline the exercise of jurisdiction in favour of the courts of a third State subject to four conditions:

1. the court of the third State must have exclusive jurisdiction according to its own legal system, which makes sense if one considers that in such a case a Spanish judgment, for example, would not be enforced in the said third State;
2. the law of the third State must base such jurisdiction on criteria analogous to those of Article 22 (this is what essentially constitutes the reflexive effect), in order to avoid the lack of jurisdiction of a court of a Member State on the basis of the Regulation, when jurisdiction of the courts of the third State would be based on an exorbitant ground of jurisdiction;
3. the foreign judgment must be able to be enforced in the Member State;
4. it must be foreseen that the judgment will be given within a reasonable period of time, this criterion being linked to the need for a fair trial. To summarise, a judge must act with great prudence before choosing to decline jurisdiction.

The reflexive effect is excluded in two cases:

1. In the case of tenancies of immovable property concluded for temporary private use for a maximum period of six consecutive months, given that the courts of the State where the defendant is domiciled have jurisdiction in line with the conditions laid out in the provision itself;
2. In relation to enforcement of judgments (Article 22 paragraph 5) given that, in accordance with CJEU jurisprudence,[18] the scope of enforcement must be interpreted in the strict sense and therefore is not appropriate to the reflexive effect.

A specific solution was required for the case of Article 22 paragraph 4, ie the question relating to the validity of patents, trademarks and other simi-

---

[18] See CJEU, Case C-261/90 *M Reichert, HH Reichert and I Kockler v Dresdner Bank AG (Reichert II)* [1992] ECR I-02149, with comments of A Borrás, (1992) Revista Jurídica de Catalunya 1121, and Case C-220/84 *AS-Autoteile Service GmbH v Pierre Malhé* [1985] ECR I-02267, in which it is clearly stated that the case must have a 'close link to the enforcement procedure', without possibility to plead a set-off between the right whose enforcement is being sought and a claim over which the courts of that State would have no jurisdiction if it was raised independently.

lar rights. Let us recall, in this instance, that in the text of the revised Lugano Convention the judgment of the CJEU on the *GAT* case was taken into consideration.[19] This related to the frequent case in which the validity of a patent arises as an incidental question, and for which the following sentence was added to the text of the Brussels I Regulation: 'irrespective of whether the issue is raised by way of an action or as a defence'. In this case, a specific rule was required for the event in which the registration of the patent was made in the registry of a third State. Thus, an exception to paragraph 1 is made, insofar as the court of the Member State may intervene even though the third State might have exclusive jurisdiction; however, there are certain self-imposing restrictions to the rule, namely that the judgment will have no effect on third parties, wherefore it is not linked to any previous judgment which might have been pronounced on the grounds of Article 22 paragraph 1, and moreover, it does not affect the registration made in the registry of the third State.

In relation to express prorogation of jurisdiction, the EGPIL Proposal, besides introducing certain amendments to Article 23 and, especially, deleting paragraph 3, provides for a new Article 23 *bis*, which also covers choice of court agreements in favour of the courts of a non-Member State.

Firstly, paragraph 3 of Article 23 is deleted, given that in the context of an extension to cases connected to third States, the exclusion, applicable in the case that neither of the parties is domiciled in a Member State, makes no sense. On the other hand, the wording of paragraph 5 adapts to the requirements of the introduction of the new Article 22 *bis*.

Article 23 *bis* refers to choice of court agreements in favour of the courts of a third State. It covers agreements which satisfy the conditions laid out in Article 23, and also contains specific conditions given that there is no common mechanism for the allocation of jurisdiction between the EU and the third State.

These specific conditions are:

1. the court of the Member State must have jurisdiction to hear the proceeding in accordance with the Regulation;
2. the chosen judge must deem himself to have jurisdiction in accordance with the internal rules on jurisdiction;
3. the court before which a party has appeared in a Member State must not immediately decline to exercise jurisdiction, as would otherwise be the case if the chosen court would have been one of another Member

---

[19] CJEU, Case C-4/03 *Gesellschaft Für Antriebstechnik mbH & Co. KG (GAT) v Lamellen und Kupplungsbau Beteiligungs KG (LUK)* [2006] ECR I-06509 (2007) Revista Jurídica de Catalunya 321.

State, but instead must wait until such time as the chosen judge declares to have jurisdiction (however, the first judge retains the right to rule on the case if he considers that the chosen judge will not pronounce his judgment within a reasonable time or if the judgment will be unable to be enforced under the law of the State of the court seised). This provision is comparable to that of Article 6 of the 2005 Hague Convention on Choice of Court Agreements.[20]

Paragraph 2 of Article 23 *bis* appears in brackets, as agreement was not reached in relation to this issue. In this paragraph, it is provided that 'the choice by the parties of a court of a non-Member State shall have no effect if all other elements relevant to the situation at the time of the choice of court are located in the same Member State'. This is more than a simple rule of applicability, given that it determines the jurisdiction of the said court if this derives from a provision of the Regulation. Furthermore, this determination may not be clear when it is debatable whether a situation is or is not of an international nature.

IV. THE RECOGNITION AND ENFORCEMENT OF JUDGMENTS GIVEN IN THIRD STATES

The Commission's Proposal does not deal with this issue. According to the opinion of the stakeholders consulted by the Commission, the recognition and enforcement of third State judgments should be left to a multilateral framework which would ensure reciprocity at the international level; this is easy to understand when it is taken into account that within the EU context, *exequatur* will be abolished. In principle, the revised Regulation would not, therefore, deal with the adoption of rules regarding the recognition and enforcement of judgments given in non-Member States.

For EGPIL, the recognition and enforcement of judgments was considered to constitute a specific question worthy of separate examination. The extension of the Regulation to cover this aspect was deemed by EGPIL to be a natural consequence of rules on direct jurisdiction in relation with

---

[20] Art 6 of the Hague Convention states: 'A court of a Contracting State other than that of the chosen court shall suspend or dismiss proceedings to which an exclusive choice of court agreement applies unless: a) the agreement is null and void under the law of the State of the chosen court; b) a party lacked the capacity to conclude the agreement under the law of the State of the court seised; c) giving effect to the agreement would lead to a manifest injustice or would be manifestly contrary to the public policy of the State of the court seised; d) for exceptional reasons beyond the control of the parties, the agreement cannot reasonably be performed; or e) the chosen court has decided not to hear the case'. See T Hartley and M Dogauchi, *Explanatory Report on the 2005 Hague Choice of Court Agreements Convention* (2007) paras 141–159.

third States. This question was dealt with in the Padua (2009)[21] and in the Copenhagen (2010) meetings.[22]

According to the EGPIL Proposal, there would be an analogous, but not identical, system of *exequatur* to the one established to date for judgments given in a Member State. The starting point for discussion is the great disparity between the national rules of the Member States regarding the enforcement of foreign judgments. Extreme positions can be identified: on the one hand, the cases of those States which provide for conditions of recognition and enforcement which are similar to those of the Regulation (such as Belgium, France or Italy); on the other hand, the cases of those which ignore the possibility of recognising or enforcing a foreign judgment in the absence of a bilateral convention (such as Finland). Thus, a judgment given in a third State might be recognised in one Member State and not in another, without the recognition decision of the first State taking effect in the second State, in accordance with the well-known adage of *'exequatur sur exequatur ne vaut'*. The so-called 'Pan-European efficacy' has not been the object of agreement.

In the Padua meeting, it was not possible to agree on a final text, however some guidelines were adopted:

1. The rules must take their inspiration from the text of the Brussels Convention of 1968, adapting the grounds for the rejection of recognition relating to public order and indirect jurisdiction. It should be emphasised that because the text is inspired by the Brussels Convention of 1968 and not by the Regulation, the proposed text is more akin to a model of cooperation among States than to a model of integration;

2. The adaptation of the rules does not depend upon a condition of reciprocity, but does not exclude the possibility of safeguarding measures as adopted by the EU;

3. The effectiveness of national and of EU mandatory laws must be guaranteed;

4. It is necessary to carefully examine the question of movement of Member States' decisions on the recognition or enforcement of a judgment given in a non-Member State throughout the EU.

---

[21] M. Fallon (n 6) 750–751; A Borrás and FJ Garcimartín, 'La XIX Sesión del Grupo Europeo de Derecho internacional privado (Padua, 18–20 Septiembre 2009)' (2009) 61 Revista Española de Derecho internacional 577; E Jayme, 'Die Vereinheitlichung des Internationalen Privat – und Verfahrensrechts in der Europäischen Union; Tendenzen und Widerstände – Tagung der 'Europäischen Gruppe für Internationales Privatrecht' (GEDIP) an der Universität Padua' (2010) 2 IPRax 185.

[22] M. Fallon (n 6) 792–819; A Borrás and FJ Garcimartín, 'La XX Sesión del Grupo Europeo de Derecho internacional privado (Copenhague, 17-19 Septiembre 2010)' (2010) 2 Revista Española de Derecho internacional 333; E Jayme, 'Tagung der Europäischen Gruppe für Internationales Privatrecht (GEDIP) in Kopenhagen' (2011) 1 IPRax 101.

The text relating to the extension of the Brussels I Regulation to the recognition and enforcement of judgments given in third States was analysed during the Copenhagen meeting of EGPIL in September 2010. This extension was deemed by EGPIL to be a natural consequence of its proposal on the rules of direct jurisdiction as these rules relate to third States.

Authentic instruments are not included in the EGPIL Proposal for a number of reasons. On the one hand, this is because the notion is not entirely clear in the laws of certain third States.[23] On the other hand, it is due to the difficulty of testing the enforceability of such instrument and the need for considerable adaptations of the text in order for it to be applicable to these types of instruments.

The main characteristics of the text adopted in Copenhagen refer to the system of recognition and enforcement and to the grounds for refusal, including a new section 4 in Chapter III of the Regulation, relating to recognition and enforcement.

The system of recognition and enforcement proposed by EGPIL follows the same scheme as the texts adopted to date, in particular the Brussels II *bis* Regulation. In effect, it is based on the following three features:

1. automatic recognition with the possibility of the interested party to apply for recognition as a main request (including the possibility of a non-recognition request) (Article 56 paragraph 2);
2. the need to follow special proceedings of *exequatur* in order to render the foreign judgment enforceable (Article 56 paragraph 8); and
3. the law of the requested Member State governing the proceedings (Article 56 paragraph 9). Unlike the European texts, the possibility of recognising and enforcing non-final judgments is excluded (Article 56-1, paragraph 2, b)). The enforcement of provisional or protective measures is also excluded, these matters being left to the national legal system.

As regards the grounds for refusal, these have been taken over from the Brussels I Regulation system, but have been adapted to allow for their operation within the extra-Community context. As a consequence:

---

[23] Although on this matter one might be led to recall the elements highlighted by the Court of Justice in Case C-260/97 *Unibank A/S v Fleming G. Christensen* [1999] ECR I-03715 regarding the interpretation of art 50 of the 1968 Brussels Convention (with note of A Borrás (2000) Revista Jurídica de Cataluña 260) and the broad definition included in art 3(e) of the 2007 Hague Convention on maintenance obligations, according to which 'e) 'maintenance arrangement' means an agreement in writing relating to the payment of maintenance which i) has been formally drawn up or registered as an authentic instrument by a competent authority; or ii) has been authenticated by, or concluded, registered or filed with a competent authority, and may be the subject of review and modification by a competent authority'.

Firstly, the control over the exercise of jurisdiction on the part of the court of the State of origin is maintained in the following terms (Article 56-3): respect is required for exclusive grounds of jurisdiction of the Member States, for choice of court agreements in favour of Member State courts and for the courts of protection (consumers, workers and insurance). For the remaining cases, a control is limited to the requirement of 'a sufficient connection' between the State of origin of the judgment and the dispute, thus excluding in all respects the concurrence of this connection when the grounds are deemed exorbitant in accordance with a non-exhaustive list of grounds of this nature included in the text (nationality of one of the parties; service on the defendant who is temporarily present in the territory of that State; presence of property belonging to the defendant unrelated to the dispute; commercial or professional activities carried out by the defendant in that State which are not connected to the dispute). A more flexible approach was preferred over a more rigid one which would consist of demanding a foreign court to base its jurisdiction on rules similar to those of the Regulation.

However, these provisions are not applied when the defendant has expressly accepted the jurisdiction of the court of origin, setting aside the exclusive jurisdiction of Article 22.

Secondly, the right to a legal defence is upheld in a similar way to that of the corresponding provision of the Regulation, by maintaining a system of respect, but without requiring the defendant to fail to commence proceedings for challenging the judgment when it was possible for him to do so (Article 56-4, paragraph 1(a). As a result, if the service was not sufficient, then the defendant may challenge the recognition of the foreign judgment in the EU even though, despite being able to do so, he chose not to lodge an appeal in the State of origin. This matter attracted much debate. It is worth recalling that Switzerland, in relation to the revised Lugano Convention of 2007, adopted the declaration provided for in Article 3, section 1 of Protocol no 1, insofar as it provides that it shall not apply the final part of Article 34, paragraph 2, which states 'unless the defendant failed to commence proceedings to challenge the judgment when it was possible for him to do so'.[24]

Thirdly, the use of the public policy clause is maintained (Article 56-6), and is complemented by the recognition of the need to respect both national and EU mandatory laws (Article 56-5). The matter of what constitutes a

---

[24] Art 3 para 1 of Protocol no 1 to the Lugano Convention of 2007 states that 'Switzerland reserves the right to declare upon ratification that it will not apply the following part of the provision in art 34(2): "unless the defendant failed to commence proceedings to challenge the judgment when it was possible for him to do so". If Switzerland makes such declaration, the other Contracting Parties shall apply the same reservation in respect of judgments rendered by the courts of Switzerland'.

novelty (the provision in relation to which a special mention is included regarding punitive non-compensatory damages as a type of judgment which is not susceptible to enforcement in the EU) thereby follows the model of the 2005 Hague Convention on choice of court agreements.[25] To this we must add the prohibition of revision as to the substance (Article 56-7), recognising the difficulty of distinguishing between the *ordre public* control and the revision as to the substance.

Finally, the ground for refusal based on the irreconcilability of an extra-European judgment with an internal one is maintained (Article 56-4 paragraphs a), b) and c)). The existence of proceedings still pending in the courts of a Member State is also maintained, although with a certain judicial flexibility. This last point was very much debated during the meeting. On the one hand, it was expressed that the observance of the rules of *lis pendens* must necessarily be reflected in all matters related to recognition and, therefore, a judgment given in a third State deriving from a case, with the same object and cause, initiated after a proceeding had been commenced in an EU Member State, must not be recognised. On the other hand, it has been deemed that this approach could give rise to strategic conduct on the part of one of the parties (what is colloquially known as the 'Italian torpedo').[26] In the end, as a compromise between the two positions, it was concluded that a certain amount of room for manoeuvre should be left to the court and, therefore, with it, the possibility of formulating this ground of refusal as being of a facultative and not of an automatic application (Article 56-4, paragraph 2).

V. THE CONCLUSION OF CONVENTIONS WITH THIRD STATES

An issue to which special focus was given is the compatibility of the text with the abundant number of existing bilateral conventions on the recognition and enforcement of judgments. It is important to recall the reference to Article 351 of the Treaty on the Functioning of the EU and the three judgments

---

[25] Art 11 of the 2005 Hague Convention states that: '(1) Recognition or enforcement of a judgment may be refused if, and to the extent that, the judgment awards damages, including exemplary or punitive damages, that do not compensate a party for actual loss or harm suffered. (2) The court addressed shall take into account whether and to what extent the damages awarded by the court of origin serve to cover costs and expenses relating to the proceedings'.

[26] T Hartley, 'art 21: Lis Alibi Pendens' (1988) 13 European Law Review 217; M Franzosi, 'Worldwide Patent Litigation and the Italian Torpedo' (1997) 19 European Intellectual Property Review 382; N Balkanyi-Nordmann, 'The Perils of Parallel Proceedings' (2001–02) 56 Dispute Resolution Journal 20; M Franzosi, 'Torpedoes are Here to Stay' (2002) International Review of Industrial Property and Copyright Law 154; T Hartley, 'The European Union and the Systematic Dismantling of the Common Law of Conflict of Laws' (2005) 54 ICLQ 813.

pronounced by the CJEU (although on the matter of investments) referring to the 'compatibility' of the agreements with EU law.[27]

In this context, there is no doubt that the EU is competent to conclude multilateral and bilateral agreements, along with the specific provisions relating to the possibility of the Member States to conclude such agreements within a system which has been qualified as one of 'supervised release'.[28] However, it is emphasised that, in respect of these 'systems of supervised release', the Brussels I Regulation is not included,[29] which means that the Member States cannot conclude bilateral conventions with third States in relation to matters falling within the scope of this Regulation.

All that remains is the survival of the pre-existent conventions on 'particular matters', to which Article 71 of the Regulation makes reference, and which Article was recently interpreted by the CJEU in a restrictive way, in a Judgment given on 4 May 2010.[30] In fact, interesting clarifications from the perspective of the creation of a European area of freedom, security and justice are included in this Judgment. The dispute was related to a contract for the carriage of goods by road from the Netherlands to Germany; this contract was submitted to the Convention on the Contract for the International Carriage of Goods by Road (CMR Convention). Article 31 of this Convention includes a *lis pendens* rule and a rule relating to enforceability. In this context, the problem was how to interpret the reference made by Article 71 of the Regulation to 'Conventions concluded by the Member States in relation to particular matters'.

The first question that arose was whether the CJEU has jurisdiction to interpret the CMR Convention. In fact, in its own words, the CJEU 'does not have jurisdiction to interpret Article 31' of the CMR Convention. Advocate General Kokott, has explained, however, in a much more flexible way, that although the CJEU has no jurisdiction to interpret the CMR Convention, 'it does, however, fall to the Court to interpret Article 71 of

---

[27] See CJEU, Cases C-249/06 *Commission of the EC v Sweden* [2009] ECR I-01335 and C-205/06 *Commission v Austria* [2009] ECR I-01301 with note in (2009) Revista Jurídica de Catalunya 905, and Case C-118/07 *Commission of the EC v Finland* [2009] ECR I-10889 with note in (2010) Revista Jurídica de Catalunya 606.

[28] A Borrás, 'Un nuevo marco jurídico para la conclusión de convenios de Derecho internacional privado entre Estados miembros y terceros Estados en materias 'comunitarizadas' (2011) 315 Noticias de la Unión Europea 119.

[29] This system deals with Regulation 662/2009 of 13 July 2009 [2009] OJ L 200/25 which establishes a procedure for the negotiation and formalising of agreements among Member States and third States on specific matters relating to the law applicable to contractual and extra-contractual obligations and Regulation 664/2009 of 7 July 2009 (published in [2009] OJ L 200/46) which establishes a procedure for the negotiation and formalising of agreements among Member States and third States on competence, recognition and enforcements of decisions on marital law, parental responsibility and the law applicable to maintenance obligations.

[30] Case C-533/08 *TNT Express Nederland BV v AXA Versicherung AG* [2010] ECR I-00000 with note of JJ Alvarez (2011) 1 Revista Jurídica de Catalunya 269.

Regulation No 44/2001 in relation to the application by the national court of those provisions of the CMR which affect the field of application of Regulation No 44/2001 and, in so doing, to take cognisance of the content of the provisions of the CMR'. Having reduced the question to the interpretation of Article 71, the CJEU ruled that:

[I]t must be interpreted as meaning that, in a case such as that giving rise to the main proceedings, the rules governing jurisdiction, recognition and enforcement that are laid down by a Convention on a particular matter, (such as the *lis pendens* rule set out in Article 31(2) of the Convention on the Contract for the International Carriage of Goods by Road, signed at Geneva on 19 May 1956, as amended by the Protocol signed at Geneva on 5 July 1978, and the rule relating to enforceability set out in Article 31(3) of that Convention), apply provided that they are highly predictable, facilitate the sound administration of justice, enable the risk of concurrent proceedings to be minimised and that they ensure, under conditions at least as favourable as those provided for by the Regulation, the free movement of judgments in civil and commercial matters and mutual trust in the administration of justice in the European Union (*favor executionis*).

To reach this conclusion, the CJEU stated that the application of a specialised Convention cannot compromise the principles which underlie judicial cooperation in civil and commercial matters in the EU, 'such as the principles of free movement of judgments in civil and commercial matters, predictability as to the courts having jurisdiction and therefore legal certainty for litigants, sound administration of justice, minimisation of the risk of concurrent proceedings, and mutual trust in the administration of justice in the European Union', principles whose observance is necessary 'for the sound operation of the internal market' and which 'constitute the *raison d'être* of Regulation No 44/2001'.[31]

In this context, the CMR Convention 'may lead to results which are less favourable for achieving sound operation of the internal market than the results to which the regulation's provisions lead'; Article 31 of the CMR Convention can therefore be applied in the EU 'only if it enables the objectives of the free movement of judgments in civil and commercial matters and of mutual trust in the administration of justice in the European Union to be achieved under conditions at least as favourable as those resulting from the application of Regulation No 44/2001'.

The consequence of the interpretation of Article 71 made by the CJEU is that the reference made by this Article is not an *in toto* reference to the specialised Conventions, but rather is conditioned by the principles which underlie judicial cooperation in civil and commercial matters in the EU and, in particular, by what is necessary for the sound operation of the internal market. On the basis of the interpretation of the CJEU, the sentence

---

[31] See points 49 to 51 and 55 of the judgment referred to in (n 30).

'Conventions concluded by the Member States in relation to particular matters', which appears in Article 71, was understood to provide exactly the contrary, taking into account the implicit conditions excluded from the text.

This interpretation is taken into account in relation to Article 82 of the Commission's Proposal, which maintains the current text, by providing that, although the Convention on a particular matter lays down conditions for the recognition and enforcement of applicable judgments, 'in any event, the provisions of this Regulation which concern the procedure for recognition and enforcement of judgments may be applied'. To clarify the situation in relation to the Lugano Convention of 2007, the new Article 84 states that the new Regulation shall not affect the said Convention.

With respect to future bilateral or multilateral conventions, we must address the question of whether it is possible to imagine a delegation in favor of the Member States, taking into account the interest that some States may have in concluding a bilateral Convention with a certain State, which may be of no interest to other Member States. On this matter, it has already been pointed out that the Commission did not want to adopt this approach in relation to the Brussels I Regulation, when it has been possible to do so, in matters of family law and contractual and non-contractual obligations. It is only possible to imagine that a change of opinion might come about when the Brussels I Regulation is being revised. For the moment, this possibility is not considered in the text of the recitals of the proposed revised Regulation, as has been the case, for example, in Recital (37) of Regulation 864/2007 on the applicable law to non-contractual obligations

VI. FINAL CONSIDERATIONS

We are faced with a revision of the Brussels I Regulation which will result, as an additional consequence, in the modification of the revised Lugano Convention of 2007, although there is hardly any practice in the application of this Convention. An important aspect of this revision concerns the topic of this paper, given that this matter constitutes an important step forward in the communitarisation of or, to use a more appropriate term for the current times, the 'Europeanisation' of rules on international jurisdiction in civil and commercial matters.

From a scientific standpoint, EGPIL has considered that this step ought to be taken, albeit on somewhat prudent terms. It is essential now to wait and see if the Member States are prepared to take this step right now, or if, on the contrary, it is to be postponed to a later date, similar to other aspects of the revision which will probably be left for a later discussion, such as the recognition and enforcement of judgments given in a third State.

The Brussels I Regulation in the International Legal Order: Some Reflections on Reflectiveness

*Alexander Layton**

I. INTRODUCTION

One of the most important features of the European Commission's Proposal ('Proposal'), and one which was perhaps less clearly anticipated than others, is the extension of the Regulation into the international legal order. It is proposed that this be achieved by the repeal of its Article 4, according to which the jurisdiction of the courts of Member States against persons not domiciled in the European Union is left to the law of the Member State in question.[1]

It is not the intention of this paper to examine that Proposal – and its many consequences – in any detail. It can merely be observed that its implications do not seem to have been fully explored,[2] and the justification for it advanced by the Commission seems distinctly shaky.[3] It must however be acknowledged that the current situation, whereby the Brussels I Regulation has mandatory application without reference to the outside world, is unsatisfactory in some respects. In three areas in particular there has long been a recognition that a purely inward-looking regime poses problems. The three areas are:

1. where there are parallel proceedings in a non-Member State;
2. where the principal subject matter of the dispute is such that there is a

---

* Queen's Counsel, 20 Essex Street.

[1] There are however two exceptions from this rule: (i) art 22, conferring exclusive jurisdiction on Member States' courts in cases with certain strong connecting factors, which applies without regard to the parties' domicile; and (ii) art 23, giving effect to jurisdiction agreements in favor of Member States' courts if either party, not just the defendant, is domiciled in a Member State.

[2] The European Parliament is skeptical: 'it would be premature to take this step without much study, wide-ranging consultations and political debate' (European Parliament Resolution of 7 September 2010 on the implementation and review of Council Regulation (EC) No 44/2001 on jurisdiction and the recognition and enforcement of judgments in civil and commercial matters (P7_TA (2010) 0304) para 15).

[3] A Dickinson, 'The Revision of the Brussels I Regulation' (2010) 12 Yearbook of Private International Law 247, 275.

strong connection with a non-Member State (the archetypal example being where the case involves rights *in rem* in immovable property in the third state); and

3.   where the parties have entered into an agreement conferring exclusive jurisdiction on the courts of a non-Member State.

Of these areas, the Proposal grapples only with parallel proceedings. This contribution looks briefly at them and comments briefly on the second area before looking in more detail at the third of these topics.

First, however, a word on terminology and on the mandatory nature of the Brussels I Regulation. The term 'reflexive effect' is often used to refer loosely to a range of proposed solutions to these problems, suggesting that the rules in Articles 27, 22 and 23 respectively of the Brussels I Regulation could be applied 'reflexively' *as if* the non-Member State were a Member State.[4] But there is little consensus on what, if any, additional conditions would be appropriate for these rules to be applied to non-Member States.

The mandatory nature of the Brussels Convention of 1968 on Jurisdiction and the Enforcement of Judgments in Civil and Commercial Matters ('Brussels Convention'), and hence of the Brussels I Regulation, appears most clearly from the decision of the Court of Justice of the European Union ('CJEU') in *Owusu v Jackson*.[5] That case involved an accident in Jamaica and there were no links with any Member State other than England, where both the claimant and the defendant were domiciled. The question was whether an English court could stay its proceedings, which had been properly brought before it under Article 2 of the Brussels Convention, even though the courts of Jamaica were more appropriate for the trial of the action. Advocate General Léger advised that it could not do so, but expressly excluded from his recommended answer these three categories of cases. Part of his proposed answer was that:

The Brussels Convention precludes a court of a Contracting State - whose jurisdiction is established on the basis of Article 2 of that Convention - from exercising a discretionary power to decline to exercise that jurisdiction on the ground that a court of a non-Contracting State would be more appropriate for the trial of the action, *where the latter court has not been designated by any agreement conferring jurisdiction, has not previously been seised of any claim liable to give rise to lis pendens or related actions and the links connecting the dispute with that non-*

---

[4] See A Layton and H Mercer, *European Civil Practice* (2nd edn, London 2004), para 15.25. The term 'reflexive effect' seems to have been first coined by GAL Droz, *Compétence Judiciaire et Effets des Jugements dans le Marché Commun* (Dalloz 1972) para 165, where the author referred only to the problem of immovable property in a third State.
[5] CJEU, Case C-281/02 *Owusu v Jackson* [2005] ECR I-1445.

Contracting State are of a kind other than those referred to in Article 16 of the Brussels Convention.[6]

The CJEU, however, in what appears to have been a deliberate rejection of that exception, stated in its judgment that 'Article 2 … is mandatory in nature and …, according to its terms, there can be no derogation from the principle it lays down except in the cases expressly provided for by the Convention'[7] and went on to rule that the Brussels Convention 'precludes a court of a Contracting State from declining the jurisdiction conferred on it by Article 2 of that convention on the ground that a court of a non-Contracting State would be a more appropriate forum for the trial of the action even if the jurisdiction of no other Contracting State is in issue or the proceedings have no connecting factors to any other Contracting State.'[8]

II. PARALLEL PROCEEDINGS IN A THIRD STATE

Article 34 of the Proposal contains a welcome provision designed to deal with the problem which may occur when proceedings in relation to the same cause of action and between the same parties are pending before the courts of a third State at a time when a court in a Member State is seised. At present in this situation, the latter court has no power to stay its proceedings, notwithstanding the parallel proceedings in the third State.[9] Under the proposed revision, the court seised in the Member State would have discretion to stay its proceedings if three conditions are satisfied. The first is that the foreign court was seised first in time, which is the same condition as applies as between the Member States under the current Article 27 of the Brussels I Regulation. The second and third conditions, however, apply only as against third States and not internally within the EU. They are that, 'it may be expected that the court in the third State will, within a reasonable time, render a judgment that will be capable of recognition and, where applicable, enforcement in that Member State' and 'the court is satisfied that it is necessary for the proper administration of justice to do so.'[10]

These are both, to a common lawyer, gratifyingly discretionary and mark something of a shift towards a flexible realism and away from a dogmatic adherence to legal certainty.

---

[6] Case C-281/02, Opinion of Advocate General Léger, 14 December 2004, para 281 (emphasis added). Art 16 of the Brussels Convention is renumbered as art 22 in the Brussels I Regulation.

[7] ibid, para 78.

[8] *Owusu* (note 5) at 1464.

[9] *Catalyst Investment Group Ltd v Lewinsohn* [2009] EWHC 1964 (Ch), [2010] Ch 218.

[10] Proposal, art 34(1)(b) and (c).

According to the revisions envisaged in the Proposal, the court would be given power to lift the stay at any time and the stay would not cause the party who seised the court in the Member State to lose the benefit of interruption of a limitation or prescription period.[11] If the proceedings in the court of the third State are concluded and they resulted in a judgment which is enforceable, or capable of recognition and (if applicable) enforcement, in the Member State in question, it is required to dismiss its own proceedings.[12]

III. CLOSE CONNECTION WITH A THIRD STATE

Article 22 of the Brussels I Regulation confers exclusive jurisdiction on the courts of Member States when the proceedings have as their principal subject matter one of a number of topics. The rule is mandatory and applies irrespective of the domicile of the parties. It is justified on the grounds that the subject matter of the proceedings has such a close connection with the territory of the Member States in question that it is inappropriate for the matter to be adjudicated by the courts of any other State. So it is surprising that an equivalent rule has not been adopted in respect of non-Member States. Indeed, the Court of Appeal of England has suggested (*obiter*) that it would be consistent with international law for Article 22(5) Brussels I Regulation, which confers exclusive jurisdiction over the enforcement of judgments on the State where enforcement is to occur, to have reflexive effect,[13] and it is at least arguable that it would be inconsistent with international law for the court of a Member State, or any State, to exercise jurisdiction over the enforcement of judgments in other States.

The Proposal maintains this distinction between Member States and non-Member States in relation to exclusive jurisdiction. Article 22 of the Proposal differs from Article 22 of the Brussels I Regulation only in some minor respects not relevant for the present discussion. But if the Brussels I Regulation is to be extended to the international legal order, one would have expected to see a rule providing for an exception to the *Owusu* principle and allowing proceedings in Member States to be stayed in favour of the courts of the non-Member State with which the proceedings have the prescribed type of close connection.

---

[11] Proposal, art 34(2) and 34(3).
[12] Proposal, art 34(4).
[13] *Masri v Consolidated Contractors SAL (No 2)* [2008] EWCA Civ 303, [2009] QB 450, paras 125–127, per Lawrence Collins LJ.

IV. CHOICE OF EXCLUSIVE JURISDICTION IN A THIRD STATE

Most surprising of all is the failure to include a rule in the Proposal which enables courts to give effect to jurisdiction agreements which confer exclusive jurisdiction on the courts of a third State, in the way that Article 23 Brussels I Regulation enables effect to be given to choice of jurisdiction agreements in favour of Member States. The problem has been recognised for many years. As far back as 1978 when the accession of the United Kingdom, Ireland and Denmark to the Brussels Convention was negotiated, the Schlosser Report referred to the problem without expressly providing a solution, but saying only that 'There is nothing in the 1968 Convention to support the conclusion that such agreements must be inadmissible in principle', citing German and French doctrine.

There is therefore a clear rule which, at least in relation to choice of court agreements, is at odds with what happens in practice; anecdotal evidence suggests that courts frequently give effect to such clauses, even where it would be contrary to the *Owusu* principle to do so.

The Nuyts Report[14] considers two different cases: where the defendant is not domiciled in a Member State, and where he is so domiciled. Where he is not domiciled in a Member State, the near-universal practice is to give effect to the agreement.[15] Where the defendant is domiciled in a Member State, there is again a large consensus that the court has power to respect the clause, although the reasons for doing so differ.[16] The Heidelberg Report[17] states that there is ongoing discussion whether the *Owusu* principle may nonetheless be inapplicable to Article 23 Brussels I Regulation and that the practice differs from state to state: 'The general reporters are convinced that this issue can and will be resolved by ECJ case law'. With respect, and especially in the light of the clarity of the decision in *Owusu* and the evidence in the Nuyts Report, this is perhaps doubtful anytime soon. But even if it is resolved by case law, the answer given by the courts may be contrary to the commercial sense and existing near-universal practice.

In England, the courts have grappled with the point in *Konkola Copper Mines PLC v Coromin*,[18] a case where reliance was placed on a Zambian choice of law and jurisdiction. Colman J held that the defendants had failed

---

[14] *Study on Residual Jurisdiction* prepared by Prof A Nuyts on 3 September 2007 ('Nuyts Report') available at <http://ec.europa.eu/justice/civil/document/index_en.htm>.

[15] ibid, 73–76.

[16] ibid, 80–84.

[17] B Hess, T Pfeiffer and P Schlosser, *Report on the Application of Regulation Brussels I in the Member States* ('Heidelberg Report') para 388, available at <http://ec.europa.eu/justice/civil/document/index_en.htm>.

[18] *Konkola Copper Mines PLC v Coromin* [2005] EWHC 898 (Comm), [2005] 2 Lloyd's Rep 555.

to establish that they could rely on the clause, but went on (*obiter*) to analyse what would have happened if he had reached a different conclusion on that point, distinguishing *Owusu* in the process. His reasoning is too lengthy and detailed to bear repetition here,[19] but in essence he decided that the methodology which led in *Owusu* to a rejection of *forum non conveniens* did not apply in the case of jurisdiction agreements, that the policy of the Brussels Convention was to be supportive of such agreements in favour of Member States, and that the reasoning of the Schlosser Report, as later recited by the CJEU,[20] was consistent with giving effect to such clauses. Colman J's decision was upheld by the Court of Appeal, on different grounds and without reference to this point.[21]

The Hague Convention on Choice of Court Agreements of 30 June 2005 ('Hague Convention')[22] regulates the effect of jurisdiction agreements as between those states which are parties to it. The EU is itself a member of the Hague Conference and has signed the Hague Convention, but has not ratified it, although it is to be expected that it will do so in due course. The Commission evidently expects the Hague Convention to resolve this issue and its officials have even observed in public that if the Brussels I Regulation were to contain a more favourable rule, then third States would have a reduced incentive to ratify the Hague Convention.[23] Ratification by the EU and by other States around the world is doubtless a desirable objective, but it is not a sufficient reason to exclude a provision from the recast Brussels I Regulation on this question. It is far from certain when, if ever, the Hague Convention will come into force at all, let alone as between the EU and enough states around the world to make any other rule of marginal significance. So far only Mexico has ratified it, and its eventual effectiveness is likely to depend to a great extent on whether the USA ratifies it; but this question is bogged down in a constitutional dispute within the USA on whether the power to ratify falls within the exclusive competence of the Federal Government, or also of the individual States. Even if it does come into effect, it will exclude a significant number of international contracts[24] and, for a significant period at least, many countries.

The case for legislation on this point is now generally agreed upon, and perhaps the simplest way of doing it would be to adopt wholesale the terms

---

[19] ibid, 570-574 (paras 86-100).

[20] CJEU, Case C-387/98 *Coreck Maritime Gmbh v Handelsveem BV* [2000] ECR I-9337.

[21] [2006] EWCA Civ 5; [2006] 1 Lloyd's Rep 410.

[22] Available on <www.hcch.net>.

[23] Informal hearing of the Legal Affairs Committee of the European Parliament (20 September 2011), viewable online at <http://www.europarl.europa.eu/wps-europarl-internet/frd/vod/player?eventCode=20110920-0900-COMMITTEE-JURI&language=en&byLeftMenu=researchcommittee&category=COMMITTEE&format=wmv#anchor1>, at 11.03.40.

[24] Hague Convention, art 2. Significantly, contracts for the carriage of passengers and goods are excluded, which will exclude a vast number of international commercial contracts.

of the Hague Convention, which, if necessary, could be done by reference, even in circumstances where that convention itself does not apply. It would, however, be sensible to extend the subject matter scope of the rule to the subject matter scope of the Brussels I Regulation, so that the difficulties which the current rules present are not perpetuated for cases which fall outside the subject matter scope of the Hague Convention, but within the Brussels I Regulation.

V. CONCLUSION

The extension of the Brussels I Regulation to the international legal order generally is a complex question and a reform which may well be put off for the time being. But whether or not this step is taken at this stage, there is a good case for legislating now not only in terms of Article 34 of the Proposal dealing with parallel proceedings in third States, but also in respect of the two other areas which have been discussed here – where there is a close connecting factor of a kind which, within the EU, would bring the case within Article 22 Brussels I Regulation; and where the parties have agreed on the exclusive jurisdiction of the courts of a third State.

Choice of Court Agreements in the Review Proposal for the Brussels I Regulation

*Ulrich Magnus**

I. INTRODUCTION

In international contracts few clauses are as common as choice of court clauses. In practice, these clauses play an important role. If validly agreed upon, they determine which court or tribunal has jurisdiction to decide a future dispute between the parties. They are designed to give the parties certainty in advance about where to sue, ie certainty with respect to eventual litigation.[1] Moreover, if the parties do not explicitly agree on a certain law, jurisdiction clauses give also a strong hint that the law at the court's seat governs the parties' contract.[2] Often therefore, choice of court agreements do not only designate the place of a possible lawsuit, but also the applicable law. They are thus often decisive to the final outcome of a lawsuit.[3] Compared to the importance and frequency of choice of court agreements, one would expect many more court decisions expressly addressing the problems of such agreements. However, the validity of a choice of court agreement is very often disputed at the beginning of a lawsuit and then settled in one way or another during the proceedings. Decisions incidentally dealing with problems of choice of court agreements are frequent; decisions exclusively dealing with them are rare.

The Brussels I Regulation addresses choice of court agreements in its Article 23. The Regulation gives a wide recognition to such agreements. In

---

* University Professor (em.) at the University of Hamburg.

[1] See B Hess, *Europäisches Zivilprozessrecht* (CF Müller 2010) para 6-128; U Magnus, 'Prorogation of Jurisdiction' in U Magnus and P Mankowski (ed), *Brussels I Regulation: European Commentaries on Private International Law* (Sellier 2007) art 23, n 5; P Mankowski, in T Rauscher (ed), *Europäisches Zivilprozessrecht* (2nd edn, Sellier 2006) art 23, n 1.

[2] See eg BGHZ 104, 268; BGH NJW-RR 1990, 183; BGH NJW 1991, 1420; BGH NJW 1996, 2569; OLG Celle RiW 1988, 137; OLG Frankfurt RiW 1989, 912; OLG Hamburg TranspR 1993, 111; OLG Frankfurt RiW 1998, 477; *Komninos S* [1991] Lloyds LR 370; *Marabenu Hong Kong and South China Ltd v Mongolian Government* [2002] 2 All ER 873; see also Recital 12 of the Rome I Regulation.

[3] See R Fentiman, '*Lis Pendens* – Related Actions, Introduction to Articles 27–30' in U Magnus and P Mankowski (ed), *Brussels I Regulation: European Commentaries on Private International Law* (Sellier 2007) para 16.

principle, it accepts full party autonomy in selecting the competent court except where the Regulation confers exclusive jurisdiction on specific courts (Article 22 of the Brussels I Regulation) or where it limits party autonomy in the interest of the weaker party.[4] Like the EU conflicts rules on contracts,[5] the Brussels I Regulation provides for specific procedural protection of those parties who typically are in a weaker position than their adversaries. The Regulation admits choice of court agreements with insured persons, consumers or employees only if the agreement opens up a wider range of competent courts to the weaker party. The jurisdiction of the courts where this party normally can sue and has to be sued cannot be ousted.

On the whole, Article 23 of the Brussels I Regulation works relatively well. Nonetheless, problems or at least questions remain. Some of these problems are even urgent. It is therefore not at all surprising that the Commission's (Review) Proposal for a Regulation of the European Parliament and the Council on jurisdiction and the recognition and enforcement of judgments in civil and commercial matters of 14 December 2010[6] ('Proposal') also includes some modifications with respect to choice of court agreements.

The Commission's Proposal must also be viewed against the background of the Hague Convention of 30 June 2005 on Choice of Court Agreements[7] ('Hague Convention'), a rival instrument. This Convention – the remains of a convention once-intended to globalise the operation of the Brussels I Regulation – sets an international standard on the treatment of choice of court agreements. The proposed changes to the Brussels I Regulation concerning jurisdiction agreements compete to a certain extent with the solutions of the Hague Convention, all the more relevant since the EU intends to ratify the latter.[8] The Brussels I Regulation and the Hague Convention therefore should be aligned as closely as possible.[9]

---

[4] Recital 14 of the Brussels I Regulation.

[5] See arts 5–8 of the Rome I Regulation.

[6] COM (2010) 748 final; see thereto B Hess, 'Die Reform der EuGVVO und die Zukunft des Europäischen Zivilprozessrechts' (2011) 2 IPRax 125.

[7] See under http://www.hcch.net. On this Convention, see in particular RA Brand and PM Herrup, *The 2005 Hague Convention on Choice of Court Agreements* (Cambridge University Press 2008); R Wagner, 'Das Haager Übereinkommen vom 30.6.2005 über Gerichtsstandsvereinbarungen' (2009) 73 RabelsZ 100.

[8] See the Council Decision 2009/397/EC of 26 February 2009 on the Signing on Behalf of the European Community of the Convention on Choice of Court Agreements [2009] OJ L133/1. Thus far (March 2012), Mexico is the only state that has ratified the Hague Convention.

[9] In the same sense, B Hess, T Pfeiffer, P Schlosser and M Weller, in B Hess, T Pfeiffer and P Schlosser, *The Brussels I-Regulation (EC) No 44/2001 – The Heidelberg Report on the Application of Regulation Brussels I in 25 Member States* (Beck 2008) para 709 ff.

The following text firstly deals with the problems and questions raised by the current Article 23; it then addresses the changes proposed in the Commission's Proposal, and finally draws some conclusions.

A. Introduction

Article 23 of the Brussels I Regulation requires two connecting factors in order for a choice of court agreements to bind the court or courts chosen: first, the parties must have chosen a court or courts in an EU Member State; second, one of the parties, irrespective whether it is the claimant or the defendant, must be domiciled in a Member State. However, it is not necessary that this Member State is the state of the chosen court(s).

Thus, Article 23(1) does not apply where neither of the parties is domiciled in the EU but a court in the EU is chosen. Where, for instance, a French and a German citizen agree on the exclusive jurisdiction of a Belgium court, Article 23 is not applicable if the two citizens have their *domicile* outside the EU (and outside of the territorial scope of the Lugano Convention). These cases have to be treated according to the national law of the Member State whose court is seised.[10] Nonetheless, paragraph 3 of Article 23 deals with a certain aspect of this situation, namely with the derogative effect of such agreements in the other EU Member States. The jurisdiction of other courts in the EU is barred in this case unless the chosen court has declined jurisdiction according to its national law. In no way does the Regulation deal with agreements that confer jurisdiction on courts outside the EU, even if such agreements oust the original jurisdiction of the courts of one or more EU Member States, and even if this jurisdiction is exclusive under Article 22.

B. Formal validity of choice of court agreements

Article 23 provides certain requirements as to the form of choice of court agreements. The provision is generous in this respect. Writing is not always mandatory; instead, a practice between the parties or a commercial usage which allows for oral agreement can suffice. As far as writing is required, reproducible electronic declarations satisfy the form.[11]

---

[10] See Hoge Raad Ned. Jur. 1985 No. 698 with note by Schultz; J Kropholler and J von Hein, *Europäisches Zivilprozessrecht: Kommentar* (9th edn, Verlag Recht und Wirtschaft 2011) art 23, para 12.

[11] See art 23(2) of the Brussels I Regulation.

Article 23 determines the form requirements, finally and conclusively.[12] No other form is admitted, nor is any further redress to national (conflicts or substantive) law allowed. The Regulation itself contains the substantive law applicable to the form of choice of court agreements.

The form requirements of Article 23 have to be interpreted in an EU-autonomous way.[13] The Court of Justice of the European Union ('CJEU') has decided on several occasions on the correct interpretation of these requirements.[14]

C. Material validity of choice of court agreements

In contrast to the requirements of form, Article 23 is not clear on the material validity of choice of court agreements. This is one of its major shortcomings. It remains open whether, and if so, how far, the provision itself regulates the material validity of the agreement or the extent to which it refers to the applicable national law. If the CJEU judgments[15] on jurisdiction clauses and in particular on their incorporation into a binding agreement between the parties are taken as a whole, it is evident that they do not only provide formal, but also certain material rules of contract formation.[16] Further, the text of Article 23 requires the existence of an agreement ('...the parties ...have agreed...'). This can be, and by the prevailing view is, understood as an autonomous regulation of the formation of the agreement,

---

[12] See CJEU, Case C-150/80 *Elefanten Schuh GmbH v Pierre Jacqmain* [1981] ECR 1671, 1688, para 25 ff.; Case C-159/97 *Trasporti Castelletti Spedizioni Internazionali SpA v Hugo Trumpy SpA* [1999] ECR I-1597, I-1653, para 37; further J Kropholler and J von Hein (n 10) art 23, n 30; A Layton and H Mercer, *European Civil Practice* (2nd edn, Thomson, Sweet and Maxwell 2004) para 20.029; P Mankowski, in T Rauscher (n 1) art 23, n 14; H Schack, *Internationales Zivilprozessrecht* (5th edn, Beck 2010) para 472.

[13] See S Auer, in A Bülow, KH Böckstiegel, R Geimer and RA Schütze (ed), *Internationaler Rechtsverkehr in Zivil- und Handelssachen* (Beck 1954 and subsequently; most recent edition 2011) art 23, n 84, 86; R Geimer and RA Schütze, *Europäisches Zivilverfahrensrecht, Kommentar* (2nd edn, Beck 2004) art 23, n 97; J Kropholler and J von Hein (n 10), art 23, n 30; U Magnus in U Magnus and P Mankowski (n 1) art 23, n 88.

[14] See in particular CJEU, Case C-24/76 *Estasis Salotti di Colzani Aimo and Gianmario Colzani v RÜWA Polstereimaschinen GmbH* [1976] ECR 1831; Case C-25/76 *Galeries Segoura SPRL v Société Rahim Bonakdarian* [1976] ECR 1851; Case C-71/83 *Partenreederei ms. 'Tilly Russ' and Ernst Russ v NV Haven en Vervoerbedrijf Nova and NV Goeminne Hout* [1984] ECR 2417; Case C-159/97 *Trasporti Castelletti Spedizioni Internazionali SpA v Hugo Trumpy SpA* [1999] ECR I 1597; Case C-387/98 *Coreck Maritime GmbH v Handelsveem BV* [2000] ECR I-9337.

[15] See cases cited above (n 14).

[16] See also R Fentiman, *International Commercial Litigation* (OUP 2010) para 2.32 ff.; J Kropholler and J von Hein (n 10) art 23, n 27; A Layton and H Mercer (n 12) para 20.083 ff.; T Pfeiffer in B Hess, T Pfeiffer and P Schlosser (n 9) para 325; H Roth, 'Internationalrechtliche Probleme bei Prorogation und Derogation' (1980) 93 ZZP 156, 162; A Briggs, *Agreements on Jurisdiction and Choice of Law* (OUP 2008) at para 7.35 advocates however the view that 'Article 23 does not require, and is not necessarily satisfied by, a contractually-binding agreement on jurisdiction'.

requiring nothing more, nor less, than the consensus of the parties.[17] In this view, Article 23 excludes further requirements for a binding agreement, such as consideration – as necessary under English law – or similar.

On the other hand, is it clear that Article 23 does not cover all aspects of contract formation. It concerns, for example, neither capacity, nor mistake, fraud, duress, agency or assignment. The provision does not allow for autonomous rules on these matters to be inferred, nor does it indicate which law should govern them.

For this reason, it has been suggested that substantive law questions concerning the formation of choice of court agreements, in particular their incorporation into a contract, *in toto* are better left to the applicable national law.[18] However, this contradicts to some extent the text of Article 23, which requires an agreement and thus covers certain material aspects of formation. It also contradicts the CJEU case law, which infers from Article 23 some rules on the material law of contract formation, and raises the question as to which domestic law should apply: the *lex fori* or the *lex causae*?

As Article 23 is silent on these aspects, they become matters to be decided in practice. The practice of the Member States is, however, not uniform.[19] The national courts follow, to varying degrees, the idea of autonomous formation rules for certain questions; for the remaining aspects, they apply partly the *lex fori* and partly the *lex causae*.[20] The majority appear to apply the substantive law designated by the private international law of the Member State whose court is seised with the case.[21]

---

[17] See CJEU, Case C-24/76 *Estasis Salotti di Colzani Aimo and Gianmario Colzani v RÜWA Polstereimaschinen GmbH* [1976] ECR 1831 para 7; R Fentiman (n 16) para 2.35; B Hess (n 1) para 6-137; J Kropholler and J von Hein (n 10) art 23, n 23, 25 ff.; U Magnus in U Magnus and P Mankowski (n 1) art 23, n 78; P Mankowski, in T Rauscher (n 1) art 23, n 39; for a good account of the differing views, see J Hill and A Chong, *International Commercial Disputes. Commercial Conflict of Laws in English Courts* (4th edn, Hart 2010) para 5.3.38 ff.

[18] P Gottwald, in T Rauscher, J Wenzel and P Wax, *Münchener Kommentar zur Zivilprozessordnung* (3rd edn, Beck 2008) art 23 EuGVVO, para 15; A Layton and H Mercer (n 12) para 20.084.

[19] T Pfeiffer, in B Hess, T Pfeiffer and P Schlosser (n 9) para 323 ff.

[20] T Pfeiffer, in B Hess, T Pfeiffer and P Schlosser (n 9) para 326.

[21] CJEU, Case C-269/95 *Francesco Benincasa v Dentalkit Srl* [1997] ECR I-3767 para 25; BGH NJW 2007, 2036 (2037); OGH ZfRV 2001, 231; GAL Droz, *Compétence judiciaire et effets des jugements dans le Marché Commun* (Dalloz 1972) para 214; R Hausmann, in C Reithmann and D Martiny (eds), *Internationales Vertragsrecht* (7th edn, Dr. Otto Schmidt 2010) para 6413; J Kropholler and J von Hein (n 10) art 23, n 23, 25 ff; A Layton and H Mercer (n 12) para 20.038; U Magnus in U Magnus and P Mankowski (n 1) art 23, n 81; P Mankowski, in T Rauscher (n 1) art 23, n 41; see also the survey on the CJEU decisions in comparison to the English common law decisions by D Joseph, *Jurisdiction and Arbitration Agreements and Their Enforcement* (2nd edn, Sweet & Maxwell, Thomson Reuters 2010) para 7.04 ff.

D. *Effects of choice of court agreements*

Article 23 gives a choice of court agreement the effect that the chosen court is exclusively competent, unless the parties have agreed otherwise and unless other provisions of the Regulation (Articles 22, 13, 17 and 21) exclude such agreements. Where an exclusive choice of court agreement is validly concluded, no other court is allowed to decide on the substance of the dispute. This does not mean that non-exclusive choice of court agreements do not fall under Article 23. The form and material requirements under Article 23 similarly apply to these agreements. However, non-exclusive choice of court agreements do not oust the jurisdiction originally founded under the Regulation.

A choice of court agreement's exclusive effect has to prove its value where one of the parties disregards the agreement and approaches a court other than that chosen. In that situation, Article 23 does not, however, take priority over Article 27 of the Brussels I Regulation. This is the most disputed and criticised shortcoming of Article 23 in relation to Article 27 of the Brussels I Regulation.[22] If a party initiates proceedings in a court other than the chosen one, this court, if seised first, must decide firstly on jurisdiction. According to Article 27(1), the court later seised, even if it is the court chosen by the parties, must stay its proceedings – if it is the same cause of action and a dispute between the same parties – until the first court has decided on its jurisdiction.[23] If the first court is a very slow court, a party can effectively undermine the exclusive effect of a choice of court agreement and delay justice considerably.

In cases of related actions, the chosen court is not obliged to stay its proceedings if another court is seised first, but has discretion to do so.[24] The same holds true for any other – non-chosen – court. However, the other court, if seised first, is obliged to decide at least on its jurisdiction (Article 28). Thus, in related actions it is possible that, despite the choice of court agreement, two or more proceedings in different Member States are entertained and lead to conflicting judgments.

The current priority rules of the *lis pendens* provisions of the Regulation do not honour choice of court agreements, but treat them on the same footing as any other jurisdictional basis. In fact, they disregard their existence.[25]

---

[22] Thereon U Magnus and P Mankowski, 'Brussels I on the Verge of Reform – A Response to the Green Paper on the Review of the Brussels I Regulation' (2010) 109 ZVglRWiss 1, 11 ff.; LG Radicati di Brozolo, 'Choice of Court and Arbitration Agreements and the Review of the Brussels I Regulation' (2010) 2 IPRax 121, 122 ff.; M Weller, in B Hess, T Pfeiffer and P Schlosser (n 9) para 369 (reporting the critique of the Member States).

[23] This is the effect of the CJEU's judgments in Case C-116/02 *Erich Gasser GmbH v MISAT Srl* [2003] ECR I-4693 and Case C-159/02 *Turner v Grovit* [2004] ECR I-3565.

[24] See art 28(1) Brussels I Regulation.

[25] In a similar sense M Weller, in B Hess, T Pfeiffer and P Schlosser (n 9) para 388 ff. (reporting also respective critique of the stakeholders of international commerce).

E. Control of misuse of choice of court agreements

Choice of court agreements can be misused to deprive a party of the forum where his or her claims would normally be decided. Articles 13, 17 and 21 prevent such misuse in respect of insurance, consumer and labour contracts. Apart from these kinds of contracts, misuse can equally occur in cases where an unexpected jurisdiction clause is nevertheless validly incorporated into a contract between, for instance, a broker and his client or a principal and his agent.[26] Neither Article 23, nor the Regulation as such, provides for a special instrument to control any misuse of a choice of court agreement in those situations. Nonetheless, it is disputed whether there is an inherent rule against any such misuse. The opinions are split.[27] In the context of the control of standard contract terms, the CJEU has stated that a jurisdiction clause can regularly be considered abusive and consequently invalid if the clause is not individually negotiated and grants, in cases of claims against a consumer, exclusive jurisdiction to the courts at the place where the professional is located (and Article 17 of the Brussels I Regulation does not apply).[28]

F. Remedies for breach of choice of court agreements

It is likewise disputed whether damages can be awarded in the case of a breach of a choice of court agreement (unless the parties have expressly stipulated damages or a penalty for such breach which they are entirely free to do).[29] On the one hand, choice of court agreements are binding civil law contracts; on the other, they exclusively concern the procedural relationship between the parties. Therefore, it is doubtful whether their breach gives rise

---

[26] See OLG München 29 U 2119/06, reported in (2007) 6 IPRax 322 with a note by G Rühl, 'Die Wirksamkeit von Gerichtsstands -und Schiedsvereinbarungen im Lichte der Ingmar-Entscheidung des EuGH (OLG München)' (2007) 4 IPRax 294.

[27] Pro such a control, see for instance P Gottwald, in T Rauscher, J Wenzel and P Wax (n 18) art 23 EuGVVO, para 15; B Hess (n 1) para 6-147; R Hüßtege, in H Thomas and H Putzo (ed), *Zivilprozessordnung* (32nd edn, Beck 2011) art 23 EuGVVO, para 18; T Pfeiffer, 'Gerichtstandsvereinbarungen und EG-Klauselrichtlinie' in FS Schütze, *Handbuch der Handelsgeschäfte* (Beck 1999) 675 ff.; however cautiously P Gottwald, in T Rauscher, J Wenzel and P Wax (n 18) art 23 EuGVVO, para 60; J Kropholler and J von Hein (n 10) art 23, para 89; contra such control for instance OLG Hamburg NJW 2004, 3126; R Geimer and RA Schütze (n 13) art 23, para 181; C Redmann, *Ordre public-Kontrolle von Gerichtsstandsvereinbarungen* (Verlag Dr. Kovac 2005) 192 ff.; sceptical P Mankowski, in T Rauscher (n 1) art 23, n 12 ff.

[28] CJEU, Case C-240–244/98 *Groupo Océano v Roció Murciano Quintero* [2000] ECR I-4941; Case C-237/02 *Freiburger Kommunalbauten v Ludger Hofstetter and Ulrike Hofstetter* [2004] ECR I-3403; Case C-243/08 *Pannon v Erzsébet Sustikné Györfi* [2009] ECR I-4713.

[29] Thereon A Briggs (n 9) para 8.01 ff.; also further U Magnus and P Mankowski (n 22) at 13; P Mankowski, 'Ist eine vertragliche Absicherung von Gerichtsstandsvereinbarungen möglich?' (2009) 1 IPRax 23 ff.

to the general contract remedy of damages or entails mere procedural sanctions. Under the current Article 23, the question is open.[30]

G. Recognition of judgments neglecting a choice of court agreement

Under the Brussels I Regulation, the recognition of a judgment cannot be refused for the reason that the judgment disregarded a choice of court agreement. Even if a court intentionally neglected a valid choice of court agreement, for instance, because it regarded the invocation of the agreement as a misuse, the final judgment of the (derogated) court must be recognised and enforced. The current Article 35(1) of the Brussels I Regulation does not allow for the judgment to be challenged for lack of jurisdiction due to the existence of a choice of court agreement, which has not been followed.[31]

H. Language of choice of court agreements

The binding force of a choice of court agreement, and in particular of a jurisdiction clause in standard contract terms, also depends on whether it is made in a language that the addressee can reasonably be expected to understand. Article 23 does not expressly mention this aspect. Again, it is open whether an inherent autonomous solution is possible or whether another law (and then the question arises as to which law) should apply in order to decide this question.[32]

I. Compliance with the Hague Convention

On a number of points, Article 23 does not correspond to the Hague Convention.[33] Thus, in contrast to the Brussels I Regulation, the Convention:

---

[30] For damages: *National Westminster Bank plc v Rabobank Nederland (No 3)* [2008] All ER 266; *Standard Bank plc v Agrinvest International Inc* [2008] 1 Lloyd's Rep 523; B Hess (n 1) para 6-146; against damages: P Gottwald, in T Rauscher, J Wenzel and P Wax (n 18) art 23 EuGVVO, para 79 (only procedural sanctions); P Mankowski (n 29) 23, 27 (but possible where specifically agreed upon by the parties).

[31] See J Kropholler and J von Hein (n 10) art 35, para 14; P Mankowski in U Magnus and P Mankowski (n 1) art 35, para 43.

[32] Thereon R Geimer and RA Schütze (n 13) art 23, para 93; U Magnus in U Magnus and P Mankowski (n 1) art 23, para 86; P Mankowski in U Magnus and P Mankowski (n 1) art 23, para 40; left open by the CJEU in Case C-288/92 *Custom Made Commercial v Stawa Metallbau* [1994] ECR 2913.

[33] As to the differences see R Wagner and JM Schüngeler, 'Das Haager Übereinkommen vom 30.6.2005 über Gerichtsstandsvereinbarungen und die Parallelvorschriften in der Brüssel I-Verordnung (EuGVVO)' (2009) 108 ZVglRWiss 399 ff.

1. requires a written or otherwise reproducible agreement;[34]
2. requires as a connecting factor only that the chosen court is located in a Contracting State;[35]
3. designates the law of the chosen court as applicable with respect to the validity of the jurisdiction clause;[36]
4. obliges any court other than the chosen court (though it must be a court of a Contracting State) to stay proceedings or to dismiss the suit for lack of competence;[37]
5. establishes some exceptions to this obligation. One exception applies where the application of the choice of court agreement would contradict the *ordre public* of the seised court.[38]

If Article 23 remains unchanged, these differences would pose a major problem because they will lead to two different systems when the EU, as intended, ratifies the Hague Convention: choice of court agreements within the EU and those subject to the Hague Convention would follow different rules.

III. PROPOSED CHANGES

With respect to choice of court agreements, the Commission's Proposal regarding the review of the Brussels I Regulation provides for few though very significant modifications. According to the Commission's explanation, the proposed modifications of Article 23 – and also those to further provisions – shall strengthen the effectiveness of choice of court agreements.[39] This is the overarching objective of the modifications of this part of the Proposal. However, while jurisdictional party autonomy is an entirely acceptable aim, it should not be forgotten that there are further objectives (such as legal certainty, protection of weaker parties etc) which need to be equitably balanced with the provision on choice of court agreements.

A. Connecting factor

The Proposal reduces the necessity of two connecting factors to one. In the future, it shall suffice that only the chosen court is located in a EU Member

---

[34] Art 3(c) of the Hague Convention.
[35] Art 5(1) of the Hague Convention.
[36] Art 5(1) and 6(a) of the Hague Convention.
[37] Art 6 of the Hague Convention.
[38] Art 6(c) of the Hague Convention.
[39] See Recital 19 of the Proposal and point 3.1.3 of the Explanatory Memorandum accompanying the Proposal ('Explanatory Memorandum').

State. No longer shall it be necessary for one of the parties to be domiciled in a EU Member State. The proposed Article 23 would therefore also cover agreements between parties who are both domiciled outside the EU, provided that they wish to seise an EU Member State's court.

This Proposal corresponds to the proposed new policy that extends the effects of the Brussels I Regulation, in principle, to parties from third States.[40] It further corresponds to the Hague Convention which states in its Article 3 a) and Article 5 that the choice of a court in a Contracting State is sufficient to found the jurisdiction of that state.

This modification is to be welcomed.[41] It avoids different treatment of choice of court agreements where persons domiciled in the EU and persons domiciled outside the EU are involved. A differentiation according to the domicile is unconvincing. Where jurisdiction is based on the parties' will, their will and not their domicile must be the decisive factor. Further, in the EU, all clauses conferring jurisdiction on a court or on the courts of a Member State should be measured according to the same yardstick and be treated in accordance with the same rules.

B. Material validity

The Proposal prescribes that a choice of court agreement confers jurisdiction, 'unless the agreement is null and void as to its substance under the law of that Member State'. 'That Member State' is the state where the chosen court is located.

The Proposal intends to remove the uncertainty as to which law governs the material validity of a choice of court agreement. The Commission wants to introduce 'a harmonised conflict of law rule on the substantive validity of choice of court agreements, thus ensuring a similar outcome on this matter whatever the court seised'.[42] The Proposal corresponds largely to the Hague Convention whose Article 6 a) refers, in respect of the validity of the agreement, to the law of the state of the chosen court.

In principle, it is to be welcomed that the proposed Article 23 designates the law which will govern the material validity of choice of court agreements. The Proposal should clarify this open and disputed question.[43] However, the proposed formulation gives rise to particular doubts.

First, it remains unclear whether Article 23 shall continue to include certain autonomous elements concerning the formation of the agreement

---

[40] See points 1.2 and 3.1.2 of the Explanatory Memorandum.

[41] In the same sense see European Group for Private International Law, 'Proposed Amendment of Regulation 44/2001 in Order to Apply it to External Situations' (2009) 3 IPRax 284 (Article 23); further U Magnus and P Mankowski (n 22) at 10.

[42] See point 3.1.3 of the Explanatory Memorandum.

[43] See also T Pfeiffer, in B Hess, T Pfeiffer and P Schlosser (n 9) para 349.20.

(namely that pure consensus suffices), which do not require any further reference to national law. The question can become relevant, for example, with respect to the concept of consideration. Under the disputed, yet prevailing, view, this and similar concepts do not form part of the consensus required under the current Article 23.[44] The autonomous formation concept within Article 23 excludes such considerations. If the reviewed Article 23 is intended to designate the applicable law for all material aspects of the formation of the choice of court agreement, the concept of consideration would have to be taken into account where English law would govern the agreement. However, the reviewed Article 23 should not change the current interpretation that the consensus aspect, as such, is entirely regulated by Article 23 itself. It would be a step backwards if national peculiarities like the consideration concept were to creep in as relevant factors. Therefore, agreement, in the sense of Article 23, should continue to require mere consensus. This would mean that a distinction between the formation and the validity of the agreement and other separate aspects like agency, assignment etc, would have to be drawn. Validity in its strict sense covers those circumstances which may invalidate an otherwise effectively formed agreement.

This leads to a second issue in relation with the proposed Article 23. It is doubtful whether the proposed new wording covers the material validity in the sense described as a whole. The ordinary meaning of the proposed inclusion 'unless the agreement is null and void as to its substance' normally comprises only those circumstances which would automatically nullify an agreement, that is, render it null and void. It normally excludes 'voidable' acts. Understood strictly, the proposed formulation would therefore cover incapacity or violation of good morals, but not error, mistake, fraud, duress etc, let alone issues relating to agency or assignment. Although error, mistake, fraud or duress also concern material validity, they do not automatically invalidate an agreement. Incapacity, on the other hand, does nullify an agreement automatically. The above-quoted reasoning of the Commission gives the impression that validity as a whole should be covered ('conflict of law rule on the substantive validity of choice of court agreements'). This would only be reasonable. It does not make sense if the law applicable to cases of voidness alone would be determined by reference to the provision. The wording should therefore be amended so as to provide 'unless the agreement is invalid as to its substance...'. The provision could be expressed even more clearly as thus: 'The material validity (concerning capacity, mistake, fraud, duress) of the choice of court agreement is governed by the law of the Member State where the chosen court or courts are located.' However, other separate questions concerning the agreement such as agency or assignment also have to be addressed. The wording

---

[44] See (n 17).

should therefore read: 'The material validity (concerning capacity, mistake, fraud, duress) of the choice of court agreement as well as matters such as agency and assignment connected with the formation of such agreement are governed by the law of the Member State where the chosen court or courts are located.'

A third issue of doubt concerns whether the Proposal refers to the substantive law of the chosen forum or to this forum's private international law. The proposed text is indifferent.[45] Ideally, reference should be made to the law that the chosen forum's private international law designates. Four reasons militate in favour of this solution. First, the solution maintains, in essence, the prevailing practice under the current Article 23. Under the current wording the forum is, however, the court seised, not necessarily the chosen forum.[46] Secondly, the proposed solution aims to ensure that all EU Member State courts involved treat a choice of court agreement according to the same rules so that – hopefully – its validity or invalidity is adjudicated uniformly, since the Rome I Regulation has unified the conflicts rules.[47] Thirdly, the solution is practical. Although the choice of court agreement and the main contract are separate agreements, which need not have the same fate, it is frequently the same law that applies to both. It is practical to determine this law according to the same conflict rules. The solution is also practical because in the end it often is, and should be, the chosen court that decides the dispute and this court will apply its own private international law. Fourthly, the *lex fori prorogati* rule complies with the Hague Convention. Article 6 a) of the Hague Convention refers to the law of the country of the chosen forum. This reference includes the private international law of that country.[48]

---

[45] It could be argued that the text would have used the expression 'the internal law of that Member State' if it intended to mean the substantive domestic law excluding private international law. However, a judge or other user of the text is unlikely to discern that.

[46] See (n 21).

[47] Although art 1(2)(e) of the Rome I Regulation excludes 'arbitration agreements and agreements on the choice of court' from its scope this exclusion reaches only as far as special rules on those agreements regulate their conclusion and validity aspects. To the extent that these special rules (like art 23 of the Brussels I Regulation) do not provide rules for the material validity of such agreements, the conflicts rules of the prior Rome Convention and now of the Rome I Regulation can and should be applied; in the same sense already BGHZ 99, 207, 209 f.; D Martiny, in K Rebmann, FJ Saecker and R Rixecker (eds), *Münchener Kommentar zum Bürgerlichen Gesetzbuch* (4th edn, Beck 2006) vor art 27 EGBGB, para 98 ff; U Magnus in J von Staudinger, *Kommentar zum Bürgerlichen Gesetzbuch mit Einführungsgesetz und Nebengesetzen* (Sellier/de Gruyter 2011) art 1 Rom I-VO, para 77; evidently contra C Heinze, 'Choice of Court Agreements, Coordination of Proceedings and Provisional Measures in the Reform of the Brussels I Regulation' (2011) Max Planck Private Law Research Paper No 11/5, 4. The fact that the Rome I Regulation does not apply in Denmark has no great importance because in Denmark the Rome Convention still applies and the Rome I Regulation only marginally deviates from the Convention.

[48] See T Hartley and M Dogauchi, *Explanatory Report on the 2005 Hague Choice of Court*

Lastly, it needs to be discussed whether the requirements for choice of court agreements established within Article 23 should apply only if an EU court has been chosen, or whether they should also be observed where the parties choose a court outside the EU and a court within the EU has to deal with that agreement. Article 23(3) of the current Regulation does not fully answer the question, but allows for the application of the EU standard by way of analogy.[49] The proposed deletion of Article 23(3) excludes the scope for this analogous reference. However, where EU Member State courts are confronted with agreements in which the jurisdiction of courts in third States is chosen, they should apply Article 23 as a yardstick with respect to the formation, the validity and further questions concerning an effective choice of court agreement.

In conclusion, in order to avoid the points of doubt to which the proposed inclusion gives rise, a new paragraph should be added to Article 23 which should read: 'The material validity (concerning capacity, mistake, fraud, duress) of a choice of court agreement as well as matters like agency and assignment connected with the formation of such an agreement are governed by the law designated by the rules of private international law of the state where the chosen court or courts are located.'

C. Effects

1. Intention of the Commission

The most decisive change that the Commission proposes is a reversal of priority. The intention of the Commission is that the chosen court should no longer be obliged to stay its proceedings if another court is seised first. Instead, 'the other court has to stay proceedings until the chosen court has established or – in case the agreement is invalid – declined jurisdiction'.[50]

This idea has to be welcomed.[51] Where the parties have validly agreed that a certain court should exclusively resolve their disputes, this court alone should decide on the merits of the case and any other court, even if seised first, should stay the proceedings.

Agreements Convention (Hague Conference on Private International Law 2007, http://www.hcch.net) para 125, para 149, n 184; R Wagner (n 7) 100, 122.

[49] See thereto J Samtleben, 'Der Art. 23 EuGVO als einheitlicher Maßstab für internationale Gerichtsstandsvereinbarungen' in S Arkan and A Yongalik (eds), *Liber Amicorum in Honour of Tugrul Ansay* (Kluwer 2006) 343, 361.

[50] See Explanatory Memorandum at 9.

[51] In the same sense U Magnus and P Mankowski, (n 22) 11 ff; LG Radicati di Brozolo (n 22) 122 ff.; contra however B Hess, T Pfeiffer and P Schlosser (n 9) para 717 (instead of a reversal of the priority rule they propose a mere release from that rule; the chosen court could then decide even if another court is first seised. This could however lead to differing judgments on the merits of the case and later to problems with the recognition and enforcement).

There is a certain danger that the defendant in the first proceedings can then use delaying tactics by not instituting proceedings in the chosen court. However, the claimant of the first proceedings is entirely free to start such proceedings in the chosen court him- or herself. The danger of the other party exercising such delaying tactics is therefore now more theoretical than real.

2. Intention achieved?

It is not clear whether the proposed change to the Regulation achieves the Commission's intention. *Sedes materiae* is not Article 23, but as in the Brussels I Regulation, the section on *lis pendens* (new Articles 29–34). However, Article 29 of the Proposal – the former Article 27 – does not mention expressly that any court other than the chosen court(s) must stay its proceedings. Article 29(1) only refers to Article 32(2) by leaving that provision untouched ('Without prejudice to Article 32(2)...'). Article 32(2) provides that other Member State courts other than the chosen court(s) 'shall have no jurisdiction over the dispute until such time as the court or courts designated in the agreement decline their jurisdiction.' This can be understood in the sense that the Commission intends, namely that the other court, which was seised first, has to stay proceedings and wait for the decision of the chosen court. However, it can also be understood in the sense that the court seised first has to dismiss the claim immediately because of a lack of jurisdiction ('...shall have no jurisdiction...'). However, taking practical aspects into consideration, in particular concerning costs,[52] an immediate stay would be the right solution where a party to a choice of court agreement institutes proceedings in a court other than that chosen. A dismissal for lack of jurisdiction could be premature: a dismissal would be justified only after the chosen court accepted jurisdiction and regarded the agreement as valid. Where the other party invokes the agreement in a court not chosen, then that court should be obliged to stay proceedings immediately (unless the defendant submits to the jurisdiction of this court). The text should say this in clear terms and should provide for it in Article 29 in a new paragraph (4) within which the *lis pendens* issue is primarily dealt. This is a far better place than Article 32(2), which could easily be overlooked.

The wording of this new Article 29(4) could be: '(4) In exception to Article 29(1) and without prejudice to Article 24(1) a court in a Member State seised of proceedings for which the parties have given exclusive jurisdiction to the court or courts of another Member State shall stay its proceedings until the chosen court has declined jurisdiction. If the chosen court has accepted jurisdiction the other court shall decline its jurisdiction.'

---

[52] A dismissal by the court first seised could lead to double costs if afterwards the chosen court declines jurisdiction and proceedings in the first court must be instituted anew.

3. Non-exclusive choice of court agreements

The proposed Article 32(2) applies only to exclusive choice of court agreements. This is more or less self-explanatory. There is no need to give priority to the chosen court where the choice of court is only optional. Where the agreement only adds another optional competent court, the court first seised shall decide first on its jurisdiction. Whether the agreement contains an exclusive or optional choice is a matter of interpretation. In the case of doubt, the choice is exclusive.[53]

In relation to this aspect, the proposed Article 32(2) excludes choice of court agreements 'governed by Sections 3, 4 and 5 of this Chapter'. This means that Article 32(2) does not apply to agreements concerning insurance, consumer and employment contracts. The reason is that in these cases choice of court agreements have no exclusive character.

The fact that the proposed Article 32(2) refers only to exclusive choice of court agreements does by no means imply that non-exclusive agreements do not fall under Article 23. The contrary is true.

4. Decision on the validity of the agreement

It could be further considered whether the court that was not chosen, but was seised first could and should decide itself on the validity of the choice of court agreement. The Hague Convention has opted for this solution.[54] Where the invalidity – according to the law of the country of the chosen court – is clearly evident and manifest, this solution could be accepted, especially where great distances and differences of law and procedure between the chosen and seised courts exist so as to entail difficulties for at least one party. In this case, a double procedure could be very burdensome and should be avoided. However, the decision of whether the invalidity is evident may be difficult and may generate uncertainty that should also be avoided. Within the EU, it appears acceptable that only the chosen court decides on the validity of the agreement according to its own law (including its private international law rules).

5. Choice of court agreements and related actions

The Proposal does not suggest modifications with respect to the regulation of related actions in EU Member States. The current Article 28 grants the later seised court discretion to stay proceedings, but does not *oblige* that court to stay. Where all related actions fall under the same choice of court agreement, the chosen court should decide on these disputes and any other court should be obliged to stay the proceedings.

The effectiveness and value of choice of court agreements could be

---

[53] See art 23(1) second sentence of the Brussels I Regulation and of the Proposal.
[54] See art 6(a) of the Hague Convention.

further improved if all other courts except the chosen one had to stay their proceedings where one of the related actions falls under a choice of court agreement. However, it has to be taken into account that the agreement does not necessarily cover the related actions. Moreover, a certain discretion is needed to decide whether there is a sufficiently close connection between the related actions. The Commission's Proposal is therefore correct to maintain the current solution.

6. Practical issues

a. Ex officio examination or invocation of a choice of court agreement?

A first problem of practical importance is the question of whether a court has to recognise a choice of court agreement *ex officio* or only when a party has invoked it. Article 27 of the Proposal, which shall replace the current Article 25 of the Brussels I Regulation, could give the impression that the court now has to decide on its own motion. Article 27 of the Proposal reads as follows: 'Where a court of a Member State is seised of a claim which is principally concerned with a matter over which it has no jurisdiction under this Regulation, it shall declare of its own motion that it has no jurisdiction.' Article 25 of the Brussels I Regulation restricts this *ex officio* examination to the exclusive jurisdiction under Article 22 of the Brussels I Regulation. The Proposal dispenses with this restriction and covers any 'matter over which it [the court] has no jurisdiction under this Regulation'. The new wording can be understood as covering also the jurisdiction conferred by a choice of court agreement.

However, the systematic and teleological interpretation of the proposed Article 27 must lead to another meaning. Where the jurisdiction depends on the parties' will, one or both parties must invoke their choice of court agreement. The court seised cannot and should not decide for the parties whether the agreement should be relied upon. The parties are entirely free to change their agreement even in the form that one party neglects the agreement and the other submits to the jurisdiction of the seised court. Only if the agreement has been invoked can the court examine whether it has jurisdiction by virtue of the agreement.

Therefore, Article 27 of the Proposal has to be interpreted so as not to cover the jurisdiction conferred by choice of court agreements. However, it would be by far preferable if the text of the provision would express this in a clear way. This could be achieved either by restoring the prior text or by listing those further provisions of the Regulation, if any, which, are relevant besides Article 22.[55]

---

[55] Since both the Regulation (art 22) and the Proposal (art 22(1)) exclude submission to the jurisdiction only in the cases of art 22, there are no further provisions which require that the seised court examines – and, as the case may be, declines – its jurisdiction *ex officio*.

b. When is a choice of court agreement invoked?

Considering the practical aspects, it can be problematic to determine whether a party has invoked a choice of court agreement. Does the mere allegation of agreement suffice to establish that a choice of court agreement has been concluded? Is it necessary that the alleging party produces a document or other proof of the agreement? Does any kind of proof suffice?

The answer depends primarily on the other party's reaction. If the other party does not contest the agreement, a mere allegation suffices. If, however, the other party contests the agreement, Article 23, does not state either in its present form or its proposed form, that it requires a certain mode or degree of necessary substantiation of how and when the choice of court agreement was concluded. The standard of proof that is required is fixed by the *lex fori*. What can be said from the EU-autonomous perspective of Article 23 is that in such a case, a mere allegation of the agreement cannot suffice. There must be some substantiation that the parties indeed concluded a choice of court agreement.

D. Addition to Article 22(1)

A further modification, though of minor importance, concerns Article 22(1). The Proposal adds another exception to the exclusive jurisdiction with respect to rights *in rem* and tenancies concerning immovable property. A new Article 22(1) b) shall allow choice of court agreements for contracts on 'tenancies of premises for professional use'. Evidently, it is the tenant who is required to intend a professional use. Indeed, there appears to be no compelling need to exclude a free choice of court where professionals on both sides conclude such contracts.[56] Whether this rule should apply as well where the landlord is a private person and only the tenant is a professional remains doubtful however. The private person who is generally less experienced than the professional may need protection against a choice of court clause that deprives him or her of the natural forum (where the premises are located). The proposed rule should therefore be limited in its application to cases where both parties act in their professional capacity.

E. Choice of court agreements and third States

The proposed modifications to the Regulation primarily strengthen the effectiveness of choice of court agreements in the EU. Moreover, to some extent they try to cover agreements which potentially affect third States as well. Insofar as third State effects are concerned, two situations have to be distinguished: first, those in which the parties have conferred exclusive

---

[56] In the same sense T Pfeiffer, in B Hess, T Pfeiffer and P Schlosser (n 9) para 319.

jurisdiction on a court or on the courts in an EU Member State and a court outside the EU is seised first; second, those in which an agreement confers jurisdiction on court(s) outside the EU and an EU Member State court is seised first. In both situations either none, one or all parties can have their domicile in the EU.

With respect to both situations, the EU cannot bind courts outside the EU, for reasons of sovereignty of the countries where those courts are located. These courts are not bound and cannot be bound by the Brussels I Regulation. They can neither be obliged to stay proceedings if they are seised first, nor can they be forced to accept jurisdiction if they are chosen. In order to circumvent a choice of court agreement, the parties can still use certain tactics to institute proceedings in countries with notoriously slow courts. Only if the court seised first is located in a Contracting State of the Hague Convention is that court obliged either to dismiss the claim or to stay the proceedings (Article 6 of the Hague Convention).

What the Brussels I Regulation can do, however, is to bind the courts in the EU. If the parties confer exclusive jurisdiction on a court in the EU, the most appropriate solution has to be that the chosen court accepts jurisdiction if the agreement is in accordance with Article 23. The court then has to decide the issue of jurisdiction on the merits, irrespective of whether another court outside the EU was seised first and whether or not a domicile of one or all parties in the EU was given.

If the parties conferred exclusive jurisdiction on a court or courts outside the EU, the proposed new Article 32(2) does not apply. Only Article 34 of the Proposal grants an EU Member State court that is seised second a limited discretion to stay its proceedings where the cause of action and the parties are the same.[57] The EU Member State court may do so if a recognisable judgment of the foreign court can be expected within a reasonable time and if, in addition, 'the proper administration of justice' so requires.[58] The new provision does not contain any express reservation in favour of an exclusive jurisdiction of EU Member States' courts (Article 22) or for the protection of weaker parties (Articles 13, 17 and 21). Nor does it apply if the EU Member State's court is seised first. The implicit assumption appears to be that the EU Member State court in the latter case shall decline jurisdiction if the choice of court agreement is valid and invoked by the defendant. Also here, the yardstick for the validity of the agreement should be the requirements set out in Article 23(1), in combination with the national law, designated by the private international law of the country of the chosen court. Articles 13, 17, 21 and 22 of the Brussels I Regulation should there-

---

[57] Although art 34 of the Proposal does not mention choice of court agreements, the provision does not exclude them and thus evidently applies to them.

[58] See art 34(1)(b) and (c) of the Proposal.

fore preclude the honouring of agreements, even if valid under the law of the chosen forum. The procedural interests and values enshrined in the cited provisions rank higher than the parties' freedom to choose a competent court. If under this perspective, the agreement is invalid, the EU Member State court would have to decide on its own jurisdiction and, as the case may be, on the merits.

In sum, it is a difficult task and one partly doomed to failure, to the extent that the Proposal attempts a one-sided regulation of choice of court agreements with links to third States, as courts in third States cannot be bound in this way. A satisfactory regulation is only possible if bilateral or multilateral conventions regulate the issue. This further supports the arguments that the EU should ratify the Hague Convention.

F. Open questions

1. Control of misuse

The Proposal does not introduce a control mechanism against the misuse of choice of court agreements. It remains open whether a general *ordre public* reservation is applicable. The fact that the Proposal does not provide for such a control militates against its existence. However, the case law of the CJEU concerning choice of court clauses in standard contract terms[59] remains untouched.

2. Breach of choice of court agreements

The Proposal does not address any remedies for the case of breach of a choice of court agreement. This question, too, remains open.

3. Recognition of judgments neglecting choice of court agreements

Finally, the Proposal does not introduce any scope for challenging the enforcement of a judgment because it neglected a choice of court agreement. The absence of any such provision must be understood to mean that the Proposal rejects this idea.

IV. CONCLUSIONS

Taken together, the proposed modifications concerning choice of court agreements are moderate. In principle, they appear to be sensible. They generally help to strengthen the effectiveness of choice of court agreements. They bring the Brussels I Regulation closer to the Hague Convention.

---

[59] See (n 28).

However, in certain respects the proposed modifications need to be improved. Insofar as this is the case, the following is suggested.

1. Instead of the Proposal's 'null and void' inclusion in Article 23(1), a new paragraph should be added to Article 23 which should read as follows: 'The material validity (concerning capacity, mistake, fraud, duress) of a choice of court agreement as well as matters like agency and assignment connected with the formation of such an agreement are governed by the law designated by the rules of private international law of the state where the chosen court or courts are located.'

2. With respect to the priority between Article 23 and the *lis pendens* rules, a new paragraph (4) should be added to the proposed Article 29 which should read as follows: '(4) In exception to Article 29(1) and without prejudice to Article 24(1) a court in a Member State seised of proceedings for which the parties have given exclusive jurisdiction to the court or courts of another Member State shall stay its proceedings until the chosen court has declined jurisdiction. If the chosen court has accepted jurisdiction the other court shall decline its jurisdiction.'

3. The proposed new Article 22(1) b) should limit itself to application in cases where both parties are acting in their professional capacity.

4. The new Article 34 of the Proposal should state that it applies also to choice of court agreements. It should however include exceptions for cases falling under Articles 13, 17, 21 and 22 of the Brussels I Regulation.

Lis Pendens and Third States: The Commission's Proposed Changes to the Brussels I Regulation

*Pippa Rogerson**

I. INTRODUCTION

The European Commission is proposing alterations to the Council Regulation 44/2001 on Jurisdiction and the Recognition and Enforcement of Judgments in Civil and Commercial Matters which affect the current Articles 27 and 28 regarding *lis pendens* and related actions. These include (a) amended Articles 29 and 30 (ex Articles 27 and 28) on *lis pendens* within the European Union ('EU'); (b) new Article 31 on the coordination of Member States' courts regarding provisional measures; (c) amended Articles 32 and 33 (ex Articles 29 and 30) on a mandatory stay in favour of a forum with exclusive jurisdiction; and (d) new Article 34 regarding *lis pendens* in the courts of a non-Member State. It is this latter proposal on which this article will focus after having outlined the current position regarding *lis pendens*.

The Commission's latest Report to the European Parliament, the Council and the European Social and Economic Committee on the Brussels I Regulation[1] was required by Article 73 of the Regulation. Two reports had been commissioned; one of a general nature from Hess, Pfeiffer and Schlosser,[2] and one specifically on the residual jurisdiction from Nuyts.[3] Proposals for reform have also come from the European Parliament,[4] and the Commission.[5]

* Senior Lecturer, Faculty of Law, Cambridge University; Fellow and Director of Studies, Gonville and Caius College.

[1] European Commission, Proposal for a Regulation of the European Parliament and of the Council on Jurisdiction and the Recognition and Enforcement of Judgments in Civil and Commercial Matters (Recast) COM(2010)748 final (14 December 2010).

[2] General Studies on the Practical Application of the Regulation <http://ec.europa.eu/justice_home/doc_centre/civil/studies/doc_civil_studies_en.htm>.

[3] A Nuyts, *Study on Residual Jurisdiction, General Report* (2007) <http://ec.europa.eu/civiljustice/news/docs/study_residual_jurisdiction_e.n.pdf>.

[4] European Parliament, Working Document on Green Paper on the Review of Council Regulation (EC) No 44/2001 on Jurisdiction and the Recognition and Enforcement of Judgments in Civil and Commercial Matters (2009) <http://www.europarl.europa.eu/sides/getDoc>; European Parliament, Draft Report on the Implementation and Review of Council Regulation (EC) No 44/2001 on Jurisdiction and the Recognition and Enforcement of

II. CURRENT POSITION ON LIS PENDENS WITHIN THE EU

Article 27 of the Brussels I Regulation currently requires any Member State's court other than the one first seised to stay its proceedings of its own motion in favour of the Member State's court which is 'first seised'. It does not matter if the parties are domiciled in Member States or not; the provision operates merely because proceedings are continuing in another Member State's court.[6] However, Article 27 is only engaged where the parties and the cause of action in both courts are the same. Article 28 deals with the situation in which related actions are commenced in more than one Member State. In such a case, courts other than that first seised are given the power to stay their own proceedings in favour of the court first seised, but are not required to do so. The operation of the existing articles is not free from difficulty.

Article 27 only takes effect where the parties to the two actions are the same. Obviously, where the parties involve identical legal persons, they are the same. However, complexities can arise, for example, it is not clear whether wholly owned companies are 'the same parties' as their owners. The Court of Justice of the European Union ('CJEU') in *Drouot Assurances*[7] held that the term 'same parties' had an autonomous meaning and that separate legal entities could be the same party. However, whether the parties were the same in a particular case was a matter for national courts to decide on the facts. One way to do this might be to consider whether a decision against one party would be *res judicata* against the other. In that case, a subrogated insurer was found not be the same party as the beneficiary of the insurance as their interests are not identical, or in the words of the CJEU, were 'not indissociable'. However, the assumption must be that in the usual case the insurer is the same party as the insured as their interests usually coincide. There is some suggestion in the English case of *Turner*[8] that a company which is controlling a majority shareholder is the same party as the shareholder for the purposes of Article 27. This is somewhat controversial in English corporate law theory, as the veil of incorpo-

---

Judgments in Civil and Commercial Matters 2009/2140 (INI) <http://www.europarl.europa.eu/sides/getDoc.> and Amendments to the Draft Report <http://www.europarl.europa.eu/sides/getDoc.>.

[5] European Commission, Green Paper on the Review of Council Regulation (EC) No 44/2001 on Jurisdiction and the Recognition and Enforcement of Judgments in Civil and Commercial Matters, COM(2009)175.

[6] CJEU, Case C-351/89 *Overseas Union Insurance Ltd v New Hampshire Insurance Co* [1991] ECR I-3317.

[7] CJEU, Case C-351/96 *Drouot Assurances SA v Consolidated Metallurgical Industries* [1998] ECR I-3075.

[8] *Turner v Grovit* [2000] 1 QB 345. This point was not considered in the House of Lords decision reported at [2002] 1 WLR 107.

ration is rarely lifted to identify a controlling shareholder as the company.[9] This case probably falls within an exception to the English domestic rule as, on the facts, the shareholder was found to be acting in bad faith by using the company as a vehicle to harass his employee by commencing the later proceedings in Spain.[10] Whether an assignee is the same party as an assignor has yet to be determined by the CJEU. The question has troubled the English court. A good example of the difficulties which might arise can be illustrated by *Kolden Holdings*.[11] A case was commenced in England by some assignors against the defendants Rodette Commerce for a declaration that Rodette was to transfer some shares. Later, an action was commenced in Cyprus by Rodette Commerce against Kolden for a declaration of non-liability under the contract of sale and purchase of the shares. The assignors had transferred their rights under the contract, including the cause of action in the English proceedings, to Kolden. The parties agreed that the causes of action were the same, but argued in the English court that Article 27 of the Brussels I Regulation prevented the English proceedings, as the parties were the same in the Cypriot proceedings which were first commenced as between those parties. The Court of Appeal held that an assignor of a cause of action was the same party as the assignee, as a judgment given against one of them would be *res judicata* against the other. Therefore the English proceedings were commenced first between Kolden (in place of the assignors) and Rodette. In fact, Rodette were not prejudiced by this. Rodette had had notice of the assignment of the English cause of action to Kolden before commencing the Cypriot proceedings, even though Kolden had not been formally named as a party in the English action until a few days after the Cypriot case had started. The Court of Appeal decided that in determining identity of interest it should look to the substance of the claim, not to the form.[12] It also held that the court was seised from the date of the commencement of the original action, not from the assignment.

---

[9] See the line of cases from *Salomon v Salomon & Co Ltd* [1897] AC 22, including the more recent *Adams v Cape Industries Plc* [1990] Ch 433. On the other hand, a liquidator of a company is probably the same party as the company in liquidation – see case *Re Cover Europe Ltd* [2002] EWHC 861 (Ch).

[10] The decision in *Berkeley Administration Inc v McClelland* [1995] ILPr 201 is not so easily explained. A French wholly-owned subsidiary was found to be the same party as its English holding company, without any explanation, in what amounted to complicated proceedings.

[11] *Kolden Holdings Ltd v Rodette Commerce Ltd* [2008] EWCA Civ 10 and [2008] ILPr 20.

[12] Therefore, in *Mecklermedia Corp v DC Congress GmbH* [1998] Ch 40 and *Mölnlycke Health Care AB v BSN Medical Ltd* [2010] ILPr 171, the interests of a licensee were found to be not identical to those of the licensor (ie not indissociable). In the former case, the defence of each defendant against the single claimant was different and in the latter, the licensee had an additional, not merely assigned, right.

Article 27 also only engages where the causes of action are the same in each court. As Fentiman argues, Article 27 is apparently concerned with the specific issue of incompatible, conflicting judgments which may compete for enforcement within the EU.[13] The main but not the only purpose of Article 27 is to avoid the possibility of irreconcilable judgments. Article 34 is a solution to irreconcilable judgments, but it is preferable to avoid having to resort to that article. Incompatibility and conflict can take place at a number of levels. Judgments may conflict as to the overall result, such that in court A one party won and in court B the other party succeeded. However, only if the claims in both courts were the same is there a real incompatibility in the result. Where the claim in one court is based on a different issue arising out of the same facts then it is possible that the two judgments are not in conflict, but are inconsistent. A different incompatibility occurs if court A decides that one party is entitled to damages in contract and court B decides that, on the facts, that party is only liable in tort. The same party is successful in both cases, but on a different ground. However, in arriving at their decisions it may be that both court A and court B agree on certain factual and even legal questions. Yet another conflict arises if court A decides that certain legal issues apply differently to the same facts than as determined by court B. A further conflict occurs if both courts come to the same conclusion on liability, but disagree as to law or fact. At the point at which the actions are commenced however, all this is in the future. Article 27 is only concerned with the possibility of conflict, which can be difficult to pin down precisely at this stage. On one argument, the purposes of Article 27 require a broad interpretation of what is meant by 'same cause of action' in order that the possibility of irreconcilable judgments is reduced as far as possible.[14] The court second seised only has to stay its proceedings, not dismiss them, and it can await the outcome of the court first seised before having to decide which matters are *res judicata*.[15]

Given the wide variety of legal systems throughout the EU, inevitably forms of legal action are very varied. In *Gubisch Machinenfabrik KG*[16], the

---

[13] R Fentiman, *International Commercial Litigation* (OUP 2010) 423–424.

[14] Consistent with the decision of the CJEU in Case C-144/86 *Gubisch Maschinenfabrik KG v Guilio Palumbo* [1987] ECR 4861.

[15] The meaning of *res judicata* also differs throughout the EU, which is a hidden problem in this discussion. English courts treat foreign judgments in the same way as English judgments and adopt a wide interpretation of *res judicata*. There are narrower versions, those of cause of action estoppel and issue estoppel – which are normally relied on as a defence to certain (new) claims. A judgment creditor will take the widest interpretation to enforce a foreign judgment. In addition, the English procedural rule requiring a claimant to bring forth the whole case on the facts at the commencement of the proceedings, leads to *res judicata* not just of those issues, but also of any other issue which may have been – but was not – pleaded (rule in *Henderson v Henderson* (1843) 3 Hare 100). Therefore in England a conflicting judgment may be much more widely interpreted than in a country with a civil law tradition.

[16] *Gubisch* (n 14).

CJEU held that proceedings do not have to be literally identical. Therefore, a case to enforce a contractual provision had the same cause of action as proceedings to annul the contract. The court held that both actions were concerned with the same factual and legal matrix and would lead to irreconcilable judgments. If the contract was invalid then it could not give rise to a claim for damages for non-performance. The CJEU later explained further in *The Tatry* that the cause of action is a double requirement: the proceedings must have the same *object* and the same *cause*.[17] Causes of action are the same if they have the same legal purpose (ie the intended legal outcome or the same end in view)[18] and the same juridical basis (ie the facts and rules of law relied on as the basis of the action[19]). The 'same end in view' can be broadly or narrowly defined. In *Gubisch Machinenfabrik KG*, the legal objective was the enforceability of the contract in one case and of an obligation arising from that contract in the other case. These were the same. In *The Tatry* the legal objective of one case was the liability of one party in damages and of the other case was a declaration of non-liability for the same damage. In *Maersk Olie & Gas AS*[20] a shipowner wished to limit its liability by establishing a limitation liability fund and the other party sought damages for loss. These were not the same causes of action as the legal rule underlying each action was different (one in an international convention and one in tort). Also the *object* was different. The first sought to limit liability and the other to establish it. This case appears to narrow the scope of Article 27. It is easy to envisage claims which constitute possible defences or counter-claims to each other which do not line up in a straightforward manner. An example: A and B enter into a contract for A to sell and deliver paper to B monthly. The contract provides for termination on 12 months' notice. B complains about the lateness of delivery in February and the poor quality of the paper when delivered. A sues in France for non-payment of invoices for January and February. B's defence is the lateness of delivery in February and the poor quality of the paper delivered in January.

What is the cause of the French action? If one simply looks at the claim, it appears to be a breach of the contractual obligation to pay. Turning to the *object*, is it the enforceability of the contract generally or of the particular obligation? Were B to sue later in England for damages for lost profit from the two deliveries as B has to source the paper from elsewhere, how should Article 27 operate? A's defence to that action is that the paper was

---

[17] CJEU, Case C-406/92 *The owners of the cargo lately laden on board the ship Tatry v The owners of the ship Maciej Rataj* [1994] ECR I-5439.

[18] ibid para 41.

[19] ibid para 39.

[20] CJEU, Case C-39/02 *Maersk Olie & Gas AS v M De Haan en W De Boer* [2004] ECR I-9657.

not late and the quality of the paper delivered was satisfactory. Simply looking at the claim to identify the cause suggests that it is the breach of obligation to provide goods of a suitable quality. However, the *object* could be
said to be the enforceability of the contract, as above. There are certain
common issues to both actions: was the delivery late giving B a defence and
a claim? Was the paper not of contract quality giving B a defence and a
claim? The issues concern the same contractual rules of law (what is the
term of the contract about payment, timing of delivery and quality) and
factual (what happened in fact). *Res judicata* would encompass both the
facts and the rules of law. But each allegation is possibly independent,
particularly those concerning the quality and the timing of delivery. A broad
interpretation of Article 27 should lead to the conclusion that the actions
are likely to result in irreconcilable judgments and that the English action
should be stayed to await the outcome of the French proceedings. The
obligation to pay only arises if the delivery obligation has been properly
fulfilled. If B is not liable to pay A, because the defence succeeds, then B is
also able to recover losses. If A can recover the payments then B has not
satisfactorily proved its claim for poor quality and late delivery.

  Further purposes of Article 27 should include the efficiency of the decision-making and the fairness to both parties. These ends are only achieved
in this case if both these claims are determined by the same court.
Nevertheless, at the point of the initiation of proceedings, it appears that
these two actions could be interpreted as different causes of action. In
particular, the focus of Article 27 is only on the claim made by each party
in their respective courts, not on the later defences.[21] This is to prevent the
problem of the claim and the defence changing over the course of the
proceedings. Only the initial claims are inspected to determine the operation of Article 27. However, in the example, the obligation to pay cannot
be independent of the obligation to perform the contract by delivering the
goods, so the two causes of action must be said to be the same. Were there
to be a claim for breach of the obligation to give 12 months' notice, that
claim would constitute a different cause of action to that for damages for
non-delivery.

  After *The Tatry*, the parties have commonly issued pre-emptive proceedings for a negative declaration in their preferred court to engage Article 27
and prevent the other party from commencing proceedings in any other
court. A widely drawn statement of claim for proceedings commenced in an
unattractive court, even when some of the claims are weak, strengthens the
hand of one party to force the other to negotiate. This might happen when,
as in England, a party can make alternative and even overlapping claims out

---

[21] CJEU, Case C-111/01 *Gantner Electronic GmbH v Basch Expolitatie Maatschappij BV*
[2003] ECR I-4207.

of the same facts[22] or where a broadly-based negative declaration is possible. For example, in *Bank of Tokyo-Mitsubishi*[23] there were complicated proceedings in England and Italy arising out of a financing arrangement granted by Bank of Tokyo (and others) to Baskan Gida. The financing was to help Baskan Gida with its cash flow difficulties during sales to Ferrero. Baskan Gida agreed to assign its rights under sales contracts to the Banks who would give notice to Ferrero and an advance would then be made to Baskan Gida by way of a Letter of Credit. Baskan Gida did not repay the advance and it became clear that the signatures of Ferrero were forgeries. Ferrero sued the Banks and Baskan Gida in Italy, seeking a negative declaration as to Ferrero's liability to the Banks. The Banks commenced later proceedings in England against Baskan Gida and other individuals and companies. These proceedings included a claim for repayment of the advance credit based on contract and claims based in fraud. Ferrero was joined to these proceedings as assignees of Baskan Gida's rights and because of the alleged involvement of a Ferrero employee in the fraud. Lawrence Collins J (as he then was) held that the contractual part of the two proceedings involved the same cause of action. Both were about Ferrero's liability to pay the Banks as a result of the assignments and undertakings. It is noteworthy that the Italian proceedings were very widely framed (seeking to establish no liability for whatever reason arising out of the contracts)[24] and encompassed the more detailed English claims. The pre-emptive strike in Italy succeeded in preventing the continuation of English proceedings. However, the fraud claims were not the same cause of action.

The result is forum shopping, albeit within the limited grounds for jurisdiction allowed in the Brussels I Regulation.[25] Forum shopping can

---

[22] The rule in *Henderson v Henderson* (n 15) requires wide overlapping and alternative claims in English proceedings.

[23] *Bank of Tokyo-Mitsubishi Ltd v Baskan Gida Sanayi Pazarlama AS* [2004] 2 LLR 395.

[24] ibid para 207.

[25] Mance LJ noted that the result of the authorities on art 27 explicitly permits forum shopping – *Tavoulareas v Tsavliris* [2004] ILPr 29 para 1. Examples of other cases which have had to consider art 27 include *Haji-Ioannou v Frangos* [1999] 2 Lloyd's Rep 337 – not the same cause of action if one action is to recover money and the other to trace the money into assets acquired; *Gamlestaden Plc v Casa de Suecia* [1994] 1 LLR 433 – action to convert loan agreement into a public document not the same cause of action as one to establish liability to pay under the agreement; *Mecklermedia Corp. v DC Congress GmbH* [1998] Ch 40 – not the same cause of action where one for infringement of a patent and the other for passing off; *Lafi Office and International Business SL v Meriden Animal Health Ltd* [2001] ILPr 19 – not the same cause of action where one for breach of contract and the other for fraud in criminal proceedings; *Molins v GD Spa* [2000] 1 WLR 1741 – same cause of action where one is for outstanding royalties and the other for rescission of the licence agreement, a declaration that no royalties due and for repayment of those already paid; *Prazic v Prazic* [2006] 2 FLR 1128 – not the same cause of action where English proceedings for a remedy under the Trusts of Land and Appointment of Trustees Act 1996 and French proceedings for ancillary relief on divorce; *Syndicate 980 v SINCO SA* [2008] ILPr 49 – not the same cause of action if one was in contract and the other in tort; *SK Slavia Praha-Fotbal AS v Debt Collect London Ltd* [2010]

be criticised for being wasteful and for encouraging improper pressure on a party to settle rather than fight in an unattractive court. This practice within the EU has even permitted exclusive jurisdiction agreements to be overridden, for example in *Erich Gasser GmbH*[26] and *JP Morgan*.[27] It is true that in each case the court first seised (which is not the court chosen by the agreement of the parties) may well, in the end, decline jurisdiction in the face of the jurisdiction agreement. Nevertheless, the defendant in that court is being deprived of the benefit of certainty negotiated in the agreement. That aspect has been addressed by other provisions in the proposed amendments to the Brussels I Regulation where the jurisdiction agreement is in favour of a Member State's court.[28]

Within the EU, Article 30 of the Brussels I Regulation provides rules on when a court is deemed to be seised. English courts are within paragraph 1, in that the rules of procedure provide that the court is seised when the claim form is issued. It is for the claimant to complete the claim form (including the statement of claim) which can be expeditiously issued by the court. The courts in other Member States may fall within paragraph 2, where the courts are seised when the authority responsible for service has received the documents which need to be served. Even though these rules could be utilized by a party whose intention is to race to the court of its choice, they are at least clearly laid down so that all litigants are aware of them. The relationship between Article 30 and Article 27 is critical and the courts should be alert to possible injustices. For example, a party who has commenced proceedings in a preferred court should not be allowed later to amend its claim so as to improve its position.[29] As actual service of the claim form is necessary to perfect Article 30, failure to pay the necessary fees to effect service must prevent Article 27 from engaging.[30]

ILPr 7 – same cause of action where English proceedings concerned the repayment of money advanced to the defendant under loan agreements and a discounted funding agreement governed by English law and in the Czech proceedings the defendant sought a declaration that its obligations had been fulfilled under the discounted funding agreement (at first instance, point not decided upon appeal); *Football Dataco Ltd v Sportrader GmbH* [2011] EWCA Civ 330 – actions in England for breach of copyright against German defendants were the same cause of action as those in Germany for a declaration that the defendants were not liable for infringement of intellectual property rights; *Masri v Consolidated Contractors International Co SAL* [2011] EWHC 1780 (Comm) – not the same cause of action (but related) where one is to make defendants personally liable for debts due to the non-registration of a company and the other to establish the defendants as parties to a conspiracy.

[26] CJEU, Case C-116/02 *Erich Gasser GmbH v MISAT Srl* [2003] ECR I-14693.

[27] *JP Morgan v Primacom AG* [2005] EWHC 508 (Comm).

[28] Proposed art 32(2).

[29] See in relation to art 28 Brussels I Regulation, *Stribog Ltd v FKI Engineering Ltd* [2011] EWCA Civ 622.

[30] *Debt Collection London Ltd v SK Slavia Praha – Fotbal AS* [2010] EWCA Civ 1250 and [2011] 1 WLR 866; in *WPP Holdings v Benatti* [2007] 1 WLR 2316, the Court of Appeal held that minor irregularities with service should not prevent art 27 from engaging.

Article 28 of the Brussels I Regulation permits a court second seised to grant a discretionary stay of its own proceedings in favour of the court first seised. This article covers related actions which lead not to incompatible decisions, but to inconsistent ones. In this case, neither the parties need to be the same, nor does the cause of action have to be the same; rather, actions are 'deemed related where they are so closely connected that it is expedient to hear them together to avoid the risk of irreconcilable judgments'.[31] In the case of Article 28, the related actions will have different legal or factual bases. The concept of related actions is also to be broadly interpreted. The CJEU held in *The Tatry*[32] that judgments may be irreconcilable even if the legal consequences are not mutually exclusive. Article 28 is therefore wider than Article 27. The English court in *Sarrio*[33] held that related actions had to be interpreted in a 'broad commonsense manner'. This case is relatively unusual as the claimant brought actions both in England and in Spain for different aspects of the dispute. It sued in Spain for amounts unpaid under a put option and in England for damages in respect of misrepresentations allegedly made during the course of negotiations of the options. The House of Lords agreed with Mance J at first instance that there were allegations common to both proceedings in relation to the negotiations leading to the sale and to the alleged misrepresentations, which meant that the two proceedings were related. In *Research in Motion UK*,[34] the Court of Appeal held that the mere possibility of irreconcilable judgments did not mean that the proceedings were inevitably related. In this case, Research in Motion had commenced proceedings in England for revocation and a declaration of non-infringement of a UK patent, and similarly in Italy for revocation and non-infringement of corresponding Italian, German, Spanish, Dutch and Belgian patents. Visto counterclaimed in the English proceedings, alleging that Research in Motion was abusing the process of the English and Italian courts by bringing the action in Italy. The Court of Appeal decided that these actions were not sufficiently related after looking not just at the claims, but also at the defences. It decided that expediency was important but that in this case it was not necessarily appropriate to hear all claims in one court. Again, the purpose of Article 28 is to avoid the possibility of irreconcilable judgments, but also to prevent the waste of time and effort in overlapping proceedings and to 'promote the proper administration of justice'.[35] It is more efficient and fairer for all parties to try to consolidate their proceedings in one court. A stay of the court second seised under Article 28 would encourage that behaviour.

---

[31] Current art 28(3) Brussels I Regulation.
[32] See (n 17).
[33] *Sarrio SA v Kuwait Investment Authority* [1999] 1 AC 32.
[34] *Research in Motion UK Ltd v Visto Corporation* [2008] ILPr 34.
[35] See (n 17) para 5478.

Nevertheless, the court may exercise a discretion in deciding whether or not to stay its proceedings. The English court in *Grupo Torras*[36] decided that the discretion was to be exercised by consideration of common law *forum non conveniens* principle. However, there is a presumption in favour of a stay being exercised.[37]

III. LIS PENDENS IN THIRD STATES

The current position regarding *lis pendens* in third States depends on whether the Brussels I Regulation engages, which will usually be the case if the defendant is domiciled in a Member State. Where the Brussels I Regulation applies, the infamous case of *Owusu*[38] has provided that no stay of proceedings in a Member State's court is possible in favour of proceedings in a third State, when the defendant is domiciled in the Member State. This decision has led to a torrent of literature and more than a few cases – some of which followed and some have not applied *Owusu*.[39] An alternative approach to declining jurisdiction might be for a Member State's court to decline to hear a case on the grounds that it is an abuse of process to bring a claim in that court when a recognisable action has been commenced or is about to be commenced in a third State's court which is appropriate. However, the CJEU in *Kongress Agentur Hagen GmbH*[40] held that national rules of procedure are for the domestic court so long as those domestic procedural rules do not impair the operation of the Brussels I

[36] *Grupo Torras v Al Sabbah* [1995] 1 LLR 374; *Cooper Tire & Rubber Co Europe Ltd v Dow Deutschland Inc* [2010] 2 CLC 104.
[37] Which may be rebutted, for example, when the court second seised has jurisdiction by virtue of an exclusive jurisdiction agreement (*JP Morgan Europe Ltd v Primacom AG* [2006] ILPr 11).
[38] CJEU, Case C-281/02 *Owusu v Jackson (t/a Villa Holidays Bal Inn Villas)* [2005] ECR I-1383.
[39] See P de Vareilles-Sommieres (ed), *Forum Shopping in the European Judicial Area* (Hart Publishing 2007); R Fentiman, 'Justiciability, Discretion and Foreign Rights' in A Nuyts (ed), *International Litigation in Intellectual Property and Information Technology* (Kluwer 2008); P Rogerson, 'Conflict of Laws – Foreign Copyright Jurisdiction' (2010) CLJ 245; J Harris, 'Understanding the English Response to the Europeanisation of Private International Law' (2008) JPIL 347; R Fentiman, 'Civil Jurisdiction and Third States: *Owusu* and After' (2006) 43 CMLR 705. Cases include: *Antec International Ltd v Biosafety USA Inc* [2006] EWHC 47 (Comm); *Gomez v Gomez-Monche Vives* [2008] 3 WLR 309; *Goshawk Dedicated Ltd v Life Receivables Ireland Ltd* [2009] ILPr 26; *Winnetka Trading Corp v Julius Baer International Ltd* [2009] Bus LR 1006; *Pacific International Sports Clubs Ltd v Soccer Marketing International Ltd* [2009] EWHC 1839 (Ch); *Equitas Ltd v Allstate Insurance Co* [2009] 1 All E.R. (Comm) 1137; *Lucasfilm v Ainsworth* [2010] Ch 503; *Catalyst Investment Group Ltd v Lewinsohn* [2010] Ch 218; *JKN v JCN* [2010] EWHC 843 (Fam); *Skype Technologies SA v Joltid Ltd* [2011] ILPr 8.
[40] CJEU, Case C-365/88 *Kongress Agentur Hagen GmbH v Zeehaghe BV* [1990] ECR I-1845 para 20.

Regulation.[41] Therefore, that alternative approach is unlikely to be possible.

There are questions thus far unresolved by the CJEU as to how far the decision in *Owusu* extends. In particular, what if the ground of jurisdiction in the third State is one of an exclusive type, for example, the proceedings in that third State involve the ownership of land?[42] Or is a stay permissible if there is an exclusive jurisdiction agreement in favour of the court of the third State?[43] Or if there are proceedings already continuing in the third State?[44] There are powerful arguments in support of a stay in favour of a third State in each case. This article focuses only on the last example, which is the subject of the proposed amendments to the Brussels I Regulation.

IV. LIS PENDENS AT COMMON LAW: THE FORUM CONVENIENS DOCTRINE

English common law doctrine has a very flexible approach to matters of *lis pendens* in third States. Freed from the rigidity of Articles 27 and 28, the courts can weigh the undesirability of actions continuing in more than one forum against wider considerations of justice between the parties. In finally deciding whether a case should continue in England many factors can be taken into account, not just the existence of the proceedings abroad, but also whether that forum is the most appropriate one in which justice can be done. There is no distinct *lis pendens* rule; it is part of the wider *forum conveniens* doctrine.[45] Generally, the English court will lean against a multiplicity of proceedings, fearing 'an unseemly race to judgment', conflicting judgments and the waste of time and effort (both by the parties and the courts) that multiple proceedings will likely entail.[46] These justifications

---

[41] See also CJEU, Case C-185/07 *Allianz SpA (formerly Riunione Adriatica di Sicurta SpA) v West Tankers Inc* [2009] ECR I 663; Case C-159/02 *Turner v Grovit* [2004] ECR I-3565 para 29.

[42] See the English decision of *Lucasfilm v Ainsworth* [2010] Ch 503, in which an action alleging infringement of a US copyright was dismissed for want of jurisdiction by the English court.

[43] In *Winnetka Trading Corp v Julius Baer International Ltd* [2009] Bus LR 1006, Norris J considered that the court did have power despite *Owusu v Jackson* to stay its proceedings in favour of Guernsey in a case where the parties had agreed a non-exclusive jurisdiction agreement for the Guernsey courts. See also *Konkola Copper Mines v Coromin* [2005] 2 LLR 555 paras 74 and 101 (Colman J) at first instance (this point not appealed).

[44] In the Irish case of *Goshawk Dedicated Ltd v Life Receivables Ireland Ltd* [2009] ILPr 26 (referred to the CJEU), the Irish Supreme Court held that *Owusu v Jackson* did not apply to such a case. Compare to the English case of *Catalyst Investment Group Ltd v Lewinsohn* [2010] Ch 218, in which *Owusu v Jackson* was followed to prevent a stay of English proceedings when there was a *lis pendens* in a third State.

[45] *Canada Trust Co v Stolzenberg (No 2)* [2002] 1 AC 1 para 20 (Lord Hoffmann).

[46] *The Abidin Daver* [1984] AC 398, 412; *Metall und Rohstoff AG v ACLI Metals (London) Ltd* [1984] 1 LLR 598; *De Dampierre v De Dampierre* [1988] AC 92.

may be unlikely in practice as few parties take more than one action to its conclusion and would prefer to settle their disputes. Once a court has declined jurisdiction or refused to do so, the parties can negotiate a settlement against a commercial assessment of the risks and costs of the proceedings. It could be argued that as jurisdictional disputes are not determinative of the substantive merits of the claim, they do not merit excessive time and care over their determination. On the other hand, jurisdictional disputes provide a framework against which the negotiations of the parties to resolve the dispute can take place and should be as carefully determined as more substantive matters. The fear of a multiplicity of proceedings remains a motivation to stay English proceedings, where appropriate, if justice can be done in foreign proceedings. To put the question differently, the English court might ask why should a case go ahead in England which is already proceeding elsewhere; that is to say, what is the justification for the duplication of effort and possible conflicting judgments? An acceptably fair answer could be based on the following observations: the foreign proceedings are too slow, too expensive, do not include all the parties, are in an inconvenient forum chosen by one party to force settlement on disadvantageous terms rather than because it was an appropriate forum,[47] the particular expertise of English lawyers and judges, better discovery rules in England or better security or costs rules or perhaps because an English judgment is more enforceable than the foreign one.[48] Unjust answers might encompass considerations reflecting the idea that England is more convenient to only one party or that proceedings in England are more likely to force the other party to settle given the inordinate cost of proceedings here.

The doctrine of *forum conveniens* operates both when a party seeks the permission of the court to serve the claim form out of the jurisdiction under Civil Procedure Rules r 6.37 and Practice Direction 6B[49] and when a defendant already served within the jurisdiction requests a stay of the English proceedings. In the first case, the claimant must show that England is the proper place for trial; in the second, the defendant must show that there is another clearly more appropriate forum in which justice can be done.[50] In either case, the existence of pending proceedings in another forum will be a factor to be taken into account in determining where the case may be tried

---

[47] *Royal & Sun Alliance Insurance Plc v Rolls-Royce Plc* [2010] LLR (I.R.) 637.

[48] Most of these justifications can be attacked on fairness grounds too. Why should a party take advantage of costs procedures in England that are more favourable to that party, but less so to the other? Likewise discovery rules, security and enforcement. Speed of the outcome, expertise of lawyers, one-stop litigation and justice at a lower cost are probably advantageous to all parties and therefore justifiable.

[49] The permission of the court is necessary to serve proceedings on a party not within the jurisdiction in a matter not within the Brussels I Regulation.

[50] Both cases are determined by application under Civil Procedure Rule r 11 which deals with challenges to the jurisdiction.

most suitably for the interests of both parties and the interests of justice.[51] First, the court looks to the 'connecting factors' between the dispute and each forum which 'will include not only factors affecting convenience or expense (such as availability of witnesses), but also other factors such as the law governing the relevant transaction, and the places where the parties respectively reside or carry on business.'[52] At common law, the appropriateness of the forum is a conglomeration of many factors, which include both the parties' expectations of likely *fora* before the events giving rise to the claim occur and what subsequently occurs.[53] One of these factors will be the existence of proceedings abroad. If the court concludes that the natural forum is the foreign one, then generally proceedings in England will be stayed in favour of the trial proceedings in that other country (or permission to serve the claim form out of the jurisdiction will be denied). Even more strongly, the court can favour the 'one-stop' determination of multi-party actions. There are clear advantages concerning efficiency and convenience in having a complex dispute decided between all the parties who might possibly be liable, in one court.[54] Such an outcome reflects not only justice between the parties, but is also more cost-effective for the administration of justice by the court. However, if the claimant can show that it will be deprived of a 'legitimate personal or juridical advantage' by trial abroad rather than in England, such that substantial justice cannot be done there, the English court will refuse to stay its proceedings (or will grant permission to serve the claim form out of the jurisdiction). That result will lead to parallel proceedings, but is acceptable, particularly where the parties have, by way of a non-exclusive jurisdiction agreement, expressly contracted for this possibility.[55]

The flexibility of the English approach means that the court can decide that the foreign proceedings are not to be given much weight in determin-

---

[51] *Spiliada Maritime Corp v Cansulex Ltd (The Spiliada)* [1987] AC 460.

[52] ibid 477.

[53] See for example, the 'Cambridgeshire' factor in *The Spiliada* [1987] AC 460. The existence of experts and lawyers in London who had acquired a huge amount of knowledge and skill especially relevant to this case in an earlier action on exactly the same type of claim, so saving both parties time and money in not having to start again with Canadian lawyers and experts, was a decisive factor making England the *forum conveniens*.

[54] In complex multi-party international cases, this is clearly the best result. See for example, the facts of *Canada Trust Co v Stolzenburg (No 2)* [2002] 1 AC 1. In *Owusu v Jackson*, part of the issue for the English court was whether to join all the defendants in an English action (which was a very inconvenient, expensive and unexpected court for most of them) or to allow the proceedings to go ahead against all the defendants in Jamaica, where the accident happened and most defendants were operated. The English defendant was possibly the least likely to be liable. The main defendants (the hotelier and manager of the resort where the accident happened) were all Jamaican and Jamaica was the court in which they could have expected to be sued, that of their domicile and that where the accident occurred.

[55] See for example, *Royal Bank of Canada v Cooperatieve Centrale Raiffeisen-Boerenleenbank BA* [2004] 1 LLR 471.

ing the *forum conveniens*. Where a party has commenced an action in a forum which has no connection with the events or the parties, and has been chosen apparently to force the other party to settle on disadvantageous terms, the court may be justified in ignoring those proceedings. Similarly, little weight will be given to the foreign action in the case where a party has merely commenced proceedings in such a court with little intention of ever bringing it to trial. On the other hand, in a case where proceedings, which are well advanced, are continuing in an appropriate forum, there is justification in not permitting a case to continue in England.[56] The timing of the commencement of proceedings is not critical, unlike the position under Article 27. In *The Coral Isis*,[57] the date of trial, rather than the commencement of proceedings, was found to be more important. Much time and effort had already been spent in proceedings almost to trial of the substantial issues in England, whilst the Dutch proceedings (commenced first) had made no progress, largely because of the inactivity of the party bringing those proceedings.[58] Therefore the court permitted the English proceedings to continue.

Taking a similar example to that above for the paper sale: A and B enter into a contract for A to sell and deliver paper to B monthly. The paper is manufactured in New York and shipped to England. The contract provides for termination on 12 months' notice. B complains about the lateness of delivery in February and the poor quality of the paper when delivered. A sues in New York for non-payment of invoices for January and February. B's defence is the lateness of delivery in February and the poor quality of the paper delivered in January.

Were B to sue later in England for damages for lost profit from the two deliveries as B has to source the paper from elsewhere, what would an English court decide? Very likely, it would determine that New York is an appropriate forum. It is the place where the paper was manufactured and so where investigations as to its quality can easily take place. It is also where A does business. On the other hand, England is also an appropriate forum as the paper is now here to be inspected (so the evidential questions as to quality can be decided conveniently) and B does business here where the paper was delivered. Neither country is definitively more appropriate. In neither country would a party suffer particular disadvantage, justice can be done equally in both. On balance, the New York proceedings were

---

[56] See eg *The Abidin Daver* [1984] AC 398, 410 and 421, *Cleveland Museum of Art v Capricorn Art International SA* [1990] 2 LLR 166 and *De Dampierre v De Dampierre* [1988] AC 92, 108.

[57] *The Coral Isis* [1986] 1 LLR 413 (decided before the 1968 Brussels Convention applied in England).

[58] See also *Arkwright Mutual Insurance Co v Bryanston Insurance Co Ltd* [1990] 2 LLR 70 (where no discovery had yet been done abroad).

commenced first and it would be more efficient for that court to decide all the matters in question before the parties. Therefore the English court would likely stay its proceedings or refuse permission to serve the claim form out of the jurisdiction. However, were there to be an argument from B that A is stalling the New York proceedings which were only commenced for tactical reasons, that the costs regime in New York is such that justice cannot be done there for B, or that B would suffer other serious injustice such as not being able to join the ship-owner, who may also be liable, in the action, the English court would permit the case to go ahead in England despite the possibility of parallel proceedings.

The doctrine of *forum conveniens* in relation to stays of English proceedings can be criticised. It may be uncertain in application[59] and without considerable experience, the principles underlying the decisions can be difficult to determine. It may give too much weight to the administrative convenience and efficiency of proceedings continuing in England, at the expense of requiring the parties to pursue their action in some objectively determined 'natural' forum.[60] The doctrine has probably been misunderstood, especially by the CJEU in *Owusu v Jackson*, as a block on the claimant's access to justice.[61] However, there are benefits in having a flexible, adaptable doctrine which can allow for account to be taken of very different circumstances in complex multinational litigation and can respond to the changes in tactics practiced by well-funded, well-advised litigants without being hidebound to strict rules of priority. It could be used as a weapon against improper forum shopping[62] in the hands of experienced judges alert to the possibility of jurisdictional game-playing.

V. THE COMMISSION'S PROPOSALS

The Commission has proposed to interpolate a new Article 34 which provides:

1. Notwithstanding the rules in Articles 3 to 7, if proceedings in relation to the same cause of action and between the same parties are pending before the courts of a third State at a time when a court in a Member State is seised, that court may stay its proceedings if:

---

[59] See (n 38) paras 40-41.
[60] See the results in *The Spiliada Maritime Corp v Cansulex Ltd (The Spiliada)* [1987] AC 460; *Lubbe v Cape Plc* [2000] 1 WLR 1545; *Connelly v RTZ Corp Plc* [1998] AC 854; *Sharab v Prince Al-Waleed bin Talal bin Abdal Aziz Al-Saud* [2009] 2 LLR 160; *Cherney v Deripaska* [2009] EWCA Civ 849.
[61] See (n 38) para 42.
[62] See however Fentiman's disagreement (n 13) para 12.08.

a. the court of the third State was seised first in time;

b. it may be expected that the court in the third State will, within a reasonable time, render a judgment that will be capable of recognition and, where applicable, enforcement in that Member State; and

c. the court is satisfied that it is necessary for the proper administration of justice to do so.

2. During the period of the stay, the party who has seised the court in the Member State shall not lose the benefit of interruption of prescription or limitation periods provided for under the law of that Member State.

3. The court may discharge the stay at any time upon application of either party or of its own motion if one of the following conditions is met:

a. the proceedings in the court of the third State are themselves stayed or are discontinued;

b. it appears to the court of the third State are unlikely to be concluded within a reasonable time;

c. discharge of the stay is required for the proper administration of justice.

4. The court shall dismiss the proceedings upon application by either party or of its own motion if the proceedings in the court of the third State are concluded and have resulted in a judgment enforceable in that State, or capable of recognition and, where applicable, enforcement in the Member State.

The effect of the proposed Article 34 is to allow the staying of actions commenced in a Member State in favour of proceedings commenced earlier on the same cause of action in a third State, where the stay is necessary for the proper administration of justice. The stay is only permitted if a recognisable (and enforceable, where appropriate) judgment of the courts of the third State is likely within a reasonable time. The article undoubtedly has some benefits. First, and most importantly, it permits a court of a Member State to stay proceedings where there is an action continuing in a third State in some circumstances. This avoids the worst excesses of the decision in *Owusu*. Secondly, the proposals contain a flexibility that the court can only stay proceedings if it is satisfied that the stay is 'necessary for the proper administration of justice'. It is not quite the mechanical rule that the existing Article 27 contains. Thirdly, the foreign judgment must be likely to be given within a reasonable time and to be recognisable (and enforceable, where appropriate). This is an important proviso. A foreign judgment which will take many years to obtain is not worth very much except to a party who wishes to avoid judgment. A foreign judgment that is not recognisable is not effective in the court deciding whether to stay its own proceedings and therefore a stay would be a waste of time and expenditure. One that is not enforceable is worthless.

There are some difficulties with the proposed Article 34. Primarily, and most importantly, there is no requirement or even a power to stay an action in a Member State where the proceedings in the third State have been commenced pursuant to a jurisdiction agreement. This is extremely regrettable and must be amended. If the proceedings in the third State are commenced first, then the action in the Member State may be stayed within the proposed Article 34. However, if proceedings have not yet been commenced in the third State, the existence of a jurisdiction agreement is not a justification to stay the action in a Member State as the proposed Article 34 is currently structured. That is an encouragement to rush to a Member State's court to frustrate a jurisdiction agreement in favour of a third State's court. Party autonomy[63] and the protection of jurisdiction and arbitration agreements from forum-shopping are strengthened in other proposed changes to the Regulation.[64] Not carrying this through to third State jurisdiction agreements is unfair on the party whose agreement is not being upheld and appears to be Euro-centric. The Hague Choice of Court Convention,[65] once ratified and brought into force in the EU, will address some aspects of this. This Convention requires courts, other than the court chosen, to suspend or dismiss proceedings except in certain circumstances, such as where the jurisdiction agreement is deemed to be void.[66] However, it only covers exclusive jurisdiction agreements. It can be argued that where the parties have entered into a non-exclusive jurisdiction agreement, this constitutes an expression that they are willing to entertain proceedings in that court. A stay would be justified in favour of proceedings in that court, particularly where there is little or no connection with the Member State's court. The Hague Convention also excludes for example, claims for personal injury and damage to property.[67] Nor are arbitration agreements with a seat in a third State protected by the possibility of a stay of a Member State's court action. Arbitration remains excluded from the Brussels I Regulation.[68] Nonetheless it is expressly referred to in some places, for example, in the proposed Article 29(4). It is quite unclear whether, by excluding arbitration generally while at the same time specifically including a requirement to stay proceedings brought in breach of an arbitration agreement where the designated seat is in a Member State, Member State's courts can continue to stay proceedings in favour of arbitration in a third State, as they are required to do by the New York

---

[63] See new Recital 15 (old Recital 14), new Recitals 19 and 20.

[64] For example in proposed art 29(4) and art 32(2), both restricted to arbitration and jurisdiction agreements in favour of Member States.

[65] Hague Convention of 30 June 2005 on Choice of Court Agreements ('Hague Convention').

[66] Art 6 Hague Convention.

[67] Art 2 Hague Convention.

[68] Art 1(1)(d) Hague Convention.

Convention.[69] Article 29(4) is intended to deal with the difficulties within the EU after *West Tankers*,[70] but those difficulties also apply to arbitration in third States.

Similarly, there is no requirement or possibility of a stay of a Member State's court proceedings in respect of a matter concerning exclusive jurisdiction in a third State. The Regulation specifically refers some matters to the exclusive jurisdiction of Member State's courts in Article 22. In the current Brussels I Regulation, this is strengthened by the non-recognition of judgments brought in other Member States.[71] However, this latter protection is deleted in the new proposals. It may be taking mutual trust and confidence too far to require a French court to enforce a judgment of the English court made in respect of ownership of French land. In relation to proceedings in England dealing with a US patent there are very strong arguments that an English court should not hear that dispute, leaving the case to go ahead in the US federal courts.[72] There may also be arguments under public international law notions of sovereignty which preclude a national court from deciding such matters. These notions are not limited to matters of exclusive jurisdiction of the Member States *inter se*.

The new Article 34 provides that the Member State's proceedings can only be stayed if the foreign proceedings are 'pending' and 'first in time'. Presumably old Article 30 (new Article 33) applies to determine when a Member State's court is seised. Therefore the English court is seised at the time of the issue of the claim form, so long as service is later effected on the defendant. However, it is also important to determine at which point the third State's court is seised. This determination could be referred to Article 34 or to that State's internal procedural rules.[73] Consistency and certainty would suggest the former.[74] However, the third State is not bound by the Brussels I Regulation, nor by any concept of mutual trust and confidence and so the determination of when its proceedings are pending may be more properly left to its internal law. As with the discussion above on the position under the current Article 30, the courts must be careful to avoid permitting abusive behaviour on the part of the claimant by means of later amendment to claims.

A further criticism which can be lodged against the proposals concerns their rigidity. The new Article 34 follows Article 27 in style. The power to

---

[69] Art II(3) of the 1958 New York Convention on the Recognition and Enforcement of Foreign Arbitral Awards.

[70] See (n 41).

[71] Current art 35(1).

[72] See *Lucasfilm v Ainsworth* [2010] Ch 503.

[73] As was the case before old art 30 was introduced (see the Brussels Convention cases such as *Dresser v Falcongate* [1992] QB 502 in which the Court of Appeal held that the court was seised when the writ was served).

[74] See also new Recital 18 (old Recital 18).

stay proceedings is limited to proceedings in relation to the same cause of action, between the same parties and arises only where the action before the courts of a third State is first in time. As we have seen, the existing case law on Article 27 permits and encourages parties to define their case tactically and race to seise their preferred court. Problems also occur in determining whether the parties or the causes of action are the same. Under the current Article 27, within the limited grounds of jurisdiction available and shored up by mutual trust and confidence, it might be argued that little harm is done. Replicating these well-known existing difficulties in a more complex world is unattractive. In the 'jungle'[75] of overlapping jurisdictional rules outside the EU it is very likely that a party may be dragged unsuspectingly into an unexpected court and stunned by potentially exorbitant costs and an extensive discovery regime and then capitulate on very unfavourable terms. In such a case, the Member State's court may conclude that it is not satisfied that a stay is necessary for the proper administration of justice. The point made here is more about the unnecessarily rigid operation of the rules. Why should justice be limited only to a stay of cases in which an action has been commenced first in a third State? Why is it limited to proceedings which involve only the same causes of action or the same parties? The rigidity appears to be unnecessary and not conducive to justice. Those Member States which do not wish to stay proceedings in favour of third States are given ample room not to do so, while those Member States which are more open to justice being achieved in other *fora* are hamstrung from following their preferred solution. This will lead to uncertainty, forum shopping within the EU (as parties race to engage their preferred court), and injustice.

The operation of the test of what is 'necessary for the proper adminis-tration of justice' is obscure. It probably introduces a form of *forum conve-niens* which could be an attractive solution to the injustices of parallel proceedings. However, there are no guidelines for Member State's courts which have no history of staying actions on this ground. The recitals explain little as to the purpose of the proposed Article 34, noting only that 'a flexible mechanism should exist'.[76] As we have seen from the common law operation of *forum conveniens*, notions of justice in relation to paral-lel proceedings include cost-efficiency to the parties and to the courts concerned, preventing abuses of process when a multiplicity of actions has been launched, facilitating the possibility of a one-stop action including all parties and discouraging inappropriate forum shopping. Achieving these ends requires a wider consideration of the justifications of the competing proceedings. Testing the appropriateness of the forum in which the actions

---

[75] Lord Goff in *Airbus Industrie GIE v Patel* [1999] 1 AC 119, 132.
[76] Proposed Recital 21.

are proceeding must be judged against the parties' expectations of the likely *fora*. It is quite probable that the policy imperatives underlying notions of 'a proper administration of justice' will point in different directions. Justice to the individual parties, efficient operation of the courts and respect for a foreign court's right to determine any dispute will not lead to the same result. As an example, is the proper administration of justice defeated where the third State court has a shorter limitation period which has expired? What if the third State has a lower damages regime or a different costs regime or a different evidentiary regime? In addition, what if the claimant in the EU court cannot make an effective counterclaim in the third State?

It is also unclear whether and on what justification an autonomous definition of the 'same cause of action' and the 'same parties' will be adopted. Where proceedings in third States are continuing under legal regimes far removed from the EU and from the interpretative judgments of the CJEU an autonomous definition should not be adopted. The twin imperatives of mutual trust and confidence and mutual recognition of judgments[77], which underpin the current Article 27, are completely lacking in relation to proceedings continuing in a third State. They are insufficiently replaced by an exhortation for the 'proper administration of justice' without further elucidation by the CJEU.[78]

In addition there is no equivalent to Article 28. It may well also be the case that the proper and harmonious administration of justice requires related actions to be stayed pending the outcome in a third State's court. However, this is impermissible under the proposals. An illustrative example: A, an English company, has contracted to deliver a cargo of oil to B, a French company, in New York and the cargo is found to be contaminated. C unloaded the cargo in New York into its storage tanks there. The contract of sale includes a jurisdiction agreement in favour of the courts of New York. There is a dispute as to whether the contamination is A's or C's fault. A sues B in France for non-payment and C commences proceedings for non-liability for damage against B and A in New York. Article 34 does not operate because the proceedings in New York were not commenced first, the causes of action are different and A and C are different parties. This will be the case despite the jurisdiction agreement. However, justice and efficiency would suggest that the French court stays its proceedings to await the outcome of the New York action. It is better that the dispute between all the parties is determined in New York, which is an appropriate place to decide the case as the place where the cargo was unloaded. Ultimately, the French court should enforce the New York judgment; this leads us to a further point.

---

[77] Ultimately to further the original purpose of the EU in free movement.
[78] Proposed Recital 21.

There are no provisions for mutual recognition and enforcement of judgments from third States. Therefore, inevitably there will be a lack of uniformity in the operation of the proposed Article 34. Member States which freely recognize and enforce third State's judgments, such as England, will also be able freely to stay proceedings under Article 34. Those which do not easily recognize or enforce third State's judgments will only rarely stay their proceedings. This potential discrepancy in the final outcome will add to the pressure to race to the court, in this case a Member State's court which does not recognize third State's judgments so as to avoid proceedings properly continuing in a third State. Another Member State's court will then also be denied hearing the action under the proposed Article 29 (ex Article 27). Presumably it is the lack of mutual recognition and enforcement of third State's judgments which supports the need for the extension of the special jurisdictional rules to defendants not domiciled in Member States and the abolition of national rules of jurisdiction over such defendants.[79] However, the justification for the extension of the EU Member States' courts' jurisdiction over cases which are minimally connected with the EU is not very strong. For example, if a New York bank agrees to lend dollars to a Japanese borrower and the deal happens to be negotiated at the London branch of the bank, the bank can now sue the borrower in London under Article 5(5). It would not be at all just if the bank can do so in breach of a Japanese jurisdiction agreement and in the face of proceedings about to be commenced in Tokyo. There is no EU interest in the dispute: neither party is domiciled in the EU, nothing significant is done in the EU and no harm is suffered in the EU or by EU parties. It may be complete happenstance that the deal was negotiated in London. The English court under current rules would stay its proceedings in favour of those in Japan. It would also recognize and enforce a Japanese judgment in such a case.

There are also less important matters of concern. The determination of a 'reasonable time' within which the third State's court is likely to come to judgment will vary from State to State. Not only is there a difficult assessment of the possible length of proceedings in a foreign third State, but there are also difficulties in determining what time is reasonable, given that it is not an autonomous concept.

---

[79] Proposed Recitals 16 and 17 articulate that the Regulation should establish a complete set of rules on international jurisdiction so as to promote the interests of claimants and defendants within the EU.

VI. CONCLUSION

In conclusion, the current proposals seem to be a strange mix of inflexibility (same cause of action, court first seised) and discretion ('necessary for the proper administration of justice'). These proposals permit courts of different legal traditions to continue with their existing traditions leading to a lack of uniformity. They will encourage, rather than discourage, satellite litigation on jurisdiction and forum-shopping by a race to the court. Without correlative provisions on the recognition of third State judgments, uniformity will not be achieved. The particular omissions of jurisdiction agreements and exclusive subject-matter jurisdiction as grounds for staying actions in the Member States' courts must be remedied. Matters relating to arbitration agreements should be included as a ground, for the avoidance of doubt.

An alternative would be to leave the staying of actions in favour of third States to national rules despite providing (either exclusive or additional) rules of jurisdiction for actions where the defendant is domiciled in a third State. However, such an approach would not resolve the *Owusu* prohibition on discretionary stays of actions commenced before a Member State's court. These proposals at least indicate that the case was wrongly decided and the CJEU must revisit it with an open mind.

The Proposed Recast of Rules on Provisional Measures under the Brussels I Regulation

*Michael Bogdan**

Imagine that a Swedish company is contemplating suing a company domiciled in Germany for payment of some goods delivered in Germany, under a contract between the two companies. As the defendant is domiciled in Germany, which is also the place of performance of the contract, there is barely any doubt that German courts would have jurisdiction pursuant to the Brussels I Regulation;[1] at least in the absence of a valid choice-of-court clause in the contract providing otherwise. In fact, German courts are probably the only courts in the European Union that are competent to make a decision on the substance of the dispute.

However, let us assume that the assets of the German defendant company consist mainly of a bank account with an English bank in London. In accordance with the Regulation, the forthcoming German judgment on the substance of the dispute will almost certainly be recognised and enforceable within the whole EU, including England, yet the Swedish company fears that by the time of the final judgment, the account may be empty; all of the money having been consumed, dissipated or moved to an off-shore account in an exotic country, where German judgments are neither recognised, nor enforced. In view of this risk, the German court can probably order certain provisional protective measures pursuant to German law, such as freezing the account, and these measures will be recognised and enforceable in England as well. However, from the point of view of the plaintiff, it may be more practical and expedient, especially if it is important that the provisional protective measures be taken and enforced quickly, to address his application for such measures directly to an English court in London.

This is where the current Article 31 of the Brussels I Regulation steps in. It provides the following:

Application may be made to the courts of a Member State for such provisional, including protective, measures as may be available under the law of that State, even

---

* Professor of Comparative and Private International Law, University of Lund.
[1] Council Regulation 44/2001 of 22 December 2000 on Jurisdiction and the Recognition and Enforcement of Judgments in Civil and Commercial Matters [2001] OJ L 12/1.

if, under this Regulation, the courts of another Member State have jurisdiction as to the substance of the matter.

Except for having replaced 'Contracting State' with 'Member State', and 'Convention' with 'Regulation', the current Article 31 of the Regulation is identical to Article 24 of the 1968 Brussels Convention on Jurisdiction and the Enforcement of Judgments in Civil and Commercial Matters (the Brussels Convention). Therefore, the existing case law from the Court of Justice of the European Union (CJEU) regarding Article 24 of the Convention also provides guidance for the interpretation of the current Article 31 of the Regulation. This is of great importance, as there are, so far, no CJEU decisions dealing with Article 31 of the Regulation alone. However, there are six CJEU judgments dealing directly with Article 24 of the Brussels Convention: *de Cavel v de Cavel*,[2] *C.W.H. v G.J.H.*,[3] *Reichert v Dresdner Bank*,[4] *Van Uden v Deco-Line*,[5] *Mietz v Intership Yachting*,[6] and *St. Paul Dairy v Unibel*.[7] There are also some other cases that are indirectly relevant for the understanding of that Article, for example *Denilauler v Couchet Frères*,[8] *Mund & Fester v Hatrex*[9] and *Italian Leather v WECO*.[10]

The relative paucity of CJEU case law must not be interpreted as evidence of the minor practical importance of provisional measures. It is a well-known fact that such measures tend to substantially strengthen the position of the applicant, and very often make the debtor amenable to a settlement, while a refusal of provisional measures shifts the balance in favour of the debtor and will often result in the discontinuation of the proceedings on the substance of the dispute.

On 14 December 2010, the European Commission presented its proposal for a recast of the whole Brussels I Regulation (the Proposal).[11] The current Article 31 is, in the Proposal, replaced with Article 36, which stipulates as follows:

[2] CJEU, Case C-143/78 *Jaques de Cavel v Louise de Cavel* [1979] ECR 1055.

[3] CJEU, Case C-25/81 *C.W.H. v G.J.H.* [1982] ECR 1189.

[4] CJEU, Case C-261/90 *M. Reichert, H.H. Reichert and I. Kockler v Dresdner Bank AG* [1992] ECR I-2149.

[5] CJEU, Case C-391/95 *Van Uden Maritime BV v Kommanditgesellschaft in Firma Deco-Line* [1998] ECR I-7091.

[6] CJEU, Case C-99/96 *H.H. Mietz v Intership Yachting Sneek BV* [1999] ECR I-2277.

[7] CJEU, Case C-104/03 *St Paul Dairy Industries NV v Unibel Exser BVBA* [2005] ECR I-3481.

[8] CJEU, Case C-125/79 *Bernard Denilauler v SNC Couchet Frères* [1980] ECR 1553.

[9] CJEU, Case C-398/92 *Mund & Fester v Hatrex Internationaal Transport* [1994] ECR I-467.

[10] CJEU, Case C-80/00 *Italian Leather SpA v WECO Polstermöbel GmbH & Co* [2002] ECR I-4995.

[11] European Commission, Proposal for a Regulation of the European Parliament and of the Council on jurisdiction and the recognition and enforcement of judgments in civil and commercial matters (Recast) COM(2010) 748 final.

Application may be made to the courts of a Member State for such provisional, including protective, measures as may be available under the law of that State, even if the courts of another State or an arbitral tribunal have jurisdiction as to the substance of the matter.

A comparison between the wording of the current Article 31 and that of the proposed Article 36 shows there are merely two differences between them. First, the words 'under this Regulation' are omitted in the Proposal. Second, the reference to 'the courts of another Member State' is replaced with 'the courts of another State or an arbitral tribunal'. However, some proposed changes concerning other Articles will also have a direct or indirect impact on the use of provisional measures.

The purpose of this chapter is to provide a summary survey of the main interpretation problems concerning the current Article 31 and discuss how they will be affected if the proposed Article 36 is adopted. The chapter thus deals merely with provisional measures ordered before or during the proceedings on the substance of the matter. There may be a practical need for provisional measures even after the judgment on the merits has been rendered, as the enforcement and/or *exequatur* (declaration of enforceability) proceedings may take some time. In such a situation, it is not Article 31, but Article 47 of the current Regulation, and not Article 36, but Articles 40 and 60 of the Proposal, that provide the legal basis for the measures. To the extent the Proposal abolishes the requirement of *exequatur*, it also limits the need for post-judgment provisional measures, which will not be dealt with further in this chapter.

It goes without saying that the current Article 31, being a component of the Brussels I Regulation, is only applicable within the scope of application of the Regulation as such, as defined in its Article 1. It can consequently only be used if the dispute concerns a civil or commercial matter, and matters of family law are in principle excluded. In the case of *C.W.H.*,[12] dealing with an application for the securing of a document to be used as evidence in an action concerning a husband's management of his wife's property directly on the basis of the marriage bond, the CJEU held Article 24 of the Brussels Convention to be inapplicable and declared that it could not be relied on to bring within the scope of the Convention provisional measures relating to matters which were excluded from it. To the extent that Article 1 of the Proposal changes the substantive scope of the Regulation, for example by excluding maintenance matters,[13] it similarly changes the scope of the application of the proposed Article 36.

---

[12] See *C.W.H.* (n 3). and *de Cavel* (n 2).

[13] In fact, this exclusion took effect on 18 June 2011, when the Council Regulation 4/2009 of 18 December 2008 on Jurisdiction, Applicable Law, Recognition and Enforcement of Decisions and Cooperation in Matters Relating to Maintenance Obligations [2009] OJ L 7/1 replaced the provisions of the Brussels I Regulation on maintenance disputes. See art 58(1) of

Pursuant to Article 1 of the current Brussels I Regulation, arbitration is also excluded from the Regulation's scope. However, this exclusion has in mind merely matters concerning the arbitration as such (for example, the appointment of an arbitrator by a court of law), but not commercial and civil disputes falling within the scope of the Regulation which are to be resolved by arbitrators. Thus, the CJEU held in the case of *Van Uden*[14] that Article 31 can be used for the purpose of obtaining provisional measures even where proceedings on the substance of the dispute have already been, or may be, commenced before arbitrators, apparently irrespective of whether the arbitration proceedings take place in a Member State or elsewhere. The CJEU pointed out that provisional measures do not concern arbitration as such and are parallel rather than ancillary to arbitration proceedings. The *Van Uden* judgment has been criticised, *inter alia*, for blurring the distinction between arbitration and judicial proceedings, but it is submitted that the decision was correct. Foreign arbitration awards are normally recognised and enforced in all Member States due to the 1958 New York Convention on the Recognition and Enforcement of Foreign Arbitral Awards, but the arbitrators are not always entitled to decide on provisional measures which can perhaps only be ordered by national courts. Even though there exists an exception regarding *lis pendens* (see Articles 29(4) and 33(3) of the Proposal),[15] the exclusion of arbitration is maintained in the Proposal and the *Van Uden* rule, permitting courts to take provisional measures even when the substance of the dispute is dealt with by arbitrators, is explicitly confirmed in the proposed Article 36.

The domicile and the nationality of the plaintiff/applicant are in principle irrelevant for the application of the current Article 31. In the introductory example above, it would make no difference if the applicant were not domiciled in a Member State such as Sweden but, for example, in Thailand. It is less certain whether the same can be said about the domicile of the defendant. It could be argued that as the current Article 31 applies only when another Member State has jurisdiction to deal with the substance of the dispute 'under this Regulation', its application presupposes that the defendant is domiciled in another Member State or that another Member State has exclusive or prorogated jurisdiction pursuant to the Regulation's jurisdictional rules. In other words, according to this view, Article 31

---

the Council Regulation 4/2009, which also contains, in art 14, its own rule on provisional measures identical to art 31 of the current Brussels I Regulation. However, Denmark is not bound by the Council Regulation 4/2009, see its Recital 48.

[14] *Van Uden* (n 5).

[15] Recital 11 of the Proposal lists the main arbitration issues that are excluded from the scope of the Regulation, in particular the form, existence, validity or effects of arbitration agreements, the powers of the arbitrators, the procedure before arbitral tribunals, and the validity, annulment, and recognition and enforcement of arbitral awards.

cannot be used when the court of another Member State, deciding on the substance of the dispute, has jurisdiction merely on the basis of its national jurisdictional rules pursuant to Article 4 of the current Regulation, for example if proceedings have been initiated in Sweden against a defendant domiciled in the USA on the basis of the presence of his assets in Sweden. It is hard to be convinced that this is the correct view, even though the wording used by the CJEU in the case of *Mietz*[16] might seem to support it. It would indeed be strange, considering that Article 31 is available to support arbitration proceedings going on in any country (see above), if it were not applicable when the substance of the dispute is adjudicated by a court of a sister Member State whose judgment will be recognised and enforced throughout the EU. In any case, if Article 31 were not applicable, it would not mean that such provisional measures are not allowed, merely that they are not governed by Article 31, but by the jurisdictional rules of the *lex fori* on the basis of Article 4. The Proposal, if adopted, will deprive this whole issue of its relevance, as the words 'under this Regulation' will be deleted, which is natural in view of the fact that the proposed Regulation is intended to regulate the jurisdiction of the Member States irrespective of whether the defendant is domiciled within or beyond the EU. In addition, the proposed Article 36 extends explicitly its application to cases where the substance of the dispute is adjudicated by the courts of 'another State' (instead of 'another Member State' in the current Article 31).

The current Article 31 does not intend to be exclusive. It provides an alternative (non-exclusive) jurisdictional ground and does not in any way limit the competence of the court deciding on the substance of the dispute to order provisional measures as well. This was made clear by the CJEU in the case of *Van Uden*,[17] and the Proposal confirms it explicitly in Article 35, which stipulates that where the courts of a Member State have jurisdiction as to the substance of a matter, those courts also have jurisdiction to issue provisional measures as may be available under the law of that State.

It follows from the wording of the current Article 31 that the substantive prerequisites of provisional measures are governed by the law of the court to which the application is made, ie the *lex fori*. This applies in the first place to the types of available measures; while some such measures are almost universally known (for example, the freezing of a bank account), other measures are available in some countries only (for example, the ordering of an interim payment to the applicant without waiting for the decision on the substance of the dispute). Further, the preconditions imposed by different legal systems vary substantially, for example, as to the requirement of urgency or of the risk of dissipation. The procedure as such is also

---

[16] *Mietz* (n 6).
[17] See *Van Uden* (n 5) para 22 and *Mietz* (n 6) paras 40–41.

governed by the *lex fori*. The wording of the proposed Article 36 makes it clear that no change is intended on this point.[18]

The *lex fori* is, however, not decisive for the classification of a measure as 'provisional, including protective'. The fact that a measure is considered provisional in the *lex fori* does not automatically bring it within the purview of the current Article 31 and the proposed Article 36. According to the CJEU in the case of *Reichert*,[19] the main feature of provisional measures within the meaning of Article 31 is that they are intended to protect a factual or legal situation so as to safeguard rights, the recognition of which is sought from another court having jurisdiction as to the substance of the matter. The measures must therefore have the effect of preserving the *status quo* and must not change it. Consequently, the CJEU held that this condition is not fulfilled by the *action paulienne* under French law, because such a measure varies the legal situation by ordering the revocation of certain dispositions made by the debtor in fraud of his creditors. In the cases of *Van Uden*[20] and *Mietz*,[21] the CJEU made clear that the ordering of an interim payment to the plaintiff does not constitute a provisional measure capable of being granted under Article 31, unless repayment to the defendant is guaranteed if the plaintiff is ultimately unsuccessful as regards the substance of the dispute. It is not quite clear what the CJEU meant by 'guaranteed'. Obviously, the mere duty of the unsuccessful plaintiff to return the money does not constitute a real guarantee of repayment. On the other hand, the requirement of a bank guarantee, or a similar security arrangement, would make interim payments very difficult and expensive to use. The problem was mentioned by the European Commission in its Green Paper on the review of the Brussels I Regulation,[22] but the Proposal does not address it.

---

[18] The application of *lex fori* is naturally subject to the general restrictions imposed by EU law, such as the prohibition of open or covert discrimination on the basis of nationality. Thus, in *Mund & Fester* (n 9), the CJEU had to deal with a German provision which only authorised provisional seizure of property when it was probable that enforcement would otherwise be made impossible or substantially more difficult, but dispensed with this requirement when the enforcement was to take place abroad (including in another Member State). Even though the German provision in question did not directly mention nationality, the CJEU noted that the great majority of enforcements abroad were against foreigners and foreign legal persons, so that the provision indirectly made it easier to procure provisional measures against foreign defendants and thus amounted to a covert form of discrimination on grounds of nationality prohibited by the Treaty. A new or amended Brussels I Regulation cannot, of course, change anything in this respect, as it cannot go against the rules of primary EU law, such as art 18 of the Treaty on the Functioning of the European Union, which prohibits any discrimination on grounds of nationality.

[19] *Reichert* (n 4).
[20] *Van Uden* (n 5).
[21] *Mietz* (n 6).
[22] COM(2009) 175 final.

Interim injunctions, for example, court orders enjoining infringements of intellectual property, fulfil the requirements and are 'provisional, including protective' measures under both the current Article 31 and the proposed Article 36. Furthermore, provisional measures can be used to preserve not only property, but also evidence. However, in the case of *St. Paul Dairy*,[23] the CJEU held that a measure ordering the hearing of a witness for the purpose of enabling the applicant to decide whether to bring a case, determine whether it would be well-founded and assess the relevance of evidence which might be adduced, is not covered by the notion of 'provisional, including protective' measures under Article 31. The CJEU stated that a provision such as Article 31, laying down an exception to the system of jurisdiction, must be interpreted strictly, and that the measure sought in the case did not pursue the aim of preserving a factual or legal situation. It is submitted that this CJEU judgment should be interpreted to mean that while measures for the purpose of preserving known evidence are in principle provisional measures under Article 31, the search for potential evidence ('evidence fishing') is not. The last-mentioned type of evidence collecting can instead often be carried out using the Regulation on Cooperation between the Courts of the Member States in the Taking of Evidence in Civil or Commercial Matters.[24] This dichotomy is maintained and confirmed explicitly within the Proposal in Article 2(b), and even more clearly in Recital (22), which clarifies that the notion of 'provisional, including protective, measures' includes, in particular, protective orders aimed at obtaining information or preserving evidence, such as the search and seizure orders referred to in Articles 6 and 7 of the Enforcement of Intellectual Property Rights Directive,[25] but does not include non-protective measures, such as ordering the hearing of a witness for the purpose of enabling the applicant to decide whether to bring a case.

Neither the wording of the current Article 31, nor that of the proposed Article 36 requires any genuine connecting link between the Member State of the forum and the measure sought. However, in the case of *Van Uden*,[26] the CJEU held that the granting of provisional measures on the basis of Article 31 is conditional on the existence of a real connecting link between the subject-matter of the measures sought and the territorial jurisdiction of the Member State which is the forum of the dispute. Such a real or genuine link consists normally of the presence of assets that are to be preserved.

---

[23] *St Paul Dairy Industries* (n 7).

[24] Council Regulation 1206/2001 of 28 May 2001 on Cooperation between the Courts of the Member States in the Taking of Evidence in Civil or Commercial Matters [2001] OJ L 174/1.

[25] Directive 2004/48 of 29 April 2004 on the Enforcement of Intellectual Property Rights [2004] OJ L 157/45.

[26] *Van Uden* (n 5).

Exorbitant jurisdictional grounds such as the nationality of the plaintiff/applicant are certainly not acceptable. As the CJEU pointed out in the case of *Denilauler*,[27] the rationale underlying this requirement in relation to Article 31 is that the courts of the country/place, where the assets subject to the provisional measures sought are located, are those best able to assess the circumstances which may lead to the granting or refusal of the measures in question. According to the CJEU in the above-mentioned case of *Van Uden*,[28] the presence of the defendant's assets is particularly important in the cases of interim payments, which cannot constitute provisional measures under Article 31, unless they relate only to specific assets of the defendant located or to be located within the confines of the territorial jurisdiction of the court to which the application is made.

The last-mentioned condition is however rather difficult to understand, as a payment order, whether interim or not, does not normally state from which particular assets the payment is to be made. What the CJEU possibly had in mind, when it provided that interim payments cannot constitute provisional measures under Article 31 unless they relate only to specific assets of the defendant in the Member State of the forum, is that an interim payment order issued pursuant to Article 31 is to be enforceable in that Member State only, ie not in the other Member States. This interpretation is, however, far from certain. It is true that extraterritorial enforcement of measures under Article 31 is normally not necessary because such measures are usually applied for in the Member State where they are to be enforced, such as the country where the defendant owns assets. On the other hand, the recognition and enforceability of provisional measures, ordered by a court not having jurisdiction as to the substance of the matter, seems to have been assumed implicitly by the CJEU in the cases of *Mietz*[29] and *Italian Leather*.[30] In any case, the Proposal stipulates in Article 2(a) that for the purposes of its Chapter III, dealing with recognition, enforceability and enforcement, the term 'judgment' includes those provisional measures that have been ordered by a court which under the Regulation has jurisdiction as to the substance of the matter (thus, *a contrario*, excluding measures under Article 36, which will not be recognised and enforced in the other Member States). This proposed restriction is obviously intended to prevent abusive forum shopping, where provisional orders under Article 36 would be obtained in one Member State for the sole purpose of having them enforced in another Member State.

On the other hand, it appears that in the presence of a genuine connecting link, the national court must not dismiss the application because of lack

[27] *Bernard Denilauler* (n 8).
[28] *Van Uden* (n 5).
[29] *Mietz* (n 6).
[30] *Italian Leather* (n 10).

of jurisdiction. On this point, the proposed Article 36 maintains the wording 'Application may be made...', in contrast to Regulation Brussels II bis,[31] whose Article 20 provides that the Regulation, under certain conditions, 'shall not prevent' the courts of a Member State from taking provisional, including protective, measures, even if the court of another Member State has jurisdiction as to the substance of the matter.

Article 2(a) of the Proposal is also aimed at overruling the CJEU judgment in the case of *Denilauler*.[32] There, the Court held that the provisions of the Brussels Convention did not apply to *ex parte* decisions on provisional or protective measures, even if delivered by the court with jurisdiction over the substance of the dispute, if they were ordered without the party - against whom they were directed - having been summoned to appear, and were intended to be enforced without prior service on the defendant. According to the proposed Article 2(a), even such a measure will be recognised and enforced, provided the defendant has the right to subsequently challenge the measure under the national law of the Member State of origin (in the case of such a challenge, the enforcement of the measure may be suspended pursuant to Article 44(3) of the Proposal). This is particularly important in light of Article 9(4) of the Enforcement of Intellectual Property Rights Directive[33], which requires the Member States to allow provisional measures to be taken without the defendant having been heard.

Finally, it is necessary to mention Article 31 of the Proposal. If proceedings as to the substance are pending before a court of a Member State and a court of another Member State is seised with an application for provisional measures, the two courts will be obliged to cooperate in order to coordinate the two proceedings, in particular in terms of the latter court seeking information from the former regarding the relevant circumstances, such as the urgency of the measure sought or any refusal of a similar measure by the court dealing with the substance of the dispute. This kind of cooperation is naturally possible and desirable even today, but the Proposal imposes such cooperative behaviour, the practical value of which remains to be seen.

---

[31] Regulation 2201/2003 of 27 November 2003 Concerning Jurisdiction and the Recognition and Enforcement of Judgments in Matrimonial Matters and the Matters of Parental Responsibility ('Brussels II bis') [2003] OJ L 338/1.
[32] *Bernard Denilauler* (n 8).
[33] Directive 2004/48 (n 25).

Free Movement of Judgments in the EU: Knock Down the Walls but Mind the Ceiling

*Andrew Dickinson**

In its Proposal, published in December 2010, to recast Council Regulation 44/2001 on jurisdiction and the recognition and enforcement of judgments in civil and commercial matters[2] ('Brussels I Regulation'), the Commission proposes the abolition, in most cases, of the intermediate declaration of enforceability procedure (*exequatur*) for the enforcement of judgments. This part of the Proposal was inevitable, having long been foreshadowed as the next stage in removing obstacles to the free movement of judgments within the European Union and, at the time, having attracted an apparently irresistible political momentum. The Commission also recommends that the power of Member State courts to resist recognition and enforcement of judgments on the grounds of a manifest incompatibility with the forum's public policy[3] should be removed, and replaced by a twin-track procedure for challenging judgments, on limited grounds, in their Member State of origin or the Member State of enforcement. Taken together, these grounds recognise a continued right of challenge on the basis of the most important 'procedural' public policy (ie the right to a fair trial), but not on other, including what might be described as 'substantive', public policy grounds. Although closely tied to the proposed abolition of *exequatur*, this element of the proposal is more controversial, and the Commission's intentions had already attracted criticism from commentators before the proposal was published.[4]

* Professor in Private International Law, University of Sydney; Visiting Fellow, British Institute of International and Comparative Law; Solicitor, England and Wales; Consultant, Clifford Chance LLP.
[1] Commission Proposal for a Regulation of the European Parliament and of the Council on jurisdiction and the recognition and enforcement of judgments in civil and commercial matters (Recast) COM(2010)748 final (14 December 2010). Unless otherwise stated, (a) references in this Article to Articles and Recitals numbers are to the Articles and Recitals of the Commission's Proposal in this COM document, and (b) the Article numbers of the Proposal are the same as those of the corresponding provisions of the Brussels I Regulation (n 2) in its current form.
[2] Council Regulation (EC) 44/2001 of 22 December 2000 on Jurisdiction, and the Recognition and Enforcement of judgments in Civil and Commercial Matters [2001] OJ L 12/1.
[3] Brussels I Regulation, art 34(1).
[4] See eg P Beaumont and E Johnston, 'Can *Exequatur* Be Abolished in Brussels I Whilst Retaining a Public Policy Defence?' (2010) 6 J Priv Intl L 249.

This chapter[5] considers the case for and against the liberalisation of the rules within the Brussels I regime for the cross-border recognition and enforcement of judgments within the EU. In so doing, it treats the questions of liberalisation of the procedural requirements (ie the abolition of *exequatur*) and liberalisation of the grounds for opposing recognition and enforcement as logically and legally distinct. It will be argued that the Commission has demonstrated a strong case for removing the procedural barriers, with appropriate safeguards to prevent fraud, but that it is on much weaker ground when it comes to restricting the right of Member State courts to refuse enforcement on public policy or other grounds. The Council and European Parliament should not, therefore, accept these elements of the Proposal.

The chapter begins with a brief summary of the current Brussels I regime (Part I), followed by an outline of the elements of the Commission's Proposal (Part II), before turning to analyse these in further detail (Part III) and concluding with a summary of the changes proposed (Part IV). Suggested amendments to the drafting of the Commission Proposal are set out in the Annex at the end of the chapter.[6]

I. THE CURRENT REGIME

The Brussels I Regulation provides for a Member State judgment to be *recognised* in the other Member States without any special procedure being required.[7] A judgment shall not, however, be recognised if any of the limited grounds of objection set out in Article 34 (public policy; default judgments; irreconcilable judgments) or Article 35(1) (limited review of jurisdiction) are applicable. Subject to these grounds, the jurisdiction of the Member State court of origin may not be reviewed,[8] and under no circumstances may a foreign judgment be reviewed as to its substance.[9] For a Member State judgment to be *enforced* in another Member State, however, it must (a) be enforceable in its Member State of origin, and (b) have been

---

[5] The chapter builds upon the author's analysis in Part II of his Article 'Surveying The Proposed Brussels I *bis* Regulation – Solid Foundations But Renovation Needed', first published in the (2010) 12 YB Priv Intl L 247, 251–269, and the author's presentation at the seminar on the review proposal organised by the British Institute of International and Comparative Law in London, 10 February 2011.

[6] These drafting proposals are taken from the author's submission to the European Parliament's workshop on the proposals to amend the Brussels I Regulation, held on 20 September and 4 October 2011. A copy of this submission is available at http://papers.ssrn.com/sol3/papers.cfm?abstract_id=1930712.

[7] Brussels I Regulation, art 33(1).

[8] ibid art 35(2).

[9] ibid art 36.

declared enforceable in the Member State of enforcement in accordance with the expedited procedure set out in Section 2 of Chapter III of the Regulation.[10] Again, enforceability may be resisted in the Member State of enforcement on the grounds set out in Articles 34 and 35(1), subject to the same restrictions.[11]

II. THE COMMISSION'S PROPOSAL

In its Proposal, the Commission recommends the abolition of the declaration of enforceability mechanism as the medium for enforcement of judgments between Member States. In its place, the Commission proposes that a judgment enforceable in its Member State of origin shall be *enforceable* and *enforced* in any Member State upon production of an authentic copy of the judgment and a certificate in the prescribed form[12] issued by the court of origin, without any intermediate procedure.[13] Thereafter, enforcement shall proceed as if the judgment were one given by the courts of the Member State of enforcement.[14] There is no requirement that the enforcing party give advance warning to the opposing party of the enforcement process. Instead, the opposing party, on learning of the judgment, has the following limited options available:

1. Article 45: If (and only if) he did not enter an appearance in the proceedings leading to the judgment, to apply to the courts of the Member State of origin[15] to review the judgment (and have it declared null and void)[16] on the ground that either (a) he was not served with the claim document in sufficient time and in such a way as to enable him to arrange for his defence, or (b) he was prevented from contesting the claim due to '*force majeure* or extraordinary circumstances without any fault on his part';[17] unless he failed to challenge the judgment when it was possible for him to do so. Such an application must be made in the prescribed form,[18] although this presently seems barely adequate for the purposes.[19]

---

[10] ibid art 38.

[11] ibid art 45.

[12] ibid Annex I.

[13] Art 38(2) and art 42(1). Additional restrictions apply to the enforcement of provisional measures (see art 2(a) and 42(2)).

[14] Art 41.

[15] Directly or via the 'competent court' in the Member State of enforcement (art 45(3)).

[16] Art 45(5).

[17] Art 45(1), a limited extension of the ground of opposition, currently found in art 34(2) of the Brussels I Regulation.

[18] Annex II.

[19] The applicant is simply required to tick a box confirming which of the two art 45(1)

2. Articles 43 and 46: In other cases, to apply to the courts of the Member State of origin for a refusal of enforcement measures if enforcement would not be permitted by the fundamental principles underlying the right to a fair trial,[20] or if the judgment is irreconcilable with a judgment between the same parties given in the Member State of enforcement or with an earlier judgment given in another Member State or in a Third State in proceedings between the same parties and involving the same cause of action and which meets the conditions necessary for its recognition in the Member State of enforcement.[21]

Notably, the Commission proposes that the current right to challenge the recognition or enforcement of a Member State judgment on the ground of manifest incompatibility with the enforcing/recognising Member State's public policy should be removed, being replaced by the limited 'fair trial' ground in Article 46.[22] Further, with one very narrow exception, no review of the jurisdiction of the court of origin would be permitted, even in the limited circumstances currently envisioned by the Brussels I Regulation (non-compliance with consumer, insurance or exclusive jurisdiction requirements).[23]

The Commission recommends, however, that the intermediate procedure should remain in certain cases, at least on a transitional basis. The draft Regulation identifies two categories of judgments in which a declaration of enforceability must still be obtained[24] by the enforcing party and served on the opposing party,[25] subject to the latter's right of appeal on limited grounds identical to those found in Article 34 (but not Article 35(1)) of the current Brussels I Regulation. These two categories are, first, judgments concerning non-contractual obligations arising out of violations of privacy and rights relating to personality, including defamation,[26] and, secondly, judgments in collective redress proceedings concerning the compensation of

---

grounds is relied upon – no additional information or evidence is required. In contrast to art 46, the text of art 45 does not expressly authorise the court to which the application is made to apply its own procedures in determining the application, and it is unclear how the application would proceed once the form is filed.

[20] Art 46(1), a provision which is intentionally narrower than the public policy ground currently found in Art 34(1) of the Brussels I Regulation, see text to n 48–118.

[21] Art 43, corresponding to the grounds of opposition, currently found in art 34(3), (4) of the Brussels I Regulation.

[22] See text to n 20.

[23] Art 35 of the Brussels I Regulation is to be removed from the new Regulation, although Member States may still fulfil treaty obligations towards third States not to recognise judgments based on the exorbitant grounds of jurisdiction set out in art 3(2) of the 1968 Brussels Convention (art 83).

[24] Art 50.

[25] Art 55.

[26] Art 37(3)(a), an exception corresponding to the exclusion of these matters from the material scope of the Rome II Regulation (n 44), according to its art 1(2)(g) (see Recital (33)).

harm caused by unlawful business practices which meet certain conditions.[27]

With less fanfare, the Commission also suggests changes to the regime for the *recognition* of judgments outside the two categories just mentioned. As before, no special procedure is to be required for recognition of a judgment.[28] Article 38(1) of the draft Regulation, however, now also states that there is 'no possibility' of opposing recognition. If this were to be believed, this would be an alarming step, as it would suggest no exceptions to the *res judicata* effect of a Member State judgment. The statement, however, appears misleading, as other provisions[29] make clear that the recognition of a judgment can be opposed by a separate application under Articles 45 or 46 under the limited grounds set out, and summarised, above.[30] The draft Regulation does not, however, address the question as to whether, and if so when, recognition of a Member State judgment may be refused on the ground of its irreconcilability with another judgment, of the Member State of recognition or elsewhere. Article 43, which addresses this issue, refers only to '[t]he competent authority of the Member State *of enforcement*'. This omission, hopefully an oversight, needs to be addressed, as this issue is too important to be left to national law or to the Court of Justice of the European Union (CJEU).

III. COMMENT

A. Introduction – the political and economic case for the abolition of exequatur

Article 81 of the Treaty on the Functioning of the European Union (TFEU), which provides the legal basis for the proposed Brussels I bis Regulation, grounds the development of judicial co-operation in civil matters upon 'the principle of mutual recognition of judgments and of decisions in extrajudicial cases'. In its 2009 Stockholm Programme, the European Council stated that the process of abolishing all intermediate measures (*exequatur*) should be continued, 'accompanied by a series of safeguards, which may be measures in respect of procedural law as well as of conflict-of-law

---

[27] Art 37(3)(b), requiring that the claim be brought by (i) a state body, (ii) a non-profit making organisation whose main purpose and activity is to represent and defend the interests of groups of natural or legal persons other than on a commercial basis, or (iii) a group of more than twelve claimants (thirteen, on this occasion, being an unlucky number for the claimants in question, at least if they are successful).

[28] Art 38(1).

[29] In particular, arts 39(3), 46(1) and 46(5). If an application is brought under arts 45 or 46, or if the judgment is contested in its Member State of origin, the proceedings in which recognition is at issue may be suspended.

[30] See text to n 15–21.

rules'.[31] The European Parliament, in turn, has described the abolition of the intermediate enforcement procedure in the Brussels I Regulation as 'a key milestone in the building of the European judicial area', while also recognising the need to ensure the protection of judgment debtors.[32]

In its Action Plan, formulated in response to the Stockholm Programme, the Commission made clear its own commitment to the abolitionist cause, in the following terms:

Cutting red tape for business is a clear priority and the cumbersome and costly *exequatur* process that is required to recognise and enforce a judgment in another jurisdiction should systematically be consigned to history whilst maintaining the necessary safeguards.[33]

Politically, therefore, the Commission's policy decision to recommend the removal of the intermediate procedure in most intra-EU enforcement scenarios was almost inevitable, and the momentum behind this development within the European machine will likely prove irresistible. In its Impact Assessment, the Commission also develops an economic case for abolition, citing data supplied to it concerning the costs and delays inherent in the *exequatur* process, suggesting that the overall annual cost of such proceedings in the EU amounts to approximately 48 million Euro.[34] The Commission suggests, with some empirical support,[35] that this is a deterrent to cross-border trade, and that the abolition of *exequatur* would be

---

[31] OJ C115/1, 4 May 2010, para 3.1.2.

[32] European Parliament Resolution of 7 September 2010 on the implementation and review of the Brussels I Regulation (2009/2140(INI)) ('EP Resolution'), Recitals C-G and paras 2–6.

[33] Communication from the Commission to the European Parliament, the Council, the European Economic and Social Committee and the Committee of the Regions COM(2010)171 final (20 April 2010) 5.

[34] The underlying data is set out in the Impact Assessment, Annex IV. The Commission's Euro 48 million figure is based on an estimate of 9,922 applications for declarations of enforceability in 2009 at an average cost of Euro 2,208 for straightforward, uncontested applications (assumed 75%) and Euro 12,791 for more complex, contested applications (assumed 25%). Some of that data, however, appears questionable. In particular, the estimate of 1,202 applications for declarations of enforceability in the UK in 2009 appears much too high, given the author's understanding that only 123 applications were recorded in the register maintained by the High Court for England and Wales in that year and that there were no such applications in Northern Ireland. In light of this, the Report's methodology, using data from France and re-basing for the UK population (CSES Report, 154), appears unreliable. In the final analysis, however, it seems unlikely that the overall cost estimate would turn out to be significantly inflated, as the above estimates of legal costs may be conservative.

[35] Impact Assessment, 18, referring to CSES Study, 59–60 and other sources. With specific reference to the proposal under discussion, 39.4% of respondents (28/71) indicated that they would be more inclined to engage in cross-border commercial activity if a judgment obtained in one Member State would be enforceable in another Member State without additional procedures. This cannot, however, be said to constitute a meaningful endorsement of the policy, particularly as more than two thirds of those surveyed chose not to answer the question and as a more favourable response was received to the following question concerning the use of written/online procedures for dispute resolution (32/71 respondents – 45.1% – being a lot more inclined to pursue cross-border litigation).

particularly beneficial for small to medium-sized enterprises (SMEs), only 25 per cent of which are found to operate internationally.[36]

B. The legal case – a matter of trust?

From a legal and practical view point, however, the case presented by the Commission for abolition of *exequatur* and, as a separate question,[37] non-retention of the public policy ground for objecting to recognition and enforcement of Member State judgments appears far weaker. The Commission suggests:

Today, judicial cooperation and the level of trust among Member States has reached a degree of maturity which permits the move towards a simpler, less costly, and more automatic system of circulation of judgments.[38]

One may ask what basis there is for this assertion of 'maturity' in the level of co-operation and trust between Member States? It must, of course, be acknowledged that the concept of 'mutual trust' is stated in Recital (16) of the current Brussels I Regulation to justify judgments given in a Member State being recognised automatically without the need for any procedure *except in cases of dispute*, and the same concept has (infamously) been deployed in recent years by the CJEU to support a strict interpretation of the first seised rule in Article 27[39] of the Regulation and the exclusion of anti-suit injunctions as a technique for regulating jurisdictional conflicts.[40]

As a matter of EU law, however, the concept of 'trust' between Member States is relevant only insofar as it relates to the application of EU law or the achievement of the EU's tasks and objectives – it is the 'mutual respect' of which Article 4(3) of the Treaty on European Union (TEU) speaks. At its highest, therefore, full observance of the legal principle of mutual trust at the enforcement stage would preclude any review of the jurisdiction of the court of origin, where based on the Brussels I regime,[41] and any challenge

---

[36] See also Eurobarometer Special Surveys, *Civil Justice* (October 2010) in which 59% of almost 27,000 EU citizens surveyed indicated, when told that a 'special declaration of enforcement (*exequatur*)' was required to enforce a judgment from another Member State, that they would be discouraged from starting proceedings in their home State against a person from another Member State, and 45% thought it very important for the EU to take additional measures to simplify enforcement procedures (Questions QC8 and QC9, at 19–21, 44–47). Both questions, however, tend towards the view of the enforcing creditor and do not appear to be sufficiently balanced towards the position of a debtor, particularly in default judgment cases.

[37] It would be perfectly possible to abolish the intermediate procedure, while retaining a right of challenge on public policy grounds.

[38] Explanatory Memorandum, 6.

[39] CJEU, Case C-116/02 *Erich Gasser GmbH v MISAT Srl* [2003] ECR I-14693, para 72.

[40] CJEU, Case C-159/02 *Turner v Grovit* [2004] ECR I-3565, paras 24–25. See also Case C-185/07 *Allianz SpA v West Tankers Inc* [2009] ECR I-663.

[41] ie ruling out even the limited review currently contemplated by art 35(1) of the Brussels I Regulation.

to the judgment based on a failure by the court of origin to apply EU law correctly.[42] It cannot, however, justify excluding the possibility of review on grounds unrelated to EU law and, in particular, a challenge based on the incompatibility of a judgment with the fundamental principles of public policy of the enforcing Member State, whether that public policy is characterised as 'procedural' or 'substantive' in nature.

Despite the creeping pervasion of EU regulation in the area of civil law, the great majority of cross-border cases will still be determined solely by the application of national law rules. It is true that the EU[43] has substantially harmonised its rules of applicable law for contractual and non-contractual obligations through the Rome I and Rome II Regulations,[44] and that the principle of mutual trust must extend to the application of these rules to identify the substantive law applicable in such cases. It must, however, be recalled that those instruments (which in any event only partially cover the landscape of civil and commercial matters) contain provisions that exclude matters of evidence and procedure from their scope[45] and that enable Member State courts to refuse to apply the law specified by the Regulation if its application would be manifestly incompatible with the public policy of the forum[46] and to give overriding effect to mandatory provisions of their own legal systems.[47] One Member State cannot, as a matter of EU law at least, be required to trust the courts of another Member State to determine cases, procedurally and substantively, in a manner that does not violate the fundamental rules and principles of the former State's legal order; and the Brussels I, Rome I and Rome II Regulations offer no guarantee that those rules and principles will be upheld.

C. The value of the public policy exception

The fact that Member States, in line with the CJEU's guidance,[48] have generally applied the public policy exception in the Brussels I Regulation restrictively and that cases involving the application of public policy with respect to the substance of the judgment are rare should not, contrary to the

---

[42] Consistently with the CJEU's ruling in Case C-38/98 *Renault SA v Maxicar SpA* [2000] ECR I-2973.

[43] Excluding Denmark, whose position on this issue will be of interest, given that it will likely be invited to adopt the new Brussels I Regulation in due course (Explanatory Memorandum, 10).

[44] Council Regulation 864/2007 on the law applicable to non-contractual obligations (Rome II) (OJ L199/40, 31 July 2007); Council Regulation 593/2008 on the law applicable to contractual obligations (Rome I) (OJ L177/6, 4 July 2008).

[45] Rome I Regulation, art 1(3) and Rome II Regulation, art 1(3).

[46] Rome I Regulation, art 21; Rome II Regulation, art 26.

[47] Rome I Regulation, art 9(2); Rome II Regulation, art 16.

[48] See, eg Case C-394/07 *Gambazzi v Daimler Chrysler Canada Inc* [2009] ECR I-2563, paras 26–29.

Commission's position, be taken as evidence that the exception is no longer required (or is required only if the right to a fair trial is breached). The Commission submits that only in a 'handful of cases' does the intermediate procedure actually lead to a refusal of recognition and enforcement[49] and that a 'substantive' public policy exception 'no longer seems necessary because to the knowledge of the Commission there has not been a single case since the entry into force of the Brussels Convention where recognition and enforcement of a judgment has been refused for this reason'.[50] The latter statement can be refuted,[51] but the lack of case law does not in any event demonstrate that the public policy exception has no value, whether as a deterrent to those seeking to export unjust or inhuman decisions or as a shield to protect the legal, social or political order of the enforcing Member State. Further, evidence of the narrowness of the exception and its limited deployment in practice would suggest that retention of the right to challenge enforcement on public policy grounds would not have a significant adverse economic impact, particularly if (as the Commission proposes) a party unsuccessfully challenging a judgment is required to pay the costs of proceedings.[52]

Public policy (*ordre public*) was described by the eminent international jurist and former judge of the International Court of Justice, Sir Hersch Lauterpacht, as 'a general principle of law in the field of private international law', one which 'may not improperly be considered to be a general principle of law in the sense of Article 38 of the Statute of the Court'[53] and which could be excluded in an international treaty in the area of private international law only by an express prohibition on its use.[54] In his view, public policy acted as an essential 'safety valve' within the private international law domain:

[T]he notion of *ordre public* – like that of public policy – is variable, indefinite and occasionally productive of arbitrariness and abuse. It has been compared in this respect, not without some justification, with the vagueness of the law of nature. Admittedly also, it has often been the instrument or the expression of national

---

[49] Impact Assessment, 12.

[50] Impact Assessment, 15.

[51] For an English case where refusal was based in part on substantive policy (the absence of a variation provision in a Greek freezing order, and the fact that the defendant would be placed in breach if she were to spend any money, including in challenging it), see *D'Hoker v Tritan* [2009] EWHC 949 (QB). See also *Malanca Motori SpA v Société des Etablissements B Savoye SA, Guirisprudenzia commerciale* 1984, II, 76, relating to a failure to apply exchange control requirements. See also the summary of national law at 49–94 of the study prepared for the European Parliament (IP/C/JURI/IC/2010-076), led by Professor B Hess and Professor T Pfeiffer, Heidelberg University. A copy of the study is available at http://ec.europa.eu/civiljustice/news/docs/study_application_brussels_1_en.pdf.

[52] Art 46(8).

[53] *Guardianship of Infants (The Netherlands v Sweden)* (1958) 25 ILR 242, 268.

[54] ibid 271.

exclusiveness and prejudice impatient of the application of foreign law. Yet these objections, justified as they are, do not alter the fact that the principle permitting reliance on *ordre public* in the sphere of private international law has become – and that it is – a general principle of law of most, if not all, civilised States. More than that: It is, on its own merits, part and parcel of the entire doctrine and practice of private international law almost from its very inception; the two are inseparable, not only as a matter of history but also of necessity; they have grown together in a mutual interaction and compromise. The purpose of private international law is to make possible the application, within the territory of the State, of the law of foreign States. This is an object dictated by considerations of justice, convenience, the necessities of international intercourse between individuals and indeed, as has occasionally been said, by an enlightened conception of public policy itself. But there is an obvious element of simplification in the view that the law of a State should be deemed to have consented or that it should reasonably be expected to consent in advance to the application of foreign law without any limitations, in any circumstances whatsoever, without a safety valve, without a residuum of contingencies in which, because of the very nature of its structure and the fundamental legal, moral and political conceptions which underlie it, it should be able to decline to apply foreign law.[55]

D. 'Mutual trust' and the EU Charter of Fundamental Rights

That said, it is clear from the recent decision in *Zarraga v Pelz*,[56] concerning the enforcement under Article 42 of the Brussels II bis Regulation of orders for the return of a child wrongfully removed from one Member State to another, that the CJEU would not subscribe to Lauterpacht's view that an express exclusion of the public policy exception is necessary where the scheme of an EU private international law instrument supports the inference that such an exception was not available. Moreover, in the following passage, the CJEU appears to suggest that the EU Charter of Fundamental Rights provides a sufficient basis for the 'mutual trust', which, in turn, justifies removal of the public policy exception as between the Member States:

[T]he systems for recognition and enforcement of judgments handed down in a Member State which are established by [the Brussels II bis Regulation] are based on the principle of mutual trust between Member States in the fact that their respective national legal systems are capable of providing an equivalent and effective protection of fundamental rights, recognised at European Union level, in particular, in the Charter of Fundamental Rights.[57]

This argument is fundamentally flawed, and cannot be accepted. The Charter of Fundamental Rights ('Charter'),[58] although it emphasises a

---

[55] ibid 270.
[56] CJEU, Case C-491/10 (PPU) *Joseba Andoni Aguirre Zarraga v Simone Pelz* [2010] ECR I-0000 (7 December 2010).
[57] ibid para 70.
[58] OJ C83/389, 30 March 2010.

commonality between the Member States in terms of their constitutional traditions and international obligations in the human rights field,[59] is addressed to the Member States only when implementing EU law and requires them, in that context, to respect the rights and observe the principles set out and to promote the application thereof.[60]

Accordingly, although the principle of 'mutual respect' does require Member States to 'trust' each other in applying EU law (including the Charter, insofar as it is relevant to the application of EU law), it cannot require them to treat the Charter as providing 'an equivalent and effective protection of fundamental rights' (to use the CJEU's words) in the determination of civil disputes, which in most cases will have nothing to do with EU law.

E. Member States' obligations under the European Convention on Human Rights

Article 53 of the Charter provides:

Nothing in this Charter shall be interpreted as restricting or adversely affecting human rights and fundamental freedoms as recognised, in their respective fields of application, by Union law and international law and by international agreements to which the Union, the Community or all the Member States are party, including the European Convention for the Protection of Human Rights and Fundamental Freedoms, and by the Member States' constitutions.

As this Article recognises, the Charter cannot in any way derogate from the Member States' obligations to meet their international and constitutional commitments, including under the European Convention on Human Rights (ECHR). In this connection, the European Court of Human Rights' 2005 decision in *Bosphorus v Ireland*[61] establishes that the member states of an international organisation (in *Bosphorus*, the EU itself) can legitimately transfer to that organisation, in the performance of their treaty obligations, sovereign powers which engage or affect Convention rights 'as long as the relevant organisation is considered to protect fundamental rights, as regards both the substantive guarantees offered and the mechanisms controlling their observance, in a manner which can be considered at least equivalent

---

[59] ibid preamble.

[60] ibid art 51. See also art 6(3) of the TEU and the Protocol on the Application of the Charter of Fundamental Rights of the European Union to Poland and to the United Kingdom. The above quoted extract in *Zarraga* may be contrasted with the CJEU's statement in Case C-400/10 (PPU) *J McB v LE* [2010] ECR I-0000 (5 October 2010) paras 51 and 52, that 'It follows that, in the context of this case, the Charter should be taken into consideration solely for the purposes of interpreting Regulation No 2201/2003, and there should be no assessment of national law as such.'

[61] *Bosphorus Hava Yolları Turizm ve Ticaret Anonim Şirketi v Ireland* [2005] 42 EHRR 1 (Grand Chamber).

to that for which the Convention provides'.[62] The same reasoning, it is submitted, is capable of being extended to the delegation of sovereign powers via the EU to another Member State, such as that contemplated in the Commission's Brussels I bis Proposal, and the fact that every Member State is also a party to the ECHR (as well as the existence of the Charter) could be treated as sufficient evidence that fundamental rights would be sufficiently protected. However, as the European Court of Human Rights emphasised, that fact would only give rise to a *presumption* that a State party has fulfilled its ECHR obligations, which presumption can be rebutted 'if, in the circumstances of a particular case, it is considered that the protection of Convention rights was manifestly deficient. In such cases, the interest of international cooperation would be outweighed by the Convention's role as a 'constitutional instrument of European public order' in the field of human rights'.[63] Accordingly, it would be a violation of the ECHR for an enforcing Member State to abrogate all responsibility for ensuring protection of ECHR rights to the Member State of origin in a case in which the judgment itself, or its enforcement, would involve a manifest violation of those rights. The rights recognised in the ECHR, of course, are not limited to the right to a fair trial (ECHR, Article 6(1)), but extensively trespass upon the area of what the Commission calls 'substantive' public policy.[64] The *Bosphorus* decision itself concerned the protection of property rights under Article 1 of Protocol 1 to the ECHR. Further, the enforcing party and the person against whom enforcement is sought must be considered as persons within the jurisdiction[65] of the enforcing Member State, whose fundamental rights must be secured by that State (and not by the Member State of origin) with respect to the processes leading to, and consequences of, enforcement of the judgment.[66] Accordingly, the Commission's Proposal, in excluding 'substantive' public policy in total, appears incompatible with the Member States' existing international obligations under the ECHR.

---

[62] ibid para 155.

[63] ibid para 156. See also the reservations expressed in the Concurring Opinions in that case.

[64] The list of ECHR rights of potential relevance in civil and commercial matters includes, for example, the rights to life (art 2), not to be tortured (art 3) or enslaved (art 4), to liberty and security of person (art 5), to respect for private and family life (art 8), to freedom of thought, conscience and religion (art 9), to freedom of expression (art 10), to freedom of assembly and association (art 11), to peaceful enjoyment of possessions (Protocol 1, art 1) and to education (Protocol 1, art 2).

[65] *Markovic v Italy* (2006) 44 EHRR 1045 para 54 (Grand Chamber, ECHR). See also *R (Smith) v Oxford Assistant Special Coroner* [2010] UKSC 29; [2010] 3 WLR 223, [295–301] (Lord Collins, UK Supreme Court). See also, with respect to the enforcement of non-contracting State judgments by an ECHR State court, *Pellegrini v Italy* (2001) EHRR 44; *Government of the United States v Montgomery* [2004] UKHL 37; [2004] 1 WLR 2241.

[66] Art 1 of the ECHR. As the ECHR has recognised, the execution of a judgment given by any court must be regarded as an integral part of the 'trial' for the purposes of art 6 (*Kalogeropoulou v Greece*, Application 59021/00, Judgment of 12 December 2002).

F. The need to maintain the public policy exception in the Brussels I regime

In its Impact Assessment,[67] the Commission draws attention to three EU private international law instruments which have enabled judgments to be enforced between Member States without any intermediate procedure and without any general public policy exception: the instruments relating to uncontested claims,[68] the Small Claims Regulation[69] and the recent Maintenance Regulation.[70] The Brussels I Regulation, however, is of a different order, in terms both of the breadth of its subject matter and the potential scale, value and complexity of the matters giving rise to enforceable judgments.

That much is evident from the Commission's reasoning supporting the retention of the intermediate procedure with respect to privacy, defamation and collective redress judgments. In supporting these exceptions, the Commission blows a sizeable hole in its case for the abolition of *exequatur*, without retaining a right of challenge to enforcement on public policy grounds. In support of the proposed exception for defamation and privacy judgments,[71] the Commission states:[72]

The proposal retains the *exequatur* procedure for judgments in defamation cases in which an individual claims that rights relating to his personality or privacy have been violated by the media. These cases are particularly sensitive and Member States have adopted diverging approaches on how to ensure compliance with the various fundamental rights affected, such as human dignity, respect for private and family life, protection of personal data, freedom of expression and information. These divergences, in combination with the absence of a harmonised conflict rule at Union level ...[73] make it premature to presume the required level of trust yet exists between legal systems in order [to] move beyond the status quo on this matter. It therefore seems preferable to retain temporarily the *exequatur* procedure for judgments in defamation cases, pending greater clarity on either substantive and/or conflict rules in this area.

It appears that the proposed exclusion of defamation and privacy actions is attributable to lobbying by the media during the consultation process.[74]

---

[67] Impact Assessment, 13.

[68] Council Regulation 805/2004 establishing a European enforcement order for uncontested claims (OJ L143/15, 30 April 2004); Council Regulation 1896/2006 establishing a European Order for Payment Procedure (OJ L399/1, 30 December 2006).

[69] Council Regulation 861/2007 creating a European Small Claims Procedure (OJ L199/1, 31 July 2007).

[70] Council Regulation 4/2009 on jurisdiction, applicable law, recognition and enforcement of decisions and co-operation in matters relating to maintenance obligations (OJ L7/1, 10 January 2009).

[71] See text to n 26.

[72] Explanatory Memorandum, 6–7. See also Impact Assessment, 15.

[73] The Commission refers here to art 1(2)(g) Rome II Regulation.

[74] Impact Assessment, 15.

Nevertheless, most, if not all, of the factors identified by the Commission as requiring the retention of *exequatur* in these cases apply to other areas of civil liability, which equally raise issues of great sensitivity, involve competing policy considerations and are addressed by the Member States' legal systems in very different ways: for example, liability for wrongful conception or 'wrongful life',[75] disputes concerning the right to life or death and other questions of medical ethics,[76] the use of gene technology,[77] the operation of nuclear installations,[78] the enforcement of contracts concerning activities which may be considered as illegal, immoral or anti-social,[79] freedom of religious expression[80] or the status or activities of religious bodies[81] and the award of punitive damages for a tort.[82]

The cases identified in the preceding paragraph are not intended as a definitive or exhaustive list of possible further exceptions to the abolition of *exequatur*, and the public policy exception to enforcement. Rather, they are intended to illustrate the point made above, that defamation and privacy actions do not merit separate and special treatment – this is only one of many controversial areas in which Member States may legitimately balance the competing policy interests in different ways, reaching solutions which may well prove unpalatable to each other despite common ties and values.

---

[75] C van Dam, *European Tort Law* (OUP 2006) 156–161.

[76] eg liability for assisted suicide, human organ donation or the duty to provide or withdraw medical treatment without the patient's consent.

[77] eg the growing of, and liability for, genetically modified crops (see COM (2006) 104 final and SEC (2006) 313 (both 9 March 2006) and COM (2009) 153 final (2 April 2009). See also CJEU, Case C-34/10, *Brüstle v Greenpeace e.V.* [2011] ECR I-0000 (18 October 2011) para 30 ('the definition of human embryo is a very sensitive social issue in many Member States, marked by their multiple traditions and value systems').

[78] See CJEU, Case C-115/08 *Land Oberösterreich v ČEZ as* [2009] ECR I-10625.

[79] eg contracts relating to internet gaming (see CJEU, Case C-42/07 *Liga Portuguesa de Futebol Profissional v Departamento de Jogos da Santa Casa da Misericórdia de Lisboa* [2009] ECR I-7633, para 57; Case C-347/09 *Dickinger v Ömer* [2011] ECR I-0000, paras 45–46) or the sale or importation of wartime memorabilia, pornographic materials or goods glorifying violence (see Case 34/79 *R v Henn and Darby* [1979] ECR 3795, para 16 and Case C-36/02 *Omega Spielhallen- und Automatenaufstellungs-GmbH v Oberbürgermeisterin der Bundesstadt Bonn* [2004] ECR I-9609), prostitution (see Case 116/81 *Adoui and Cornuaille v Belgian State* [1982] ECR 1665, para 8) or the promotion of abortion (see Case C-159/90 *Society for the Protection of Unborn Children v Grogan* [1991] ECR I-4865, discussed below (see text to n 87–95), or contracts with counterparties upon whom a Member State has imposed unilateral trade sanctions. As to the relationship between public policy in this area, and limits on the fundamental freedoms under EU law see below (text to n 113–117).

[80] eg the right of an employee to wear a symbol of his or her religious faith. See also the decision of the European Court of Human Rights in *Lautsi v Italy,* Application 30814/06, Judgment of 18 March 2011.

[81] eg the right to use a building for the purposes of worship.

[82] Art 40(3) of the German EGBGB; Rome II Regulation, Recital (32).

G. Relationship with the Rome I and Rome II Regulations

Contrary to the Commission's apparent view to the contrary,[83] the fact that, subject to limited exceptions,[84] civil and commercial disputes involving contractual and non-contractual obligations are likely to fall within the scope of the Rome I and Rome II Regulations, whereas defamation and privacy actions do not, is not a sufficient point of distinction. As noted above,[85] both the Rome I and Rome II regimes retain exceptions for the public policy and overriding mandatory provisions of the forum, allowing the Member State before which proceedings are brought to preserve its own fundamental values. If the Member State of origin can do so, there seems to be no reason why the Member State of enforcement should not equally have this entitlement. To enable public policy to be applied by one court, but not the other, appears likely to encourage forum shopping to obtain a favourable public policy regime, which would undermine one of the primary aims of the Brussels I, Rome I and Rome II regimes.[86]

H. Illustrating the need for a public policy exception

Three sets of hypothetical examples based on the facts of past decisions of European courts may serve further to highlight the above points.

First, the CJEU's well-known decision in *Society for the Protection of Unborn Children Ireland (SPUC) v Grogan*,[87] which involved proceedings brought in the Irish High Court by SPUC, a company incorporated under Irish law with the purpose of preventing the de-criminalisation of abortion in Ireland, against members of student associations giving advice about the availability of legal terminations in the UK. On a preliminary reference, the CJEU ruled that 'it is not contrary to Community law for a Member State in which medical termination of pregnancy is forbidden to prohibit students associations from distributing information about the identity and location of clinics in another Member State where voluntary termination of pregnancy is lawfully carried out and the means of communicating with those clinics, where the clinics in question have no involvement in the distribution of the said information'.[88] Since that decision, the relevant provision in the

---

[83] Explanatory Memorandum, 6–7.

[84] Of the examples given above, non-contractual obligations arising out of nuclear damage also fall outside the scope of the Rome II Regulation by reason of its art 1(2)(f).

[85] See above, text to n 46–67.

[86] Brussels I Regulation, Recital (11); Rome I Regulation, Recital (6); Rome II Regulation, Recital (6).

[87] CJEU, Case C-159/90 *Society for the Protection of Unborn Children Ireland Ltd v Grogan* [1991] ECR I-4685.

[88] ibid para 32.

Irish Constitution has been amended.[89] Nevertheless, the basic constitutional principle recognising the right to life of the unborn child remains,[90] and the margin of appreciation allowed to Ireland in criminalising abortion, subject only to limited exceptions, has recently been affirmed by the European Court of Human Rights.[91] In this area, Ireland's policy approach is opposed to the consensus within the Contracting States of the Council of Europe, who allow abortion on broader grounds than currently permitted under Irish law.[92]

As neither SPUC, nor the defendants were public authorities, the proceedings in that case involved a 'civil and commercial matter', within the material scope of the Brussels I Regulation.[93] Suppose, therefore, that in a similar case the Irish court were to grant an injunction against a student domiciled in another Member State, but studying in Ireland, preventing him from (for example) offering to make arrangements for a foreign termination.[94] Should courts in every other Member State be obliged to enforce that injunction against the student irrespective of their own laws and public policies concerning abortion? Alternatively, suppose that an abortion carried out unlawfully in Ireland results in proceedings in another Member State, for example for the recovery of unpaid fees or commissions or for negligently caused injury. Should an Irish court be bound to recognise a judgment in such proceedings even if a defence of illegality under Irish law were rejected by the foreign court?[95]

Secondly, in *Hillside (New Media) Limited v Baasland*,[96] the English High Court granted declaratory relief to an English online gaming company (H) that it was not liable to a Norwegian domiciled defendant (B), whether in contract, tort or otherwise, for significant losses (almost £3 million) suffered by him as a result of placing bets and wagers online. The Court

---

[89] Following the amendment, art 40.3.3 of the Constitution of Ireland acknowledges that this section shall not limit the freedom to travel between Ireland and another state, or to obtain or make available, in the State, subject to such conditions as may be laid down by law, information relating to services lawfully available in another state.

[90] ibid.

[91] *A, B and C v Ireland*, Application 25579/05, Judgment of 16 December 2010, paras 233–241.

[92] ibid para 235.

[93] CJEU, Case C-167/00 *Verein für Konsumentinformation v Henkel* [2002] ECR I-8111.

[94] The author offers no view as to whether such acts would be unlawful as a matter of Irish law. The proposition is that there is a point at which Irish law and public policy concerning abortion is fundamentally opposed to that of other Member States.

[95] The reason for rejection of the illegality defence may vary: for example, because (1) the applicable law is held to be a law other than Irish law, (2) adequate evidence of Irish law is not presented to the court, (3) the court misapplies Irish law, or (4) because the court considers Irish law to be manifestly contrary to local public policy. The last of these presents the 'conflict of public policy' issue most acutely.

[96] *Hillside (New Media) Limited v Baasland* [2010] EWHC 3336 (Comm).

concluded, with reference to the Rome I and Rome II Regulations,[97] that any claim by B against H was governed by English law,[98] under which H could not be liable.[99]

Nevertheless, as the CJEU has acknowledged, 'legislation on games of chance is one of the areas in which there are significant moral, religious and cultural differences between the Member States'.[100] In these circumstances, in a similar case involving a defendant based in the EU, should a court in a Member State taking a very different position on the morality of gambling be bound to recognise the English judgment as preventing proceedings by a locally domiciled party to recover gaming losses?[101]

Thirdly, in *Viking v International Transport Workers' Federation (ITWF)*,[102] the English High Court granted permanent injunctions restraining the ITWF, an international trade union based in London, and the Finnish Seamen's Union from instituting or encouraging others to institute legal action against Viking, a company incorporated in Finland whose vessels operated on routes between Finland and neighbouring states. Subsequently, on appeal, the Judge's order was set aside and certain questions were referred to the CJEU as to the impact of the EC Treaty (as then was) on the activities of trade unions.[103]

In *Viking*, the injunction was based on EU law, and the Judge considered that she was as well placed to rule on this as any Finnish court.[104] What would be the position, however, if an injunction in a similar case had been based on national industrial relations law? In this connection, the special rule of applicable law for industrial action in Article 9 of the Rome II Regulation may help to reduce the possibility of a conflict with the public policy of the enforcing Member State in a cross-border cases – in most cases, the law applicable will be that of the country where the action is to be, or has been, taken and that will be a principal place of enforcement of

---

[97] See above, n 44.

[98] *Hillside* (n 96) paras 21–52 (Smith J).

[99] ibid paras 53–57. Whether these decisions are correct as a matter of English (and EU) law is not in point here.

[100] *Liga Portuguesa* (n 79) para 57. See also *Dickinger* (n 79) para 45 ('moral, religious or cultural factors, as well as the morally and financially harmful consequences for the individual and for society associated with betting and gaming, may be capable of justifying a sufficient margin of discretion for the national authorities for them to determine, in accordance with their own scale of values, what is required in order to ensure consumer protection and the protection of society').

[101] Norway, although not a Member State of the EU, is a party to the Lugano Convention.

[102] *Viking Line ABP v International Transport Workers' Federation* [2005] EWHC 1222 (Comm).

[103] *International Transport Workers' Federation v Viking Line ABP* [2005] EWCA Civ 1299. As it is well known, those questions were answered (adversely to the trade unions) in Case C-438/05 *International Transport Workers' Federation v Viking Line ABP* [2007] ECR I-10779.

[104] *Hillside* (n 96) paras 55–82.

an injunction. Article 9 cannot, however, eliminate conflicts: in particular, the court giving judgment may determine that the industrial relations law of the country where the action is threatened is manifestly contrary to local public policy, and refuse to apply it.[105] In such a case, would a court in the Member State where the industrial action takes place be required to enforce the injunction even if it would be lawful under local law, giving greater emphasis to the 'right to strike'?

In the first two examples (abortion; internet gaming), the Commission Proposal would require Member State courts to recognise and enforce judgments notwithstanding the evident conflict of public policy. This suggests not only a lack of sensitivity for the 'different legal systems and traditions of Member States', as TFEU Article 67 requires, but also a somewhat careless disregard for the role that national courts play in the legal and democratic orders of the Member States. Depriving those courts of the 'safety valve' that the public policy exception offers may, when controversial cases inevitably arise, have the undesired result of removing public 'trust' not only in other Member State courts, but also in the EU itself.

In the third example (industrial action), it may be that a different answer could be given according to the terms of the Commission Proposal, but only because of a curious and unheralded new provision in the boilerplate section. Article 85 of the Proposal (to be read with Recital (27)) provides that:

This Regulation shall not affect the right of workers and employers, or their respective organisations, to engage in collective action to protect their interests, in particular the right or freedom to strike or to take other actions, in accordance with Union law and national law and practices.

As a matter of first impression, it is difficult to see how a Regulation, which deals only with questions of jurisdiction and the recognition and enforcement of judgments, could affect the 'right to strike', or what precise function Article 85 is intended to serve. One possibility, however, is that it is intended to provide an additional (substantive public policy) ground for refusal to enforce a Member State judgment, such as the injunction restraining industrial action in the above example. If that is the intention, this should be clearly and precisely stated, and not deduced from a hidden provision tucked away in the boilerplate of the Regulation. More fundamentally, it is submitted that the EU's best interests are not well served by a provision which appears to value the 'right to strike' above the rights to

---

[105] Art 9 of the Rome II Regulation also remains subject to the 'common habitual residence' exception in art 4(2), and this may create particular difficulties in the case of international trade unions such as the ITWF (see A Dickinson, *The Rome II Regulation* (Oxford 2008) para 9.32).

life, liberty and security and other fundamental values recognised by the Charter. There is no good reason for a provision of this kind. Article 85 should be deleted and only the first sentence of Recital (27) maintained, as a signal that the EU values equally all fundamental rights. Instead, 'substantive public policy' should be addressed in the Regulation without giving special treatment to particular subject areas.

I. Divergences in procedural law, and the collective redress exception

In support of the proposed exception for collective action judgments,[106] the Commission offers the following explanation:[107]

Concerns relating to the abolition of *exequatur* have also been raised with respect to collective redress … In this area, the procedural law of Member States diverges widely; in some countries, legislation on collective redress has only been introduced very recently, thereby not allowing to fully assess the practical application of these rules and their economic effect on foreign companies. It seems therefore preferable to retain the *exequatur* procedure for judgments in collective redress proceedings for the time being to maintain all existing controls on foreign judgments in such proceedings.

Procedural divergences between the Member States are not, however, restricted to collective redress actions. What is said by the Commission about this area ('Essentially, every national system of compensatory redress is unique and there are no two national systems that alike in this area')[108] could be applied to civil procedure in general. The following comments of Professor Snijders, in a 1996 study on comparative procedural law within the EC, remain valid today notwithstanding the proliferation of EU instruments in the civil justice area:[109]

A brief look at the legal systems discussed in this book[110] will lead to the inevitable conclusion that there are enormous differences between the various nations. The differences are particularly remarkable between the rules of procedure applying in England and Wales on the one hand and those applying in continental Europe on the other hand. If you would want to transport the *huissier de justice* or *gerechrs-deurwaarder* (process-server) with his writ across the North Sea, you would receive as warm a welcome as the Armada, let alone if you want to transport the Netherlands court system.

---

[106] See above, text to n 27.
[107] Impact Assessment, 16. See also Explanatory Memorandum, 7.
[108] ibid. See also the recent Commission Consultation Document, 'Towards a Coherent European Approach to Collective Redress' (SEC (2010)173 final, 4 February 2011).
[109] HJ Snijders et al (eds), *Access to Civil Procedure Abroad* (Kluwer Law International 1996) 7.
[110] Belgium, England, France, Germany, Italy, Luxembourg and the Netherlands.

This is not a call for unification of civil procedure as a necessary pre-requisite for the abolition of *exequatur*.[111] Such a move would, it is submitted, be catastrophic, destroying with a single blow both the Member States' legal heritage[112] and commercial certainty. Rather, and again, the point made is that there is nothing unique about collective redress proceedings which justifies their being given special treatment in the Commission's Proposal. Further, and more specifically, there is nothing special about collective redress proceedings relating to 'unlawful business practices', which is all that the Commission's proposed carve-out would apply to. No reason is given as to why, even if the Commission's reasoning is accepted, judgments in collective redress proceedings relating (for example) to environmental damage or alleged human rights abuses should flow freely around the EU despite the wide divergence in collective redress procedures.

J. Disharmony with the fundamental freedoms under EU law

There is a further, and more fundamental, discord in the Commission's Proposal to remove the public policy exception. Although the principle of mutual recognition of judgments has now taken its place at the high altar of EU law, by its inclusion in the text of Article 81 of the TFEU, on the 'free movement of judgments', it remains a derivative principle. It exists, as the recitals to the Brussels I Regulation[113] and the proposed Brussels I bis Regulation[114] acknowledge, to promote the effective functioning of the internal market, ie 'an area without internal frontiers in which the free movement of goods, persons, services and capital is ensured in accordance with the provisions of the Treaties'.[115] Its continuing subservience, although no longer servitude, to these basic freedoms is emphasised by the reference in Article 81(2) of the TFEU to the EU's power to civil justice measures being available 'particularly when necessary for the proper functioning of the internal market'.

Against this background, and however one views the current relationship between the 'area of justice' and the fundamental freedoms of EU law, the following question arises: why should the public policy exception be taken away from the Member States with respect to the free movement of judgments when they remain entitled under the Treaties to impose unilateral

---

[111] In his opening paragraph (n 109 at 7), Professor Snijders describes the uniformity of civil procedure as 'a utopia for the time being'. Whether utopia or dystopia, all can agree that it is an imaginary world.

[112] See art 67 of the TFEU, requiring respect for the 'different legal systems and traditions of the Member States'.

[113] Brussels I Regulation, Recital (2).

[114] ibid Recital (3).

[115] TFEU, art 26(2).

controls on the free movement of goods, persons, services and capital based on public policy or other mandatory requirements?[116] In these areas, the CJEU has long recognised that EU law 'does not impose upon the Member States a uniform scale of values as regards the assessment of conduct which may be considered as contrary to public policy'.[117] The Commission gives no good reason for treating the cross-border recognition and enforcement of judgments any differently.

K. The public policy exception – conclusion

The preceding arguments have focussed upon the Commission's Proposal to abolish the public policy exception to enforcement. It is respectfully submitted that, for the reasons given, the case for retention of the exception for all types of dispute is overwhelming. That, however, does not address the wider question as to whether the Commission's Proposal to abolish the intermediate enforcement procedure (*exequatur*) should be supported. It would be possible, with minimal adjustment to the text of Article 46 of the Commission's Proposal,[118] to widen the right of challenge to enforcement of a judgment by application in the enforcing Member State to include any manifest breach of that State's public policy, not limited to a breach of the fundamental principles underlying the right to a fair trial, as the Commission currently proposes.

L. Reviewing the jurisdiction of the court of origin

The question whether *exequatur* should be removed can also be separated from the question whether, as the Commission proposes,[119] the enforcing court should not be entitled to review the jurisdiction of the court of origin. As noted above,[120] the 'mutual trust' principle (as derived from Article 5(3)

---

[116] ibid arts 36, 45(3), 52(1), 62, 65(1), 202. These derogations are, of course, restrictively interpreted (see eg CJEU, Case C-441/02 *Commission v Germany* [2006] ECR I-3349, paras 34–35).

[117] *Adoui and Cornuaille v Belgian State*, (n 79) para 8. It should be noted that the concept of 'public policy' as used in the TFEU (n 114) carries a narrow meaning (see, eg C Barnard, *The Substantive Law of the EU* (3rd edn, OUP 2010) 151, but is supplemented by other, related concepts (eg 'public morality,' 'public security', the 'protection of life of humans') and by the CJEU's own concept of 'mandatory requirements' (see eg C Barnard, ibid 165 ff.). All, it is submitted, are capable of falling within the definition of 'public policy' as used in the Brussels I Regulation and other private international law instruments, subject to the limits laid down by the CJEU (see text to n 48 and 51).

[118] See Annex, Proposal 3, art 46. If the Commission is unsuccessful in its proposal to harmonise the rules of jurisdiction for non-EU domiciled defendants, it would also be necessary to reinstate the prohibition (currently, in art 35(3) of the Brussels I Regulation) on the use of public policy grounds with respect to the rules of jurisdiction of the court of origin.

[119] See text to n 33.

[120] See text to n 41.

of the TEU) can justifiably be invoked as a justification for the removal of
the limited review currently permitted by Article 35(1) of the Brussels I
Regulation: the enforcing court should be bound by the court of origin's
assumption of jurisdiction over the substance of the matter and must trust
that it acted in accordance with the requirements of the Regulation in so
doing. In the case of consumers, however, it is submitted that this justification should not prevail. Article 12 TFEU requires consumer protection to
be taken into account in defining and implementing EU policies and activities and Article 169 of the same Treaty targets a high level of consumer
protection. Consumers currently enjoy a high level of protection with
respect to the bringing of legal proceedings against them as a consequence
of Article 16(2) and Article 17 of the Brussels I Regulation, requiring that,
in general, proceedings against a consumer in relation to the listed categories of consumer contracts be brought in the Member State of the
consumer's domicile and limiting the consumer's ability to contract out of
that regime. These protections would remain under the proposed Brussels I
bis Regulation.[121] Nevertheless, the protection given would potentially be
rendered illusory or of little value in individual cases if, in the event that
proceedings are commenced by a counterparty in a Member State court
outside the consumer's domicile in violation of Article 16(2), the consumer
is required to travel, and/or to instruct a legal representative, to make a
jurisdictional plea and, perhaps, to participate in the proceedings up to trial
in a legal system with which he or she will likely have no familiarity.
Enabling a judgment to be challenged in the Member State of enforcement
on the ground of a breach of the rules set out in Section 4 of the proposed
Brussels I bis Regulation would reinforce the effectiveness of the consumer
protection afforded by those rules, and deter vexatious proceedings. Again,
a small amendment to the text of Article 46 is all that would be needed to
achieve this (see Annex, below, Proposal 3, art 46).

A further right to review jurisdiction at the enforcement stage could be
supported in the case of judgments relating to rights *in rem* in immovable
property, where the Member State of origin has violated the exclusive jurisdiction of another Member State where the land in question is situated.[122]
The reason why this situation may be considered to stand apart from the
other grounds of exclusive jurisdiction in Article 22, is that Article 345 of
the TFEU provides 'The Treaties shall in no way prejudice the rules in
Member States governing the system of property ownership.'

The automatic recognition and enforcement of judgments of another
Member State court concerning title to land situated in the enforcing

---

[121] Also art 16(2) and 17.
[122] Brussels I Regulation and Proposal, art 22(1)(a).

Member State would appear liable to cross the line drawn by this Article.[123]

M. Removing the procedural barriers – does exequatur serve a useful purpose?

This leaves the question of the proposed abolition of the declaration of enforceability procedure to be considered on its own merits. The Commission's economic case for taking this step[124] appears robust, and the safeguards proposed by the Commission (with the modifications proposed in the preceding paragraphs) would appear sufficient to allay most legal concerns, particularly in terms of the protection of fundamental rights. Nevertheless, a strong practical case can equally be made for the retention of some form of intermediate procedural requirement, even if it is streamlined and enhanced, most obviously by the use of improved technology.[125] The Commission's focus is upon the function of the intermediate procedure as a means of enabling the respondent to oppose recognition or enforcement.[126] If that were its only function, the case for reversing the procedural burden and placing it upon the party seeking to oppose recognition or enforcement would, it is submitted, be compelling. On closer examination, however, the intermediate procedure may be argued also to serve the following functions, which will not adequately be replicated within the proposed Brussels I bis Regulation.

First, it may provide a means of ensuring that the respondent is actually aware of the judgment and able to take steps to challenge it before his rights are irreparably affected. Under the Brussels I Regulation, as it currently stands, a party in whose favour a judgment is given may seek protective measures under the law of the enforcing Member State, without obtaining a declaration of enforceability, provided that the judgment is one which

---

[123] See A Dickinson, 'European Private International Law: Embracing New Horizons or Mourning the Past?' (2005) 1 J Priv Intl L 197, 204–205.

[124] See text to n 34–36.

[125] For example, it might be possible to create a clearing system within which the enforcing party could simultaneously make applications for a certificate of enforceability (to be served on the opposing party) in several Member States either (a) though the designated court in the Member State of origin, or (b) a centralised website. In its Impact Assessment, at 14, 17–18, the Commission considers, but discards, proposals for alleviating the burden upon applicants, including 'a system of co-operation between courts ... which would allow EU claimants to introduce the application in their own Member State, after which the courts of the Member State of origin would transmit it to the Member State where enforcement is sought'. This proposal, which the Commission does not specifically reject, appears worthy of further consideration.

[126] In its Impact Assessment, at 12, the Commission argues that 'in 93% of the cases, the intermediate step is a pure formality as there are no reasons to refuse recognition and enforcement of the foreign judgment ...Only in a handful of cases does the procedure actually lead to a refusal of recognition and enforcement'.

must be recognised under the Regulation.[127] He cannot, however, proceed to take any other enforcement measures until the declaration of enforceability has been served on the respondent[128] and either the time for lodging an appeal has expired or any appeal has been determined.[129] By contrast, under the Commission's Proposal, it is clear that the first time a party may hear of a judgment is when an enforcement measure is taken against his property.[130] By the time the respondent is able to react, that measure, or its effects, may be irreversible – the property (depending on local procedures in the place of enforcement) may have been sold or damaged and the respondent may have been unable to meet contractual or other obligations relating to that property. At that stage, the possibility of applying to limit the enforcement proceedings to protective measures, to make enforcement conditional on the provision of security or to suspend enforcement[131] may offer little comfort.

Secondly, as a means of ensuring that foreign court orders, particularly those involving non-monetary remedies, are effectively assimilated into the legal order of the enforcing Member State. Currently, the intermediate procedure provides a judicial mechanism for any doubts as to the legal effect of a judgment to be addressed before any enforcement measures[132] are taken. Under the proposed Brussels I bis Regulation, the enforcement of a judgment is placed immediately in the hands of the 'competent enforcement authorities', where no judicial process may be required[133] and where the responsibility for enforcement may lie with persons with no formal legal qualifications or experience of judgments from outside their own legal systems. The Regulation does not provide any explicit mechanism enabling those authorities to resolve doubts as to the legal effect of a judgment. The problem of assimilation is, however, acknowledged in Article 66 of the Commission's Proposal under which:

If a judgment contains a measure or an order which is not known in the Member State of enforcement, the competent authority in that Member State shall, to the extent possible, adapt the measure or order to one known under its own law which has equivalent effects attached to it and pursues similar aims and interests.

The 'competent authority' may not, however, be competent to adapt the measure in this way.

---

[127] Brussels I Regulation, art 47(1).
[128] ibid art 42(2).
[129] ibid art 47(3).
[130] Commission Proposal, art 45(4).
[131] ibid art 44(1).
[132] Other than protective measures, if available extra-judicially.
[133] For example, in England and Wales, by the execution of a writ of *fieri facias* or warrant of execution against the debtor's goods, which is in most cases an administrative process.

Thirdly, judicial scrutiny also serves as a deterrent to fraudulent enforcement proceedings. The Commission's economic case for abolition of *exequatur* does not address the possibility that removal of the protection afforded to judgment debtors by the intermediate procedure and the use of standard forms, containing only an extract of the judgment, may increase the potential for forgery and fraud in the enforcement process. This is something that will need to be closely monitored if the Proposal is adopted in its present form.

N. Adjusting the Commission's proposal – protecting the judgment debtor and avoiding fraud

These three functions of the current intermediate procedure are important, but are not adequately addressed in the Commission's Proposal. Nevertheless, it must be acknowledged that alternative, less burdensome solutions can almost certainly be found. The problem of notice and effective protection of the respondent's property could be addressed by a requirement that a copy of the judgment or certificate of judgment be served on the respondent a certain period (perhaps 7 or 14 days) before any enforcement measures other than provisional measure are taken, unless it is not practicable to take this step (because, for example, the respondent cannot be found or would be likely to take steps to frustrate enforcement), and for the enforcing party to certify compliance with this requirement to the competent authority of the Member State of enforcement (see Annex, below, Proposal 1). That requirement, it is submitted, would likely also serve as a deterrent to fraudulent enforcement proceedings. As to the problem of assimilation of judgment, this could be satisfactorily addressed by adding a second paragraph to Article 66 to enable the competent enforcement authorities, or any interested person, to apply to the designated court of the Member State of enforcement for a declaration as to the judgment's effect within that State's legal order (see Annex, below, Proposal 4). With these additional protections, abolition of the intermediate procedure could be supported.

A further difficulty, which arises from the division of responsibility between the Member States of origin and of enforcement in Articles 45 and 46,[134] is that the person against whom enforcement is sought may be required simultaneously to pursue two applications in two different jurisdictions. This could be addressed by a requirement that any application under Article 46 be stayed while an application under Article 45 is pending before the Member State of origin.[135]

---

[134] See above, text to n 15–21.
[135] See Annex, below, Proposal 2. Art 46(7) enables the court seised of an art 46 application

Suggested amendments to the text of the Commission's Proposal, reflecting these proposals, are set out in the Annex at the end of this chapter.

O. Authentic instruments – far enough, already

Whether or not the intermediate procedure (*exequatur*) is abolished for Member State court judgments, it should remain for authentic instruments, which are not the product of a judicial determination and appear even more open to abuse as the instruments of fraud. Arguably, the existing regime in Article 57 of the Brussels I Regulation already goes too far in giving a cross-border effect to these instruments, and their privileged position should advance no further. Accordingly, the amendments proposed in Article 70 of the Commission's Proposal should be rejected in any event.[136]

IV. CONCLUSIONS

The Commission must be commended for the way in which it has conducted the review of the Brussels I Regulation. Its proposed reforms with respect to the recognition and enforcement of judgments are, however, a mixed bag. Overall, the recommendation to abolish the intermediate procedure for enforcement of Member State judgments (*exequatur*) can be supported, provided that the following adjustments are made to the Commission's proposed Brussels I bis Regulation:[137]

1. First, and most importantly, parties should retain the right to challenge, and Member State courts should retain the right to refuse, the recognition or enforcement of a judgment on the ground that such recognition or enforcement would be manifestly incompatible with the public policy of the recognising/enforcing Member State.[138]
2. Secondly, the consumer should have the right to challenge the recognition or enforcement of a judgment on the ground that the court of origin breached the requirements of Section 4 of the Chapter I of the Regulation concerning jurisdiction over consumer contracts.[139]

---

to stay the application if an ordinary appeal has been lodged against the judgment in the Member State of origin or if the time for lodging such an appeal has not yet expired, but does not address the effect of a parallel application under art 45.

[136] See also J Fitchen, 'Authentic Instruments and European Private International Law in Civil and Commercial Matters: Is Now the Time to Break New Ground?' (2011) 7 J Priv Intl L 33.

[137] See the amendments suggested in the Annex below.

[138] See above, text to n 48–118.

[139] See above, text to n 119–121.

3. Thirdly, to respect Member States' systems of property ownership, a further ground of jurisdictional review should be considered to address situations where the court of origin has taken jurisdiction in circumstances where another Member State court has exclusive jurisdiction under Article 22(1)(a) (rights *in rem* in immovable property).[140]
4. Fourthly, to protect the judgment debtor and deter fraud, it should be a pre-condition to enforcement measures, other than provisional measures of enforcement, that the enforcing party should certify to the competent authority of the Member State of enforcement that a copy of the certificate of judgment has, where practicable, been served upon the respondent and that a specified period (say, 7 or 14 days) has elapsed following service.[141]
5. Fifthly, the competent enforcement authorities, and any interested party, should have the right to apply to the designated court in the Member State of enforcement to clarify the effect of the judgment within the legal order of that State.[142]
6. Sixthly, the relationship between simultaneously pending applications under Articles 45 and 46 should be addressed, to ensure efficient procedural co-ordination.[143]
7. Seventhly, the available grounds of challenge should apply equally to both the enforcement and the recognition of a judgment.[144]
8. Finally, the *exequatur* procedure must remain in any event for authentic instruments, which move freely enough in the EU already.[145]

So to conclude: the walls can come down, provided that the EU legislature takes care to ensure that the ceiling does not crumble.

ANNEX

Possible amendments to the text of the Commission Proposal[146]

Proposal 1 – Requirement for service on respondent before taking enforcement measures other than provisional measures

Article 40

<u>1.</u> An enforceable judgment shall carry with it by operation of law the

---

[140] See above, text to n 122–123.
[141] See above, p 159.
[142] See above, text to n 132–133 and p 159.
[143] See above, text to n 135.
[144] See above, p 139.
[145] See above, text to n 136.
[146] The suggested amendment are shown underlined (with deletions also shown).

power to proceed to any protective measures which exist under the law of the Member State of enforcement.

<u>2. With the exception of protective measures under paragraph 1, no measures of enforcement shall be taken unless either:</u>

<u>(a) the applicant has, not less than [7 or 14] days before the date upon which the enforcement measure is sought, served on the party against whom the enforcement measures is sought a copy of the certificate referred to in Article 42(1) or (2) in accordance with the requirements of Regulation (EC) No. 1393/2007, where applicable;[147] or</u>

<u>(b) it is impracticable to serve judicial documents on the party against whom enforcement measures are sought, and the applicant has taken reasonable steps to notify the contents of the judgment to the party against whom enforcement measures are sought.</u>

Article 42

1. For the purposes of enforcement in another Member State of a judgment other than those referred to in paragraph 2, the applicant shall provide the competent enforcement authorities with:

(a) a copy of the judgment which satisfies the conditions necessary to establish its authenticity; ~~and~~

(b) the certificate in the form set out in Annex I issued by the court of origin, certifying that the judgment is enforceable and, containing, where appropriate, an extract of the judgment as well as relevant information on the recoverable costs of the proceedings and the calculation of interest~~.~~; and

<u>(c) if the competent authority of the Member Stare of enforcement requires, a certificate using the form set out in Annex [ ] confirming that the requirements of Article 40(2) have been satisfied.[148]</u>

Proposal 2 – Relationship between parallel Art. 45 and Art. 46 applications

<u>*Article 46 bis*</u>

<u>1. A party who makes applications under both Article 45 and Article 46 with respect to the same judgment shall promptly notify the courts in the</u>

---

[147] The Annex I certificate should contain a statement that the applicant intends to proceed to enforcement measures in accordance with the Regulation, and a summary of the recipient's rights under Articles 45 and 46.

[148] In the case that service of the certificate is impractical, the Annex I certificate would request information as to the steps taken to serve these documents on, or bring them to the notice of, the person against whom enforcement measures are sought.

Member State of origin and the Member State of enforcement of that fact. 2. Upon receiving the notification under paragraph 1, the court in the Member State of enforcement shall stay the application under Article 46 until the court in the Member State of origin determines the application under Article 45.

3. If paragraph 1 applies, the court in the Member State of origin shall promptly notify the court in the Member State of enforcement of the outcome of the application under Article 45.

Proposal 3 – Broader grounds for opposing recognition or enforcemen

Article 43 deleted

~~The competent authority in the Member State of enforcement shall, on application by the defendant, refuse, either wholly or in part, the enforcement of the judgment if~~

~~(a) it is irreconcilable with a judgment given in a dispute between the same parties in the Member State of enforcement;~~

~~(b) it is irreconcilable with an earlier judgment given in another Member State or in a third State involving the same cause of action and between the same parties provided that the earlier judgment fulfils the conditions necessary for its recognition in the Member State of enforcement.~~

Article 46

1. In cases other than those covered by Article 45, ~~a party shall have the right to apply for a refusal~~ the Member State of enforcement shall refuse ~~of~~ recognition or enforcement of a judgment ~~where such recognition or enforcement would not be permitted by the fundamental principles underlying the right to a fair trial.~~ if:

(a) such recognition or enforcement is manifestly contrary to public policy (*ordre public*) in the Member State in which recognition is sought;

(b) it is irreconcilable with a judgment given in a dispute between the same parties in the Member State in which recognition is sought;

(c) it is irreconcilable with an earlier judgment given in another Member State or in a third State involving the same cause of action and between the same parties, provided that the earlier judgment fulfils the conditions necessary for its recognition in the Member State addressed in which recognition is sought; or

(d) the judgment was given in breach of the requirements of Section 4 of Chapter I or of Article 22(1).

1a. In its examination of the grounds of jurisdiction referred to in paragraph 1(d), the court or authority applied to shall be bound by the findings of fact on which the court of the Member State of origin based its jurisdiction.

1b. Subject to paragraph 1(d), the jurisdiction of the court of the Member State of origin may not be reviewed. The test of public policy referred to in paragraph 1(a) may not be applied to the rules relating to jurisdiction.

*Article 37(2)-(3) and Articles 47-63 **deleted**[149]*

Proposal 4 – Adjustment to clarification mechanism in Art. 66

Article 66

1. If a judgment contains a measure or an order which is not known in the Member State of enforcement, the competent authority in that Member State shall, to the extent possible, adapt the measure or order to one known under its own law which has equivalent effects attached to it and pursues similar aims and interests.

2. The competent authority or any interested party may apply to the court of the Member State of enforcement, listed in Annex III for a declaration as to whether and if so how paragraph 1 applies to a judgment.

---

[149] Note: If, as proposed above (p 160), the requirement of *exequatur* is to remain for authentic instruments, arts 47–63 would need to be adapted for this purpose and incorporated within Chapter IV.

The Brussels I Review Proposal: Challenges for the Lugano Convention?

*Andreas Furrer**

I. A SURVEY OF THE BRUSSELS AND LUGANO SYSTEMS

A. Introduction

The revision of the Brussels I Regulation[1] has had a major impact on the Lugano Convention[2] because of the unique concept of parallelism between this regulation of the EU, and the Lugano Convention, signed between the EU and a limited number of non-EU States. The most important goal of the Lugano Convention was to extend the legal effect of the Brussels I Regulation to the Lugano Contracting States.

In this chapter, the term 'Lugano States' refers to the three Contracting States remaining outside the EU: Iceland, Norway, and Switzerland. Under the term 'EU Member States', all Member States of the EU are referred to, except Denmark, whose special status in the Brussels/Lugano systems will not be addressed.[3]

This chapter will first sketch a short historical survey showing how the concept of parallel legal sources has been developed. This will be followed by a focus on the relevant changes set out in the Commission's Proposal ('Proposal'),[4] in order to outline the new legal and political background of the revised Lugano Convention. The status of the Lugano Convention in the system of the Brussels I Regulation, and the implications of the proposed changes will then be discussed, concluding with a summary.

---

* Professor of Private, Comparative, Private International and European Law, University of Lucerne, Switzerland; Partner, Meyer Müller Eckert, Zurich.
[1] Council Regulation 44/2001 of 22 December 2000 on Jurisdiction and the Recognition and Enforcement of Judgments in Civil and Commercial Matters [2001] OJ L 12/1, 16 January 2001.
[2] Council Decision concerning the Conclusion of the Convention on Jurisdiction and the Recognition and Enforcement of Judgments in Civil and Commercial Matters [2009] OJ L 147, 10 June 2009.
[3] U Magnus and P Mankowski (ed), *Brussels I Regulation: European Commentaries on Private International Law* (Sellier 2007) intro.
[4] Commission, Proposal for a Regulation of the European Parliament and of the Council on Jurisdiction and the Recognition and Enforcement of Judgments in Civil and Commercial Matters (Recast), COM(2010) 748 final.

B. *Short historical survey*

The Lugano Convention was signed on 16 September 1988 ('Lugano I') and came into force between the initial signatory states on 1 January 1992. It aimed to extend the rules of the 1968 Brussels Convention to certain members of the European Free Trade Association (EFTA).

It is worth noting that in the four years between the date of signature of the Lugano Convention and the date of entering into force in 1992, the political map of Europe had completely changed: not only did the Iron Curtain fall during these groundbreaking years but most of the Member States of the EFTA decided to join the EU. Thus, in 1992, most Contracting States of the Lugano Convention were already EU Member States.

Towards the end of the century, the Contracting States discussed a coordinated revision of the Brussels Convention and of Lugano I. However, in 1998/99, after the competence of the EU to legislate in the field of civil law and procedural law was established (see Articles 61 lit c and 60 of the EC Treaty), the European Commission gave up this joint effort in favour of the transformation of the Brussels Convention into the Brussels I Regulation. Further, the European Commission froze these negotiations and focused on the other projects in this field and promoted related regulations including, for example, the Brussels II Regulation, the Regulation on taking evidence, the Regulation on undisputed claims, and the Regulation on serving documents.[5] Therefore, after the Brussels I Regulation entered into force on 1 March 2002, Europe was again divided in two different legal areas with significant substantive differences. The negotiations to align the Lugano I Convention with the Brussels I Regulation took more than seven years, and concluded with the signing of the Lugano Convention on 30 October 2007 ('revised Lugano Convention'). There were two important reasons for this delay. First, the Court of Justice of the European Union (CJEU) had to decide whether the EU has exclusive competence to sign the revised Lugano Convention. After three years, in its legal opinion 1/03 of 7 February 2006,[6] the CJEU affirmed the exclusive competence of the EU.

---

[5] Council Regulation 2201/2003 of 27 November 2003 Concerning Jurisdiction and the Recognition and Enforcement of Judgments in Matrimonial Matters and the Matters of Parental Responsibility, Repealing Regulation 1347/2000; Council Regulation 1206/2001 of 28 May 2001 on Cooperation Between the Courts of the Member States in the Taking of Evidence in Civil or Commercial Matters; Regulation 805/2004 of the European Parliament and of the Council of 21 April 2004 Creating a European Enforcement Order for Uncontested Claims; Regulation 1393/2007 of the European Parliament and of the Council of 13 November 2007 on the Service in the Member States of Judicial and Extrajudicial Documents in Civil or Commercial Matters (Service of Documents), and Repealing Council Regulation 1348/2000.

[6] Opinion 1/03 of the Court on the Competence of the Community to Conclude the New Lugano Convention [2006] ECR I-1145. See T Baumé, 'Competence of the Community to Conclude the New Lugano Convention on Jurisdiction and the Recognition and Enforcement

Secondly, the Lugano States and the EU had a lengthy and difficult discussion on the consequences of the fact that the CJEU would be – and now is – authorised to interpret the revised Lugano Convention in the preliminary ruling proceeding (Article 234 of the EC Treaty). Since non-EU Lugano States like Switzerland were not represented in the CJEU, the Contracting States had to find an appropriate system to safeguard the uniform interpretation of the revised Lugano Convention by all the national courts and the CJEU. These negotiations resulted in a compromise, which can be found in the Protocol 1 on Certain Questions of Jurisdiction, Procedure and Enforcement, and in the Protocol 2 on the Uniform Interpretation of the Convention and on the Standing Committee.

In the EU, the revised Lugano Convention entered into force on 1 January 2010 and on 1 January 2011 in Switzerland.[7] For Switzerland, this day was also a landmark in the history of procedural law because, for the first time, Switzerland had implemented a uniform civil and criminal procedural law that superseded the 26 different procedural laws of the cantons. This fundamental change of the procedural foundations of Swiss law has been – and still is – a major challenge for Swiss lawyers. In the next few years, Swiss lawyers will be occupied in developing a new body of case law, bridging the procedural gaps and lacunae and discussing the legal questions in dispute.

II. RELEVANT CHANGES IN THE COMMISSION'S PROPOSAL

A. *The Commission's goal to simplify access to justice within the EU for EU residents and companies*

One of the major goals of the Commission is to simplify the access to justice within the EU for EU residents and companies in their legal relationships with third country residents. The Commission's concerns are as follows:

Access to justice in the EU is overall unsatisfactory in disputes involving defendants from outside the EU. With some exceptions, the current Regulation only applies

---

of Judgements in Civil and Commercial Matters: Opinion 1/03 of 7 February 2006' (2006) 7 German Law Journal 705 <http://www.germanlawjournal.com/index.php?pageID=11& artID=752>; A Borrás, 'Competence of the Community to Conclude the Revised Lugano Convention on Jurisdiction and Enforcement of Judgements in Civil and Commercial Matters – Opinion C-1/03 of 7 February 2006: Comments and Immediate Consequences' (2006) 8 Yearbook of Private International Law 37.

[7] Confédération Suisse, Traités internationaux pour lesquels la Suisse assume les fonctions de dépositaire: Convention concernant la competence judiciaire, la reconnaissance et l'exécution des decisions en matière civile et commerciale <http://www.dfae.admin.ch/etc/medialib/downloads/edazen/topics/intla/intrea/depch/misc/conlug2.Par.0007.File.tmp/ mt_110114_lug2 part_f.pdf>.

where the defendant is domiciled inside the EU. Otherwise jurisdiction is governed by national law. The diversity of national law leads to unequal access to justice for EU companies in transactions with partners from third countries: some can easily litigate in the EU, others cannot, even in situations where no other court guaranteeing a fair trial is competent. In addition, where national legislation does not grant access to court in disputes with parties outside the EU, the enforcement of mandatory EU law protecting e.g. consumers, employees or commercial agents is not guaranteed.[8]

The Commission refers in this passage to four alleged problems. First, the Commission notes that in disputes involving defendants from outside the EU, the access to justice within the EU is unsatisfactory.

Secondly, it argues that the current Brussels I Regulation only applies where the defendant is domiciled inside the EU. It points out that when the defendant is domiciled in a third country, it is still national law that applies; therefore, the access to justice for EU companies varies according to jurisdiction. Thus, the Commission advocates a fully harmonised regulation which excludes national jurisdiction rules in relation to third countries.

Thirdly, the Commission is concerned that the principle of fair trial is endangered without such an exclusive and extensive jurisdiction in relation to third countries.

Fourthly, the Commission highlights that the enforcement of mandatory laws protecting consumers, employees or commercial agents is not guaranteed. For these four reasons, the Commission wishes to expand the field of application of the Brussels I Regulation. This raises the question of whether these concerns also affect the operation of the revised Lugano Convention. Specifically, are these four grounds taken into consideration for privileging EU residents and companies also relevant for the Lugano States?

B. Most important issues of the Proposal in relation with third countries

The Commission suggests that the goal to simplify the access to justice for EU residents and companies shall be done by three measures:

First, the Proposal extends the jurisdiction rules of the Brussels I Regulation to third country defendants. For that purpose, the Commission proposes a revised mechanism in Article 4 of the Proposal, which reads:

1. Persons domiciled in a Member State may be sued in the courts of another Member State only by virtue of the rules set out in Sections 2 to 7 of this Chapter.
2. Persons not domiciled in any of the Member States may be sued in the courts of a Member State only by virtue of the rules set out in Sections 2 to 8 of this Chapter.

---

[8] Proposal (n 4) at 1.2.

Article 4(2) of the Proposal widens the field of application of the Brussels I Regulation, because all special and exclusive jurisdictions are now applicable, irrespective of the domicile of the claimant. This extension is consistent with and consequential to the EU's exclusive competence in the field of the Brussels I Regulation, as established by the CJEU in its Opinion 1/03.[9] The aim of this rule is to waive all national jurisdiction clauses. In its Opinion 1/03, the CJEU further held that the reference to national law in Article 4(1) of the Brussels I Regulation qualifies the applicable national rules to be an integral part of the EU rules:

Given the uniform and coherent nature of the system of rules on conflict of jurisdiction established by Regulation No 44/2001, Article 4(1) thereof, which provides that 'if the defendant is not domiciled in a Member State, the jurisdiction of the courts of each Member State shall, subject to Articles 22 and 23, be determined by the law of that Member State', must be interpreted as meaning that it forms part of the system implemented by that Regulation, since it resolves the situation envisaged by reference to the legislation of the Member State before whose court the matter is brought.[10]

It has to be stressed that this interpretation of Article 4(1) of the Brussels I Regulation is not applicable in respect of the Lugano States, because these States are not Member States of the EU and, therefore, are not subject to the EU rules.[11]

Secondly, the Commission proposes two more additional *fora* for disputes outside the EU: According to Article 25 of the Proposal, a claim can be filed at the court where the property belonging to the defendant is located, provided that the value of the property is not disproportionate to the value of the claim and that the dispute has a sufficient connection with the Member State of the court seized. Such a forum is generally considered to be an exorbitant forum, with the result that this basis of exorbitant jurisdiction shall now be formally established at the EU level.

According to Article 26 of the Proposal, the courts of a Member State will be able to exercise jurisdiction if no other forum guaranteeing the right to a fair trial is available and the dispute has a sufficient connection with the Member State concerned. The first exorbitant forum should not be applicable under the revised Lugano Convention because of the specific rules in Article 22 thereof. This exception is also expressly provided for in Article 64(2) lit a of the revised Lugano Convention, which will be discussed subsequently. The second forum should not be applicable because the preconditions established should never be fulfilled within the field of

---

[9] Opinion 1/03 (n 6).

[10] Opinion 1/03 (n 6) para 148.

[11] A Buhr, *Europäischer Justizraum und revidiertes Lugano-Übereinkommen – Zum räumlich-persönlichen Anwendungsbereich des europäischen Rechts über die internationale Zuständigkeit in Zivil- und Handelssachen* (Stämpfli Verlag 2010) para 938 ff.

application of the revised Lugano Convention. Thus, the concern that exorbitant *fora* might become applicable is not justified under the Lugano system.

Thirdly, the Proposal introduces a discretionary *lis pendens* rule for disputes on the same subject matter and between the same parties where these disputes are pending before the courts in the EU and in a third country.

This specific rule would not be applicable under the revised Lugano Convention because Articles 27 to 30 thereof already provide certain specific rules applicable to these matters. This is the reason why Article 64(2) lit c of the revised Lugano Convention expressly refers to this exception: every change to this system must be facilitated by a revision of the Convention itself. These proposals of the EU show the Commission's reservations towards third countries' jurisdictions. It seems that it is the European Commission's firm view that citizens and companies are not to be expected to file claims outside the EU and to bear the consequence that third countries' laws will be applicable without guaranteeing the EU minimal standards of protection reflected in the mandatory rules (ie in respect of employment law or consumer protection).

This very reluctant attitude towards third countries raises concerns in view of the well-established *Savigny principle*, which constitutes the basis of European private international law in general. The *Savigny principle* relies on the legal presumption of the equality of legal systems: if a person has entered a legal relationship in a foreign (or in terms of the EU, a 'third') country, this person has to be aware that a foreign judge can be competent to hear a case and that this foreign judge might apply foreign law to this legal relationship. It seems that this well-acknowledged fundamental principle is questioned by the Commission, and that this development is applauded by legal authorities like Johannes Weber:

> It is hard to explain why an insurance policyholder, a consumer or an employee domiciled in a Member State can benefit from the European Jurisdiction ... favourable to them only in relation to defendants from Member States and deserve less protection if they enter into a transaction with a non-EU party.... This issue is delicate with regard to guaranteeing the application of mandatory secondary law.[12]

Based on the *Savigny principle*, the consequence of applying foreign (third countries') law is not that difficult to explain: if a person enters into a contract with a party from a third country, it may encounter some advantages such as better prices. However, one of the risks of such a transaction is that a foreign judge will hear the case and apply foreign law. Depending on the specific circumstances and the applicable law, the consumer or the

---

[12] J Weber, 'Universal Jurisdiction and Third States in the Reform of the Brussels I Regulation' (2011) Max Planck Private Law Research Paper 11/7, 6.

employee may even enjoy greater protection under a foreign jurisdiction. On the basis of the *Savigny principle*, this risk has to be borne unless the applicable foreign law contradicts the international *ordre public*.

However, the Commission seems to consider this fundamental principle to be questionable. It is one further example which seems to support the idea that the EU continues its efforts in constructing a European fortress in the field of jurisdiction and applicable law. This again raises the question of the implications of this development on the revised Lugano Convention.

III. RELATIONSHIP BETWEEN THE BRUSSELS I REGULATION AND THE REVISED LUGANO CONVENTION

A. *Different interpretation of Article 54b of the Lugano I Convention and Article 64 of the revised Lugano Convention*

The aforementioned transformation of the Brussels Convention into the Brussels I Regulation has delayed the negotiations on a revised Lugano Convention, and one of the main issues in the discussion between the EU and the non-EU Lugano States was – or should have been – the clarification of the new relationship between these two sources of law.

There have been two starting points for these negotiations: on the one hand, Article 54b of Lugano I was the relevant norm to regulate the relationship between the Brussels I Regulation and Lugano I, and between Lugano I and any further directives or regulations of the EU.[13] On the other hand, based on the CJEU's Opinion 1/03, it was undisputed that the revised Lugano Convention shall be part of EU law because the EU has an exclusive (internal and, therefore, external) competence to rule on questions of jurisdiction, recognition and enforcement. Consequently, as an international convention of the EU, the revised Lugano Convention is the higher source of law and has priority over the parallel rules of the Brussels I Regulation. It is therefore important to note the different legal setting and purpose of Article 54b of Lugano I compared to the subsequent Article 64 of the revised Lugano Convention: whereas Article 54b of Lugano I was designed as a conflict rule to coordinate two international conventions with the same content, Article 64 of the revised Lugano Convention coordinates the field of application of an international convention in relation with an internal EU regulation. This coordination mechanism not only had to observe the transformation of the Brussels Convention into a regulation of the EU, but also take into account the exclusive competence of the EU mentioned above. However, the parties have not made any substantial

---

[13] See (n 5).

changes to Article 64 of the revised Lugano Convention apart from some formal adaptation to the Brussels I Regulation. They have concretised the relationship between the revised Lugano Convention and the Brussels I Regulation as follows:[14]

First, as a general rule, according to Article 64(1) of the revised Lugano Convention, the Brussels I Regulation shall prevail over the Convention if the proceeding is filed at a court of an EU Member State. This is an exception from the aforementioned EU rule of precedence of international law. Thus, even though the wording is quite similar, the different tasks of the coordination mechanisms in Article 54b of Lugano I and Article 64 of the revised Lugano Convention have to be taken into account.

Secondly, Article 64 of the revised Lugano Convention is restricted by several exceptions. The two main exceptions are listed in its Article 64(2): In matters of jurisdiction, where the defendant is domiciled in a non-EU Lugano State and where an exclusive competence according to Article 22 applies or where the contracting parties had agreed upon a place of jurisdiction according to Article 23, the rules of the revised Lugano Convention shall apply (Article 64(2) lit a). Further, when the proceedings are instituted according to Articles 27 and 28 of the revised Lugano Convention, its rules shall apply, too (Article 64(2) lit b).

---

[14] Art 64: '1. This Convention shall not prejudice the application by the Member States of the European Community of the Council Regulation (EC) No 44/2001 on jurisdiction and the recognition and enforcement of judgments in civil and commercial matters, as well as any amendments thereof, of the Convention on Jurisdiction and the Enforcement of Judgments in Civil and Commercial Matters, signed at Brussels on 27 September 1968, and of the Protocol on interpretation of that Convention by the Court of Justice of the European Communities, signed at Luxembourg on 3 June 1971, as amended by the Conventions of Accession to the said Convention and the said Protocol by the States acceding to the European Communities, as well as of the Agreement between the European Community and the Kingdom of Denmark on jurisdiction and the recognition and enforcement of judgments in civil and commercial matters, signed at Brussels on 19 October 2005.
2. However, this Convention shall in any event be applied: (a) in matters of jurisdiction, where the defendant is domiciled in the territory of a State where this Convention but not an instrument referred to in paragraph 1 of this Article applies, or where Articles 22 or 23 of this Convention confer jurisdiction on the courts of such a State; (b) in relation to *lis pendens* or to related actions as provided for in Articles 27 and 28, when proceedings are instituted in a State where the Convention but not an instrument referred to in paragraph 1 of this Article applies and in a State where this Convention as well as an instrument referred to in paragraph 1 of this Article apply; (c) in matters of recognition and enforcement, where either the State of origin or the State addressed is not applying an instrument referred to in paragraph 1 of this Article.
3. In addition to the grounds provided for in Title III, recognition or enforcement may be refused if the ground of jurisdiction on which the judgment has been based differs from that resulting from this Convention and recognition or enforcement is sought against a party who is domiciled in a State where this Convention but not an instrument referred to in paragraph 1 of this Article applies, unless the judgment may otherwise be recognised or enforced under any rule of law in the State addressed.'

These rules are protected by the right of the courts of the Lugano States to refuse the recognition and enforcement of judgements which are based on the Brussels I Regulation, if this jurisdiction differs from the revised Lugano Convention and if no other national law would allow such recognition and enforcement (Article 64(3) of the revised Lugano Convention). In the merely formal adaptation of Article 64 of the revised Lugano Convention, the parties have not made any concessions to the new function of this Article compared to Article 54b of Lugano I. There is no reference to the problem of the primacy of international law over the secondary legislation of the EU and no further reflections have been made in respect of the EU's exclusive competence in the field of jurisdiction, recognition and enforcement. Therefore, it is necessary to analyse how Article 64 of the revised Lugano Convention should be interpreted with respect to these two fundamental changes.

B. Five examples

The problem to be discussed shall be addressed with the help of the following examples:

Case 1: A claimant domiciled in Switzerland files a claim against a respondent domiciled in Spain.

Case 2: A claimant domiciled in Spain files a claim against a respondent domiciled in Switzerland.

Case 3: In a proceeding concerning an unlimited tenancy agreement of a Spanish cottage, a claimant domiciled in Switzerland files a claim against a respondent domiciled in Greece.

Case 4: A Spanish consumer files a claim in Spain against a company incorporated in Switzerland.

Case 5: A company incorporated in Germany files a claim at the place of performance in Spain against a company incorporated in Switzerland.

The first two cases are not in dispute because they unquestionably fall within the field of application of Article 64(1) of the revised Lugano Convention. Article 2 of the Brussels I Regulation is directly applicable if the defendant is domiciled in a Lugano State and no other rules of jurisdiction of the Lugano/Brussels systems can be applied. Under the same conditions, the revised Lugano Convention is applicable if the jurisdiction of Article 2 of this Convention is based on the respondent's domicile in a Lugano State. Thus, in the first case, the Brussels I Regulation is applicable, and in the second case, the revised Lugano Convention is applicable.

In the three other cases, Article 2 of the Brussels I Regulation/revised Lugano Convention is not directly applicable. In a narrow interpretation of Article 64(1) of the revised Lugano Convention, these cases do not fall within the field of application of Article 2 and, accordingly, these cases are not directly covered by Article 64(1) of the revised Lugano Convention. It has therefore to be considered whether Article 64(1) or (2) of the revised Lugano Convention is applicable to these three cases.

C. *Narrow interpretation of Article 64(1) of the revised*
Lugano Convention

In its Opinion 1/03, the CJEU held that it is 'apparent from an analysis of Regulation No 44/2001 alone that, given the unified and coherent system of rules on jurisdiction for which it provides, any international agreement also establishing a unified system of rules on conflict of jurisdiction such as that established by that regulation is capable of affecting those rules of jurisdiction'.[15] Thus, on the one hand, the most important consequence of Article 64(1) of the revised Lugano Convention is safeguarding the EU's freedom to develop its internal law on jurisdiction, recognition and enforcement. On the other hand, it is also in the EU's exclusive competence to specify the field of application of the Brussels I Regulation in relation to the revised Lugano Convention, which is the second important function of the latter's Article 64(1) and (2).

In considering this second question concerning the field of application of the Brussels I Regulation in relation to the revised Lugano Convention, a first reading of Article 64 of the revised Lugano Convention gives the reader the impression that the Brussels I Regulation prevails in all cases to which the exemption rules listed in Article 64(2) do not apply. Such a reading of Article 64 would have a rather surprising legal consequence: in most cases where the exception rules of Article 64(2) are not applicable, the courts of the EU Member States would apply the Brussels I Regulation, whereas in the same cases when the claimant files the claim at a court of a Lugano State, the revised Lugano Convention would be applicable.

However, a closer analysis of Article 64 of the revised Lugano Convention leads to another conclusion: there are mainly three reasons for such a narrow interpretation of Article 64(2), which narrows down the field of application of Article 64(1) of the revised Lugano Convention. These reasons are set forth below:

Firstly, it is a widely acknowledged principle (also in EU law) that exceptions from general rules must be interpreted in a narrow way. This raises the question of whether para 1 or 2 of Article 64 constitutes such an excep-

---

[15] Opinion 1/03 (n 6) at para 151.

tion to the general rule. Referring to the general rule that an international convention normally prevails over internal law, Article 64(1) of the revised Lugano Convention is a clear exception from this rule; therefore, it must be interpreted in a narrow way. Article 64(2) of the revised Lugano Convention is an exception to the exception of Article 64(1) and must be interpreted in a broad way. This leads to the conclusion that Article 64(2) has to be understood as a non-exhaustive enumeration narrowing down the field of application of Article 64(1). The revised Lugano Convention applies in all cases of special and/or an exclusive jurisdiction.

Secondly, one important goal of the revised Lugano Convention is to liberalise, facilitate and guarantee the recognition and enforcement of foreign judgements in the field of application of the revised Lugano Convention. As mentioned, Article 64(3) endangers the recognition and enforcement of judgements from EU Member States in Lugano States: in order to avoid refusals of the recognition and enforcement of judgements, Article 64(1) of the revised Lugano Convention has to be interpreted in a narrow way.

Thirdly, it would be inconsistent with the fundamental principles regarding international conventions if the principle of reciprocity would not be guaranteed. One important consequence of this principle of reciprocity is that the field of application is the same for both contracting parties. Therefore, if a claimant domiciled in an EU Member State files a claim against a defendant domiciled in a non-EU Lugano State and based on a narrow interpretation of Article 64, the revised Lugano Convention shall apply.

This narrow reading of Article 64(1) reflects the importance of safeguarding the jurisdiction at the domicile of the defendant, an internationally acknowledged rule that is also the basic rule of jurisdiction underlying the Brussels I Regulation and the revised Lugano Convention. Article 64(2) of the revised Lugano Convention reflects the common intentions of the parties to agree upon some specified exceptions which are listed in Sections 2 to 7 of this Convention. Thus, Article 64(2) shall be read as a provision with a non-exhaustive list of examples which confirms the general priority rule of international conventions. There are no reasons to consider that the Lugano States would have accepted a rule that would allow courts of the EU Member States to apply the Brussels I Regulation in the field of application of the revised Lugano Convention, outside the exceptional rule in its Article 64(1).

D. Implications of this understanding on the five examples

Returning to the five examples mentioned above, we can draw the following conclusions: as mentioned, case 1 and case 2 are ruled by Article 64(1) of the revised Lugano Convention. Article 2 of the Brussels I Regulation is directly applicable if the defendant is domiciled in a Lugano State and no other rules of jurisdiction of the Lugano/Brussels systems are applicable. Under the same conditions, the revised Lugano Convention is applicable, if the jurisdiction of Article 2 of this Convention is based on the respondent's domicile in a Lugano State. Thus, in case 1, the Brussels I Regulation is applicable, in case 2, the revised Lugano Convention is applicable. In case 3, the jurisdiction of the Spanish court is based on Article 22(1) of the revised Lugano Convention. This rule is expressly listed in Article 64(2) of the revised Lugano Convention and, therefore, undisputed. In case 4, according to Article 64(2) of the revised Lugano Convention, the jurisdiction of the Spanish court is based on Article 16(1) of the revised Lugano Convention because the defendant has its seat in a Lugano State. In case 5, according to Article 64(2) of the revised Lugano Convention, the jurisdiction of the Spanish court is based on Article 5(1) of the revised Lugano Convention because the seat of the defendant is in a Lugano State.

IV. STATUS OF THE REVISED LUGANO CONVENTION IN THE
COMMISSION'S PROPOSAL

As discussed above, the most important concern of the Commission's Proposal in relation to third countries is to expand the EU jurisdiction against respondents not having a domicile or seat in the EU.

This goal of the Commission illustrates that the dispute concerning the field of application of the revised Lugano Convention will gain importance after the revision of the Brussels I Regulation. A broad interpretation of Article 64(1) of the revised Lugano Convention would increase the cases in which a court from a Lugano State would not recognise and enforce a judgment of a court in a EU Member State, as there will be scope for a growing number of cases in which the courts could establish their jurisdiction on a Brussels I Regulation basis, different to the jurisdiction rule in the revised Lugano Convention.

In light of this close relationship between the Brussels I Regulation and the revised Lugano Convention, it is interesting to note how the Commission wishes to develop or at least safeguard the parallelism of these two important sources of law. This raises the question of the extent to which the revision of the Brussels I Regulation can be done in coordination with the Lugano States.

The analysis of the preparatory documents leads to a sobering conclusion. Neither in the report of Hess/Pfeiffer/Schlosser of September 2007,[16]

---

[16] B Hess, T Pfeiffer and P Schlosser, *Report on the Application of Regulation Brussels I in the Member States* (2007), Study JLS/C4/2005/03, at 1.

nor in the Commission's Report of 2009[17] to the European Parliament, nor in the analysis of the Centre for Strategy & Evaluation Service of December 2010[18] have any substantial efforts been made to include the revised Lugano Convention in the respective research. At the very least, there are some (limited) references in the 2010 report of the European Commission:

In the seventh consideration of the preambles, the Commission updated the history of the Brussels I Regulation and made reference to the Lugano Convention. It confirms that the 'continuity in the interpretation of these Conventions and this Regulation should be ensured'.

In Article 77 (which is the revised Article 66 of the Brussels I Regulation), the transitional provision privileging proceedings instituted before the entry into force of the Brussels I Regulation and of Lugano I shall be deleted.

The most prominent reference to the revised Lugano Convention can be found in the new Article 84 of the Proposal: 'This Regulation shall not affect the application of the Convention on jurisdiction and the recognition and enforcement of judgments in civil and commercial matters, signed on 30 October 2007 in Lugano.' Does this new Article 84 of the Proposal clarify anything in relation to the difficult and controversial question of the relationship between the Brussels I Regulation and the revised Lugano Convention? The answer is probably not: rather, it can be read as a confirmation of both alternative interpretations of Article 64 of the revised Lugano Convention.

V. CONCLUSION

The implications of the Commission's Proposal for the non-EU Lugano States depend on the interpretation of Article 64 of the revised Lugano Convention. In a broad interpretation of Article 64(1) – and a narrow literal interpretation of the exceptions to these exceptions in Article 64(2) of the Convention – a revised Brussels I Regulation would destabilise the goal of a common area of jurisdiction guaranteed by the revised Lugano Convention. On the basis of this international convention between the EU and the non-EU Lugano States, it seems appropriate that the underlying rules should not be changed unilaterally by the Commission.

---

[17] Report from the Commission to the European Parliament, the Council and the Economic and Social Committee on the Application of Council Regulation (EC) No 44/2001 on Jurisdiction and the Recognition and Enforcement of Judgments in Civil and Commercial Matters (COM (2009) 174 final).

[18] Centre for Strategy & Evaluation Service, Data Collection and Impact Analysis – Certain Aspects of a Possible Revision of Council Regulation No. 44/2001 on Jurisdiction and the Recognition and Enforcement of Judgments in Civil and Commercial Matters ('Brussels I') (2010).

It would therefore be important to clarify the open issue of the delimitation of the fields of application of the Brussels I Regulation and of the revised Lugano Convention. Bound to an international convention, the EU cannot unilaterally narrow the field of application of the revised Lugano Convention – however, it accepts unilaterally the precedence of the revised Lugano Convention, in terms of a general rule of precedence of international conventions over internal EU law. This should be clarified in Article 84 of the Proposal. Irrespective of such a clarification in the Proposal, for the reasons mentioned above, a narrow interpretation of Article 64(1) of the revised Lugano Convention – and therefore a broad interpretation of Article 64(2) of this Convention – is appropriate.

It goes without saying that such an interpretation will trigger a parallel revision of the revised Lugano Convention in order to ensure the parallelism of these two sources of law, which is one of the central goals of all parties of the revised Lugano Convention, including the EU. Therefore, it would be wise for the European Commission to consider the parallelism of the revised Lugano Convention when proposing the revision of the Brussels I Regulation and to involve the non-EU Lugano States into this preparatory work.

As discussed above, the European Commission is determined to improve the legal status of respondents in disputes with claimants domiciled outside the EU. This manifests the fundamental distrust of the European Commission towards third countries' legal systems, an approach which undermines one of the cornerstones of international private law, that is, the *Savigny principle* and the assumption of the equality of all legal systems. It seems that Europe is on the way back to the theory of statues of the Renaissance with the applicable laws of the cities of Florence, Bologna or Amsterdam.

In this context, the revised Lugano Convention could serve as a bridge to those third countries, providing for the establishment of a close legal and commercial relationship with the EU. The circle of possible Contracting States should therefore be opened to such countries. For that purpose, it might be wise to transfer the revised Lugano Convention under the umbrella of the Hague Conference and to set out an appropriate catalogue of criteria for legal systems in order to become Contracting States of this Convention. However, looking at the fundamental problems of certain Member States of the EU,[19] it will be difficult to apply a very high standard to the jurisdictions of countries interested in ratifying the revised Lugano Convention.

---

[19] EU Anti-Corruption Report.

Protection against Abuse of Process in the Brussels I Review Proposal?

Luboš Tichý *

I. INTRODUCTION

This chapter highlights a topic which is rarely discussed in the context of EU private international law: abuse of process and how to protect against it. It is particularly worth considering this subject in relation to the proposed recast of the Brussels I Regulation[1] (the 'Proposal') and its intended aims: to shift towards the liberalisation of the recognition regime (mainly by abolishing *exequatur*), and to open up the entire system to third countries. However problems which have arisen in cases like *Gasser*[2] also show the need to focus on the question of abuse under the Regulation.[3] Moreover, any introduction of a control mechanism to protect against the abuse of process under Brussels I will affect EU procedural law more generally, given the Regulation's fundamental significance for other instruments of EU procedural law.

This contribution will first outline the phenomenon of abuse of process in the context of the Brussels I Regulation (Part II). It will then deal with categories of abuse of process in national legal orders, along with the tools to resolve this problem (Part III). The article next reflects upon the advantages and disadvantages of the introduction of new control mechanisms against abuse within the context of the Brussels I review process (Part IV). It will conclude with a proposed 'model' solution (Part V).

---

* Professor of Law, Charles University, Prague.
[1] European Commission, Proposal for a Regulation of the European Parliament and of the Council on Jurisdiction and Recognition and Enforcement of Judgments in Civil and Commercial Matters (Recast), COM (2010) 748 final, 14 December 2010; see also European Commission, Green Paper on the Review of Council Regulation (EC) No 44/2001 on Jurisdiction and the Recognition and Enforcement of Judgments in Civil and Commercial Matters (COM (2009) 175) and European Commission, Report from the Commission to the European Parliament, the Council and the EESC on the Application of Council Regulation (EC) No 44/2001 (COM (2009) 174 final). The volume R de la Feria, S Vogenauer, *Prohibition of Abuse of Law* (Hart 2011) has not yet been available when this article was drafted.
[2] CJEU, Case C-116/02 *Gasser v MISAT* [2003] ECR I-14693. See further details under Part III.D.
[3] B Hess, *Europäisches Zivilprozessrecht* (CF Müller 2010) 328; B Hess, T Pfeiffer and P Schlosser, *The Brussels I Regulation (EC) No 44/2001 – The Heidelberg Report on the Application of Regulation Brussels I in 25 Member States* (Beck, Hart, Nomos 2008) paras 657-665; D Stauder, 'Die internationale Zuständigkeit in Patentverletzungsklagen – Nach drei Jahrzehnten' in A Ohly et al (eds), *Festschrift für Gerhard Schricker* (Beck 2005) 919, 927.

II. THE PHENOMENON OF ABUSE OF PROCESS UNDER THE BRUSSELS I REGIME

A. Definition

Legal doctrine relating to the Brussels I Regulation makes reference to the notion of abuse of process, albeit infrequently,[4] but without defining the term any further.[5]

For the purposes of this essay, without claiming completeness, the abuse of process will be defined as an undertaking that is in conflict with good morals and pursuing an unlawful, and at times even harmful purpose. Frequently, the abuse of process arises out of illegal activities or particular circumstances which conflict with the law.[6] Perpetrated by one party, it will harm either the other party or the public.

B. The Brussels I Regulation and abuse of process

Abuse of process within the scope of application of the Brussels I Regulation can be related to controversial court and arbitration agreements.[7] It can also be related to cases of *forum non conveniens*; so-called 'torpedo' actions,[8] pre-emptively brought by a potential defendant to block claims brought by the other side through the Brussels I *lis pendens* mechanism; and proceedings where claims rest upon false evidence, counterfeit documentation or otherwise falsified proof.[9] It may also involve cases which lead to the violation of the principles of a fair trial, and consequently to unfair treatment and harm to the other side.[10]

The most notable examples[11] of abuse of process in international litigation have so far occurred within the context of cross-border cases between the so-called 'old' Member States, ie within well-developed and stabilised court systems and legal cultures. As a result of the opening up of the

---

[4] See B Hess (n 3); S Leible and E Röder, 'Missbrauchkontrolle von Gerichtsstandsvereinbarungen in europäischen Zivilprozessrecht' (2007) RIW 481.

[5] M Taruffo, *Abuse of Procedural Rights: Comparative Standards of Procedural Fairness* (Kluwer 1999).

[6] F Bydlinski, 'Skizzen zum Verbot des Rechtsmissbrauchs im österreichischen Privatrecht' in J Lazar (ed), *Zákaz zneužitia práva* (Iura edition 2001) 83, 98.

[7] U Magnus and P Mankowski, 'Brussels I on the Verge of Reform' (2010) 109 ZVglRWiss 1, 18; S Leible and E Röder (n 4).

[8] See *Gasser* (n 2).

[9] See Section IV.

[10] See eg *Sürmeli v Germany*, Application No 75529/01, Judgment of 8 June 2006, para 98; see also W Frenz, *Handbuch Europarecht, Europäische Grundrechte*, vol 4 (Springer 2009) 1520. For further details, see S Iseburg-Epple, *Die Berücksichtigung ausländischer Rechtshängigkeit nach dem europäischen Gerichtsstands - und Vollstreckungsübereinkommen vom 27.9.1968* (Lang 1992).

[11] See *Gasser* (n 2); see also CJEU, Case C-4/03 *Gesellschaft für Antriebstechnik mbH und Co KG v. Lamellen- und Kupplungsbau KG* [2006] ECR I-6509 and Case C-539/03 *Roche Nederland B.V. v Primus and Goldbery* [2006] ECR I-6535.

European area of justice to third countries, one can expect that such situations will arise much more frequently. The increased scope for abuse, together with the upcoming liberalisation of the Brussels I system, represents a real threat to legal certainty and law enforcement within the EU: it could potentially put the fundamental procedural right of fair trial in jeopardy.

C. The Proposal's incomplete intentions

Although one of the intentions of the Commission's Proposal is 'avoiding abusive litigation tactics', the Proposal does not guarantee sufficient protection against procedural abuse. Even though this objective is mentioned twice in the Proposal's preamble (Recitals (19) and (20)),[12] seemingly referring to the reform of the *lis pendens* and other provisions, [13] the objective has not been fulfilled because the Proposal lacks, whether intentionally or unintentionally, both a general clause conferring protection against the abuse of process, and more specific regulations which would protect against unfair clauses conferring jurisdiction (which are not dealt with in this paper).

III. ABUSE OF PROCESS: HOW TO PREVENT OR AVOID IT

A. Categories of abuse of process in national systems

The abuse of process or procedural rights is a phenomenon which is known in all legal cultures. It is not an illegal action, but a so-called "negation" of law, ie achieving a result which is contrary to the law. It occurs when there is an ulterior purpose or motive underlying the use of process, and some act within the use of the legal process is not proper in the regular course of the proceedings

In national procedural law, the meaning of the prohibition of the abuse of procedure differs significantly from jurisdiction to jurisdiction, even though all European jurisdictions acknowledge the principle that civil proceedings should be conducted in a reasonable and fair manner.[14] According to *Rechberger*,[15] for instance, civil proceedings which cannot

---

[12] See Recitals 19 and 20 which focus only on jurisdiction and arbitration agreements as measures for avoiding abusive litigation tactics.

[13] For an overview of the proposals, see B Hess, T Pfeiffer and P Schlosser, *Heidelberg Report* (n 3) 203–212.

[14] M Taruffo, 'General Report' in M Taruffo (n 5).

[15] WH Rechberger and DA Simotta, *Grundriss des österreichischen Zivilprozessrechts* (7th edn, Manz 2009) para 26.

fulfil their purpose, ie the provision or maintenance of legal peace, should not be allowed to continue. Such processes should be forestalled or otherwise prevented from taking place.[16]

Throughout national legal systems, there is neither a single definition of abuse of process, nor a legal delineation of this term.[17] The definitions of the abuse of process concept are usually very vague. They include gross procedural unfairness, breach of loyalty, bad faith, fraudulent conduct, dilatory tactics and the notion of improper purpose.[18] In English proceedings, for instance, procedural abuse takes on four forms:[19]

1. intended manipulation or frustration of the proceedings;
2. negative impact without separate culpability;
3. arbitrary type of action inconsistent with procedural rules; and
4. any other digression from proper procedures.

Legal systems also differ in their protection against procedural abuse, specificfally in the way in which such protection mechanisms are anchored in the procedural orders. Legal systems based on the French legal culture[20] contain relatively specific legal regulations including sanctions for abuse of process.[21] Other legal orders, which are oriented along the English common law approach, make reference to the principle of decency, which also applies to abuse of process.[22]

A relatively independent group is made up of those European states whose civil procedure is modelled along the lines of the German tradition.[23] There, the prohibition of procedural abuse is not in itself a general principle, even though some sources in the literature consider it to be so.[24] Instead, the good faith principle also pertains to procedure and is a criterion for the assessment of procedural abuse. The practical application of

---

[16] M Taruffo (n 5) 6–7.

[17] ibid 9–10.

[18] See N Andrews, 'Abuse of Process in English Civil Litigation' in M Taruffo (n 5) 69–70 and N Andrews, *Principles of Civil Procedure* (Sweet and Maxwell 1994) 241.

[19] See N Andrews, 'Abuse of Process in English Civil Litigation' (n 18) 65 ff.

[20] A Dondi, 'Abuse of Procedural Rights: Regional Report for Italy and France' in M Taruffo (n 5) 109.

[21] See art 46 and art 100 of the Italian CPC (Codice di procedura civile), according to which 'Per proporre una domanda o per contraddire alla stessa e necessario avervi interesse' and art 31 of the French CPC (Code de Procédure Civille) according to which 'L'action est ouverte à tous ceux qui ont un intérêt légitime au succès ou au rejet d'une prétention [...]'. See also L Cadiet, *Code de Procédure Civile* (LexisNexis 2007).

[22] N Andrews, 'Abuse of Process in English Civil Litigation' (n 18) 65 ff.

[23] B Hess, 'Abuse of Procedure in Germany and Austria' in M Taruffo (n 5).

[24] L Rosenberg, KH Schwab and P Gottwald, *Zivilprozessrecht* (17th edn, Beck 2010) 491; R Greger, in R Geimer et al (eds), *Zöller Zivilprozessordnung, Kommentar* (25th edn, Dr Otto Schmidt 2005) 753, para 18.

this principle is relatively rare, both in Germany[25] and Austria.[26] Swiss procedural law[27] has developed on the basis of the French tradition in respect of protection from abuse of procedure, while many Central European states, like the Czech Republic, do not even use the term "prohibition of the abuse of procedure".

However, one thing that all Member States have in common is that they have abandoned the previously very popular and widely accepted principle set out by *Goldschmidt*,[28] which dictated that there cannot be an abuse of process, because procedure itself is neutral, so any abuse occurring during the proceedings can only concern substantive law.

Just as rectitude, fairness and good faith are not synonymous with legality, nor is abuse of procedure necessarilly equal to illegality.[29] Generally speaking however, one can group together terms like dishonesty, loyalty, bad faith, harmful actions, inexcusable abuse of law, gross error, and fraudulent behaviour, under a concept of abuse of process. In this respect, certain specific categories of abuse of process stand out: lack of legitimate interest in filing a lawsuit; charges without any legal or factual ground; and arbitrary justification of an alleged violation of the law with the aim of obtaining legal information from the court (or actions with any other unsuitable or illegitimate purpose).[30]

B. Qualification of abuse according to objective criteria

Two relevant notions or principles are interwoven with the abuse of procedural rights or civil process. The first notion is the principle of good faith,[31] which acquires a special feature in the legal process; the second is the legitimate interest in legal protection[32] (German: *Rechtsschutzbedürfnis*). Occasionally, reference may, in addition, be made to good morals (*bonos mores*). Both notions are of an objective nature. Sometimes, they are applied simultaneously as a single principle,[33] but the two notions should

---

[25] L Rosenberg, KH Schwab and P Gottwald (n 24) 491–492; HJ Musielak, *Grundkurs ZPO* (9th edn, Beck 2007) 84; R Greger (n 24) 753.

[26] WH Rechberger and DA Simotta (n 15) para 27.

[27] Art 128 of the Swiss Act of Civil Procedure of December 19, 2008 (AS 1739 (2010)).

[28] H Goldschmidt, *Der Prozess als Rechtslage* (Berliner Juristische Fakultät 1925) 292.

[29] M Taruffo (n 14) 3 ff.

[30] N Andrews, *Principles of Civil Procedure* (n 18) 245.

[31] M Taruffo (n 14) 11.

[32] L Rosenberg, KH Schwab and P Gottwald (n 24), HJ Musielak (n 25), R Greger (n 24). Sharply against of any use of this criterion is E Schumann, 'Kein Bedürfnis für das Rechtsschutzbedürfnis – Zur Fragwürdigkeit des Rechtsschutzbedürfnisses als allgemeiner Prozessvoraussetzung', in R Holzhammer et al (eds), *Festschrift für HW Fasching* (Manz 1988) 439.

[33] D Holthausen, *Theorie und Praxis einer allgemeinen Rechtsmissbrauchsschranke für Prozessparteien* (Peter Lang 2005) 65–80.

be considered autonomously. One can apply them independently and even cumulatively. On the contrary, a subjective criterion, such as fault (French: *faute*),[34] is not a relevant measuring tool for the purposes of classifying a procedural action.

The following observations can be made in relation the principles of good faith and of a legitimate interest in legal protection:

1. Typically, the creation of an artificial procedural situation (eg 'establishing' an artificial connecting factor as basis for the seised court's jurisdiction)[35] is in contradiction with the good faith principle and shows a lack of legitimate interest in legal protection.
2. A procedural act of one party which is aimed at causing damage to the other party contradicts the principle of good faith.[36]
3. Querulous law suits which are targeted at the other party, are in their substance mala fide law suits and may sometimes be classified as actions which lack a legitimate interest in legal protection.
4. The prolongation of proceedings by abusing the appeal system or by filing an action in a jurisdiction either known for its time-consuming proceedings or known as a court-locking jurisdiction in order to gain time contradicts the good faith principle.[37]

C. Procedural sanctions in national legal systems

National legal systems also differ with regards to the sanctions or consequences of abuse of process. The sanctions vary depending on the person at whom they are aimed (party or attorney).[38]

The first category of sanctions involves sanctions of a monetary nature, ie damages, fines and the reimbursement of procedural costs.[39]

A number of legal orders penalise the relevant abusive proceedings or legal actions with the sanctions of invalidity, prescription, illegality etc.[40]

[34] D Holthausen (n 33), L Cadiet (n 21), J Normand, 'Final Report: The Two Approaches to the Abuse of Procedural Rights' in M Taruffo, *Abuse of Procedural Rights* (n 5) 237–243.
[35] eg N Andrews 'Abuse of Process in English Civil Litigation' (n 18) 69; B Hess (n 23) 155, 158, 159 and CJEU, Cases C-104/79 *Foglia v Novello* [1980] ECR 745, 244–80; *Foglia v. Novello (No.2)*, [1981] ECR 3045 and, more recently, C-367/96 *Kefalas v Greece* [1998] ECR I-02843, paras 20, 21–23. One way of avoiding an abuse is by listing the exorbitant jurisdictions and excluding their application (Brussels I Regulation, art 3(2) and art 4(2) with the reference to Annex I).
[36] An example of such actions could be the search orders, see N Andrews, 'Abuse of Process in English Civil Litigation' (n 18) 69.
[37] ibid 69, 71; P Schlosser in B Hess, T Pfeiffer and P Schlosser, *Heidelberg Report* (n 3) para 657. Typically, preventive torpedo actions are filed in the field of patent law.
[38] M Taruffo (n 14) 4 ff.; N Andrews (n 18) 69 ff.; Hazard Jr in M Taruffo, *Abuse of Procedural Rights* (n 5) 35–40; B Hess (n 23) 151 ff.
[39] Fines are typically applied according to French civil procedure, whereas damages are characteristic for the Anglo-Saxon proceedings.
[40] M Taruffo (n 14) 22 ff.

Another sanction is the termination of the proceedings. It applies, albeit of a limited scope, in Germany and Austria as a result of an insufficient legitimate interest in legal protection (*Rechtsschutzbedürfnis*).[41]

D. *Abuse of process in the cross-border context*

In international proceedings, the possibilities for abuse are more wide-ranging: the more relevant the international element and the broader the factual or legal dimension of the case is, the more significant the scope for abuse becomes.

1. *Jurisdiction*

An abuse of process can primarily occur regarding jurisdiction, whether or not there exists exclusive or non-exclusive jurisdiction.

The connecting factor for jurisdiction, which derives from either the character of the legal relationship between the parties or the character of the parties themselves, such as their location, is the decisive element.[42] It is possible to artificially create the circumstances which dictate the connecting factor, through outright fraudulent behaviour or other actions, even where the primary purpose of this action may not be to to affect the court's jurisdiction. The question arises therefore whether this kind of behaviour is sufficiently serious and significant that it should be supervised and sanctioned. To assess the severity of the abuse, the already-mentioned legitimate interest in legal protection (*Rechtsschutzbedürfnis*) is most suitable. Any other criterion, which would be based on the protection of the other party or on other values, would probably not be applicable.

In cases where the artificial creation of circumstances dictating the connecting factor cannot be said to have any connection with the legal issues at hand, but are made solely to establish the jurisdiction of a particular court, such actions must be regarded as having been taken in bad faith.

2. *Parallel proceedings*

The doctrine of *lis pendens* is based on a broad definition of the object of litigation[43], and aims to prevent parallel proceedings ,to enhance legal certainty and to guarantee procedural economy. However, because the object of litigation is so broadly defined, it can hinder the initiation of legitimate claims.

---

[41] B Hess (n 23).

[42] P Wautelet, in U Magnus and P Mankowski (eds), *Brussels I Regulation: European Commentaries on Private International Law* (Sellier 2007) arts 32–33; R Fentiman in U Magnus and P Mankowski (eds), ibid arts 27–30; T Pfeiffer in B Hess, T Pfeiffer and P Schlosser, *Heidelberg Report* (n 3) paras 156, 158, 162.

[43] See the interpretation of art 27 Brussels I Regulation in Case C-159/02 *Turner v Grovit* [2004] ECR I-3565.

Therefore, greater emphasis should be placed on the investigation of the legitimate interest in the legal protection of the parties at an early stage of the proceedings.[44]

E. Critique of the status quo

The current situation is unsatisfactory for two reasons. First, the Brussels I Regulation itself does not include an explicit general rule which would allow for the sanctioning of procedural abuse. The second weakness is the current case law of the Court of Justice of the European Union (CJEU), which has adopted non-uniform definitions of the obstacles of *lis pendens* and the finality of court decisions:[45] it interprets the first category autonomously, and allows for a national interpretation of the second.[46] It is submitted that the CJEU adopts an overly liberal approach in cases which constitute clear procedural abuses, be it through torpedo suits abusing the institution of *lis pendens*, or through the artificial delay of proceedings. The CJEU interprets the use of procedural rights too benevolently, ie without sufficient analysis of the need for legal protection, and without sanctioning almost vexatious delays to proceedings.[47]

An example of this can be seen in the *Gasser* case,[48] in which the defen-

---

[44] It is characteristic that such a behavior of the alleged infringer of intellectual property rights is called 'preventive torpedo action' (T Pfeiffer (n 42) para 657). Such actions seeking declaration of non-infringement filed in jurisdictions known for their time consuming proceedings or even with a court lacking jurisdiction are a typical examples of abuse of international process. Such actions are not less abusive than the very striking torpedo case *Boston Scientific v Johnson and Johnson*, 647 F.3d 1353 (2011) (for details see M Zigunn, *Entscheidungen inländischer Gerichte über ausländische gewerbliche Schutzrechte und Urheberrechte* (Beck 2002) 13 ff.). See further B Hess (n 3); S Leible in T Rauscher, *Europäisches Zivilprozess – und Kollisionsrecht EuZPR/EuIPR*, vol 1 (2nd edn, Sellier 2011) art 27.

[45] S Iseburg-Epple (n 10).

[46] S Sepperer, *Der Rechtskrafteinwand in den Mitgliedstaaten der EuGVO* (Mohr Siebeck 2010).

[47] The attitude of the CJEU regarding the identity of the proceedings, as per art 27 of the Brussels I Regulation, deserves criticism also from another perspective, namely that of the identity of the parties. Even the existence of the same parties in two proceedings, but in opposite roles (the plaintiff in one proceedings is in the position of a defendant in the other) cannot lead to the conclusion that the proceedings are identical (see also S Leible, in T Rauscher (n 44) para 651. My criticism does not mean that I would advocate the doctrine of *forum non conveniens*. On this point I fully share the view of the CJEU denying the application of this doctrine even under the Brussels Convention (Case C-281/02 *Owusu v Jackson* [2005] ECR I-1383 para 24) See also comments of Vlas (P Vlas in U Magnus and P Mankowski (n 42) art 2, para 72.

[48] The rule in art 27 is extremely relevant for preventing irreconcilable judgments and ensuring procedural efficiency. It is however the subject of abuse in the sense of the 'forum shoppers charter', as the critics call the Brussels I jurisdiction regime (F Juenger in M Taruffo, *Abuse of Procedural Rights* (n 5) 354, 357). Those who abuse this rule may also apply the 'main object' doctrine developed in the CJEU rulings (eg Case C-144/86 *Gubisch v Palumbo* [1987] ECR I-4905 and Case C-159/02 *Turner v Grovit* [2004] ECR I-3565) in filing the 'preventive' torpedo actions (not only in the field of intellectual property rights). This doctrine

dant considered the action of the plaintiff to constitute an abuse of procedure because it prevented the defendant from judicial protection. He argued that the plaintiff's law suit caused a blockage effect through the *lis pendens* provisions. The CJEU, in its reasoning, rejected this argument. In the view of the CJEU, the applicability of the *lis pendens* provisions, which considers lawsuits in a chronological order according to which court was seised first or second, cannot be called into question. The CJEU regards the principle of mutual trust highly. Furthermore, there are no established criteria for assessing the prolongation of proceedings as an abuse of procedural law.

The potential for abuse of process permitted by this jurisprudence is unacceptable, and it is necessary to consider possible alternatives to the status quo.

IV. SANCTIONS AGAINST ABUSE IN THE CROSS BORDER CONTEXT

A. Existing sanctions

A number of traditional lines of reasoning (including those underlying the Brussels I Review Proposal itself[49]) support the introduction of effective control mechanisms against abuse of process.

In light of the suggested abolishment of *exequatur* and the opening up of the Brussels I system to third State jurisdictions, there is an increased risk of further abuse and a mechanism is needed to reduce the scope for such abuse. This mechanism does not yet exist, because the current means of procedural protection are insufficient.

Certain existing mechanisms can ensure a certain protection against procedural abuse in cross-border cases, such as public policy, the principle of fair trial, counterclaims and other tools. However, they do not necessarily provide an effective protection against abuse of process as they are not specifically designed to apply to the above described cases of abuse. This will be shown below for each of these mechanisms.

1. Counterclaim

The possibility of a counterclaim is used as an argument against the introduction of special protection in the case of torpedo actions. It bases on the assumption that the other party can assert its claim even in proceedings

---

is a barrier in the efforts to overcome an abuse. Some courts did their best in vain (see for example, The Rechtsbank Den Haag, *DSM v NOVO Nordisk*, IER 200, 39; Tribunal de Grande Instance Paris, *Schaerer, Schweiter v Fadis*, II C 2002, 325; Landgericht Düsseldorf, Inst GE 3,8). See on this point P Schlosser (n 37) paras 657, 660, 661, 662; R Fentiman in U Magnus and P Mankowski (n 42) paras 483–486.

[49] See (n 1).

which were initiated through a torpedo action. Whether the affected party is really able to do so in such an instance is a matter to be decided by the *lex fori*. However, not every procedural system permits participants to lead a counterclaim alongside the defence of the original claim. In this respect, the argument against introduction of special protection does not succeed. Moreover, the counterclaim may fail, because of a lack of jurisdiction.

2. Monetary sanctions

Certain sanctions already exist in respect of abuse of process, such as the reimbursement of procedural costs and the imposition of fines. It is obvious, however, that even here the arguments that these protect against abuse of process are not fully convincing. Not every procedural system includes the 'principle of victory' in a dispute in respect of procedural costs. [50] Even the award of procedural costs to the winning party does not solve the problem completely. First of all, it might be the case that the winning party has previously suffered damage which cannot be covered by the award of procedural expenses, where such damage would have been averted if it had not been for the torpedo suit. Similarly, actions against vexatious torpedo actions and sanctions in the form of procedural fines may be unable to redress damage caused by abuse of process.

3. Ordre public

The public policy exception becomes relevant at the stage of recognition of decisions. It is obvious that this protection is not effective, as procedural abuse does not necessarily lead to the application of *ordre public*, except in the case of fraudulent behaviour.[51] For instance, public policy does not consider the issue of court competence, as Article 35(3) Brussels I Regulation shows.

4. Protective tools in enforcement proceedings

Even though the enforcement proceedings itself may offer a whole number of legal tools,[52] their use cannot prevent the negative effects of torpedo actions and those negative effects cannot be rectified retrospectively.

---

[50] J Pfennigstorf, 'The European Experience with Attorney Fee Shifting' (1984) 34 Law and Contemp. Probl. 36, 66 ff.

[51] The attitude of the CJEU towards the access to justice is debatable (*Gasser* (n 2) paras 70-72). It is questionable whether the theory of justice in this ruling complies with art 6 of the European Convention on Human Rights. The CJEU considers that the fundamental human rights aspects can not moderate the strict interpretation of art 27 of the Brussels I Regulation (see also Fentiman's comments on arts. 27–30 in U Magnus and P Mankowski, *Brussels I Regulation* (n 45) para 32. However, the delays in proceedings are not regarded as a reason for the application of the *ordre public* clause (see eg OLG Hamburg EuLF 2009 II-10 and J von Hein, *Europäisches Zivilprozessrecht* (9th edn, Verlag Recht und Wirtschaft 2011) 500).

[52] HF Gaul, 'Treu und Glauben sowie gute Sitten in der Zwangsvollstreckung oder Abwägung nach Verhältnismässigkeit als Massstab der Härteklausel des § 765a ZPO' in

5. The public interest element of proceedings – Pandora's box

An automatic refusal of a vexatious suit constitutes a very serious infringement of procedural rights. It is submitted that, as a result, a situation is created which opens itself up for abuse. It can also be argued that the autonomous will of the claimant is curtailed for reasons of public interest.[53] However, these arguments are not convincing, as in fact each and every procedural institution can be opened to abuse.

6. Compensation for damages

The argument that compensation for damages can be claimed to sanction abuse of process stems especially from the experiences within the Anglo-American procedural systems, in which it is possible to bring a suit for compensation for damages as a result of a vexatious abuse of proceedings.[54]

However, damages are a weak consolation for the affected participant who acts in good faith, as again he must bring the suit and has to prove the occurrence of a damage which could have been prevented.

B. The need for the introduction of specific procedural protection

In addition to the options considered above in Sections III and IV.A, procedural abuse can be challenged contrary to what the CJEU case law suggests.[55] To achieve a certain balance against abuse through a torpedo action, a narrower interpretation of the cause of action[56] allows the commencement of a powerful interlocutory or another action, in particular a compensation lawsuit against the plaintiff of a torpedo action. However, this approach also has a negative side, in that the narrowing of the definition could be abused by initiating parallel procreedings in relation to actions which were brought in good faith. For these reasons, the mere shift in interpretation does not seem to be an effective and reliable tool.

The other sanctions mentioned in the previous sections are completely ineffective, apart from the counterclaim which could be admissible at the EU level. Also, all arguments in opposition to the introduction of protection against the abuse of process have one common feature. Except for the possibility of bringing a counterclaim, they all deal with an *ex post* protection,

---

H Prütting (ed), *Festschrift für Gottfried Baumgärtel* (Heymanns 1990) 75; AK Bitter, *Vollstreckbarerklärung und Zwangsvollstreckung ausländischer Titel in der Europäischen Union* (Mohr Siebeck 2009); I Bach, *Grenzüberschreitende Vollstreckung in Europa* (Mohr Siebeck 2008).

[53] E Schumann (n 32) 439 ff.

[54] But in recent years a tort has been of slight importance. See N Andrews, 'Abuse of Process in English Civil Litigation' (n 18) 76, 77 and *Metall und Rohstoff v Donaldson Lujkin* [1990] 1 QB 391 at 469.

[55] See the criticism of R Fentiman in U Magnus and P Mankowski (n 42) paras 11–13.

[56] See B Hess on the need for reform (n 3) 329.

which requires further effort for the affected party and additional procedural costs, which in the end might not necessarily be paid by the vexatious claimant.

However, specific protection should provide a mechanism to *prevent* the occurrence of damage, which would make all other mechanisms unnecessary that are aimed at the *ex post facto* awards for damages resulting from procedural abuse.

V. A MODEL SOLUTION FOR THE BRUSSELS I REGULATION

A. *A measure of abuse – basis for the prohibition of abuse of process*

Above we considered that the reference to an artificial connecting factor for the purposes of creating exorbitant jurisdiction can be considered as procedural abuse, but without any particular relevance which would deserve a special regulation. The torpedo action and the delays in proceedings are, on the contrary, relevant procedural abuses. Whilst the second type of abuse needs to be dealt with at the national level through fines, the abuse of the actual substance of the proceedings requires a legislative solution on the EU level. If a decision was achieved fraudulently, this is a case to which the application of *ordre public* is relevant, but non-fraudulent torpedo suits and delays in proceedings cannot be effectively prosecuted under the current legal framework.

The basic criterion for the prohibition of abuse is the legitimate interest in legal protection. This requires the consideration of the objectives of the claim and the degree to which the interests of the claimant are affected. Fault is not a decisive factor. It is also irrelevant whether the improper intention of a party covers the whole connecting factor or only a part of it. If the unfair goal of the action pursues, at least to some extent, a different goal than that which is implied in its wording, this is an abuse that has to be sanctioned. The sanction for abuse is the dismissal of the action or the stay of proceedings. Such an approach has only one line of reasoning underlying it, which is the inadmissibility of a lawsuit which is in conflict with the actual goal of civil proceedings.

In order to challenge effectively the abuse of cross-border proceedings in the EU, it is necessary to impose, at the EU level, a duty on the court to review the fairness (in terms of good faith and a legitimate interest in legal protection) of each lawsuit.

It is necessary to introduce into the general provisions of the Brussels I Regulation the following clause:

'Actions of parties, which aim at circumventing the law, which contradict good morals and which, in their result, abuse the law, are considered ineffective.'

B. Assessment

Conformity with the law, be it the *lex fori*, the *lex causae* or otherwise, including good faith, needs to be evaluated *objectively*. This means that it is not primarily necessary to take the procedural situation or the intention of the parties into consideration. Such a consideration is an additional element.

C. Review competence of the courts/sanctions

The responsibility of an *ex officio* examination of abuse of process pertains to any court, including national and EU courts, and this responsibility must be engaged throughout the entire proceedings. Further, it is necessary to establish a sanction for the abuse of law, which should be the dismissal of the lawsuit. The application of this sanction, ie a dismissal of a suit or the stay of proceedings, should be left to the national legal system.

The Revision of the Brussels I Regulation: A View from the Hague Conference

Marta Pertegás*

I. INTRODUCTION

The Council Regulation of 22 December 2000 on Jurisdiction and the Recognition and Enforcement of Judgments in Civil and Commercial Matters ('Brussels I Regulation')[1] is a cornerstone of private international law in the European Union,[2] with past and present connections to the work of the Hague Conference on Private International Law (Hague Conference).

As an intergovernmental organisation comprising over seventy Member States (including all twenty-seven EU Member States and the EU) charged with working 'for the progressive unification of the rules of private international law',[3] questions of international jurisdiction and the recognition and enforcement of judgments have featured prominently in the work programme of the Hague Conference for over 85 years,[4] and are set to continue to do so in the near future. A number of Hague Conventions drawn up since 1951 deal with questions of jurisdiction or recognition and enforcement in specific fields, for example: recognition of divorce decrees;[5] jurisdiction relating to the wrongful removal of children;[6] enforcement of

* First Secretary at the Hague Conference of Private International Law; Professor, University of Antwerp. The views expressed in this paper are those of the author, who gratefully acknowledges the assistance of Mr Alexander Kunzelmann, Legal Officer at the Permanent Bureau, for the preparation of this paper.

[1] Council Regulation (EC) 44/2001 of 22 December 2000 on Jurisdiction, and the Recognition and Enforcement of Judgments in Civil and Commercial Matters [2001] OJ L 12/1.

[2] For example, U Magnus and P Mankowski (eds), *Brussels I Regulation: European Commentaries on Private International Law* (Sellier 2011) 12.

[3] See art 1 of the Statute of the Hague Conference on Private International Law <http://www.hcch.net/index_en.php?act=conventions.text&cid=29> and HCCH (ed), *Collection of Conventions 1951-2009* (Intersentia 2010).

[4] See K Lipstein, 'One Hundred Years of Hague Conferences on Private International Law' (1993) 42 ICLQ 553, 570–572.

[5] Hague Convention of 1 June 1970 on the Recognition of Divorces and Legal Separations.

[6] Hague Convention of 25 October 1980 on the Civil Aspects of International Child Abduction.

orders for payment of costs and expenses of proceedings;[7] recognition of orders relating to the adoption of children;[8] jurisdiction and recognition and enforcement of orders concerning the protection of children,[9] and concerning vulnerable adults;[10] and decisions concerning child support and other forms of family maintenance.[11]

In relation to judgments in civil and commercial matters generally, the Hague Convention of 1 February 1971 on the Recognition and Enforcement of Foreign Judgments in Civil and Commercial Matters, which was concluded in 1967 and completed by a Supplementary Protocol concluded in 1971, established uniform rules on recognition and enforcement of judgments only (*'Convention simple'*), but did not directly regulate the assumption of jurisdiction by the court of origin (unlike a *'Convention double'*).[12] The Supplementary Protocol requires the Contracting States to refuse the recognition and enforcement of judgments based on certain 'exorbitant' grounds of jurisdiction, rendered against persons located in a Contracting State. The Convention and its Protocol have however remained inoperative, due to the fact that the Contracting States[13] have not concluded 'supplementary agreements', as provided by Article 21 of the Convention, a necessary condition for the recognition and enforcement of judgments between them. Nevertheless, the Convention was influential in the development of subsequent European instruments, such as the 1968 Brussels Convention (the precursor to the Brussels I Regulation).

More recently, the entry into force of the Brussels I Regulation, in March 2002, coincided with a significant turning point in the Hague Conference's work in the area of international litigation. At this time, the Hague

---

[7] Hague Convention of 25 October 1980 on International Access to Justice; Hague Convention of 1 March 1954 on Civil Procedure.

[8] Hague Convention of 29 May 1993 on Protection of Children and Co-operation in Respect of Intercountry Adoption.

[9] Hague Convention of 19 October 1996 on Jurisdiction, Applicable Law, Recognition, Enforcement and Co-operation in Respect of Parental Responsibility and Measures for the Protection of Children.

[10] Hague Convention of 13 January 2000 on the International Protection of Adults.

[11] Hague Convention of 23 November 2007 on the International Recovery of Child Support and Other Forms of Family Maintenance; Hague Convention of 2 October 1973 on the Recognition and Enforcement of Decisions Relating to Maintenance Obligations; Hague Convention of 15 April 1958 concerning the recognition and enforcement of decisions relating to maintenance obligations towards children.

[12] See CN Fragistas, 'Explanatory Report on the Hague Convention of 1 February 1971 on the Recognition and Enforcement of Foreign Judgments in Civil and Commercial Matters' in *Actes et documents de la Session extraordinaire: Exécution des Jugements* (Imprimerie Nationale 1969) 360, in which reference is also made to the work of the Hague Conference on judgments prior to 1951.

[13] At present, Albania, Cyprus, Kuwait, the Netherlands and Portugal are Contracting States to the Convention. See Status Table <http://www.hcch.net/index_en.php?act=conventions.status&cid=78>.

Conference decided to suspend work on the so-called 'Judgments Project', which had been launched in the 1990s with the purpose of developing a comprehensive global instrument covering jurisdiction as well as the recognition and enforcement of foreign judgments, and to refocus efforts on negotiating a new instrument on a specific basis of jurisdiction, that is, jurisdiction founded on choice of court agreements.[14] This resulted in the conclusion of the Hague Convention of 30 June 2005 on Choice of Court Agreements ('Choice of Court Convention'), which the EU (then the European Community) signed on 1 April 2009. The EU's ratification of the Choice of Court Convention is currently linked to the ongoing revision of the Brussels I Regulation.

Given the connections between the Brussels I Regulation and the work of the Hague Conference on international litigation, it is not surprising that the Permanent Bureau of the Hague Conference is following the review process, to the extent that the (proposed) changes to the Regulation might impact on the Hague Conventions or the current work programme of the Hague Conference.

II. THE BRUSSELS I REVIEW PROCESS SEEN FROM THE HAGUE CONFERENCE

As contemplated in Article 73 of the Brussels I Regulation, the European Commission released in April 2009 a Report on the application of the Regulation.[15] The Report was accompanied by a Green Paper, which launched a consultation process with interested parties on possible ways to improve the operation of the Regulation. Following this consultation process, the European Commission published in December 2010 its proposal for a revised Brussels I Regulation ('Proposal'),[16] accompanied by a detailed Staff Working Paper explaining the policy decisions underlying the proposed amendments to the text of the Regulation.[17] The Commission Proposal launched a legislative process which will eventually lead to a Regulation being adopted by the European Parliament and the Council in

---

[14] A Schulz, 'The Hague Convention of 30 June 2005 on Choice of Court Agreements' (2005) 7 Yearbook of Private International Law 1.

[15] European Commission, Report to the European Parliament, the Council and the European Economic and Social Committee on the Application of Council Regulation (EC) No 44/2001 on jurisdiction and the recognition and enforcement of judgments in civil and commercial matters (COM(2009)174 final).

[16] Commission Proposal for a Regulation of the European Parliament and of the Council on jurisdiction and the recognition and enforcement of judgments in civil and commercial matters (Recast), COM(2010)748 final.

[17] Commission Staff Working Paper, Impact Assessment – Accompanying document to the Proposal for a Regulation of the European Parliament and of the Council on jurisdiction and the recognition and enforcement of judgments in civil and commercial matters (Recast), SEC(2010)1547 final.

the future.[18] Meanwhile, a rapidly growing body of academic commentary on the Brussels I Regulation review process is influencing the decision-making process within the EU institutions.[19]

From the perspective of the Hague Conference and its global membership, two specific points addressed in the review process are primarily important: (a) the operation of the revised Regulation in the international legal order and (b) the revised section on choice of court agreements. This contribution, largely based on the official response of the Permanent Bureau to the European Commission's Green Paper,[20] only comments on these two points.

A. *The operation of the Regulation in the international legal order*

The Brussels I Regulation, as currently formulated, provides the jurisdiction rules to be applied by Member State courts when the defendant is domiciled in a Member State. For most cases involving defendants domiciled outside the EU (non-EU defendants), the current Brussels I Regulation leaves in place national rules of the various EU Member States on the conferral of jurisdiction and on the recognition and enforcement of foreign judgments.[21]

1. *Extension of jurisdiction rules*

The Proposal amends the Brussels I Regulation to allow non-EU defendants to be subject, in principle, to the same jurisdiction rules as EU defendants

---

[18] In accordance with the 'ordinary legislative procedure', set out in art 294 of the Treaty on the Functioning of the European Union. While negotiations at the Council are progressing, the European Parliament's first reading is expected around September 2012. See <http://www.europarl.europa.eu/oeil/file.jsp?id=5890332>.

[19] In addition to this publication, see for instance: C Kessedjian, 'Commentaire de la refonte du règlement n° 44/2001' (2011) 47(1) Revue trimestrielle de droit européen 1; C Heinze, 'Choice of Court Agreements, Coordination of Proceedings and Provisional Measures in the Reform of the Brussels I Regulation' (2011) Max Planck Private Law Research Paper No 11/5; J Weber, 'Universal Jurisdiction and Third States in the Reform of the Brussels I Regulation' Max Planck Private Law Research Paper No 11/7, both available online at SSRN; B Hess, 'Die Reform der EuGVVO und die Zukunft des Europäischen Zivilprozessrechts' (2011) 2 IPRax 125-130; A Dickinson, 'Surveying the Proposed Brussels I *bis* Regulation – Solid Foundations but Renovation Needed' (2010) 12 Yearbook of Private International Law 247–309; F Pocar, 'Revision de Bruxelles I et ordre judique international: quelle approche uniforme?' (2011) Rivista di diritto internazionale privato e processuale 591–600 and the forthcoming proceedings of the Milan Conference that took place on November 25 and 26, 2011.

[20] See letter from Permanent Bureau to the Commission dated 13 July 2009, <http://ec.europa.eu/justice/news/consulting_public/0002/contributions/civil_society_ngo_academics_others/hague_conference_on_private_international_law_en.pdf>.

[21] For a thorough study on these national provisions and how they interact with EU legislation and objectives, see A Nuyts, *Study on Residual Jurisdiction, General Report* (2007) <http://ec.europa.eu/civiljustice/news/docs/study_residual_jurisdiction_en.pdf>, in particular 84 ff.

(sections 2 to 7 of Chapter II).[22] Moreover, the Proposal inserts a new section 8 into that Chapter with two new jurisdiction rules that apply solely to non-EU defendants: one subsidiary rule based on the place where property belonging to the defendant is located, and the other based on the doctrine of *forum necessitatis*. These new rules should be understood as the 'lowest common denominator' of currently applicable jurisdictional grounds under national rules. In addition, a new Article 34 in the Regulation would enable a court in a Member State to stay and dismiss its proceedings when proceedings 'in relation to the same cause of action and between the same parties' are pending before the courts of a third State, or have been concluded and have resulted in an enforceable judgment.

From the Hague Conference's perspective, these proposed changes are significant developments.

Firstly, the European Commission has opted for a unilateral, outward-looking revised Regulation to pursue the essential policy of enhancing the legal security of EU citizens when engaging in cross-border trade and commerce. Admittedly, the option of multilateral negotiations leading to a global instrument on international litigation was considered as a possible alternative avenue for attaining this goal.[23] In the European Commission's Staff Working Paper accompanying the Proposal,[24] the European Commission noted the option to 'negotiate an international agreement which would establish common rules on jurisdiction and the recognition and enforcement of judgments on an international level'. This would ensure that 'States only take jurisdiction on the basis of internationally accepted criteria'. However, the European Commission decided not to pursue this option as its only action 'because it [did] not seem to be realistic that agreement on a multilateral convention on this issue could be reached in the short or medium term'.

Interestingly, the unilateral action proposed by the European Commission has proven to be a catalyst for renewed interest in a multilateral initiative. In contrast with the cautious approach taken in 2010 by the Council on General Affairs and Policy of the Hague Conference regarding the possible continuation of the Judgments Project,[25] in April 2011 the

---

[22] New art 4(2).

[23] According to the Commission (n 17), this option received significant support from stakeholders in the public consultation. In addition to the Permanent Bureau (n 20), these stakeholders include the governments of Austria, Czech Republic, Estonia, Germany, Finland, the Netherlands and the United Kingdom <http://ec.europa.eu/justice/news/consulting_public/news_consulting_0002_en.htm>.

[24] Commission (n 17) 23.

[25] The Council on General Affairs and Policy is charged with the operation of the Hague Conference, including determining its work programme (see art 4 of the Statute (n 3)). See Hague Conference on Private International Law, Conclusions and Recommendations adopted by the Council (Council on General Affairs and Policy of the Conference, 7–9 April 2010) <http://www.hcch.net/upload/wop/genaff2010concl_e.pdf>.

Council 'concluded that a small expert group should be set up to explore the background of the Judgments Project and recent developments with the aim to assess the possible merits of resuming the Judgments Project'. In April 2012 the Council welcomed the findings of the expert group and endorsed a two-track approach for conducting future work in the area. A working group shall be established to develop proposals for consideration by a Special Commission in relation to provisions on the recognition and enforcement of judgments, including jurisdictional filters (ie indirect grounds of jurisdiction), while the expert group is reconvened to consider and make recommendations on the desirability and feasibility of making provisions in relation to matters of jurisdiction (including parallel proceedings).[26]

Secondly, in view of forthcoming discussions at the international level, it is interesting to reflect on the substance of the proposed changes. Do existing jurisdiction rules in the Brussels I Regulation, as well as the new proposed grounds, and the proposed *lis pendens* rule of Article 34, reflect internationally accepted standards? The European Commission comments in this regard:

[T]he envisaged creation of a forum of necessity and a 'mildly exorbitant' rule of jurisdiction, e.g. based on the location of assets provided that the case has a sufficient link with the forum, is hardly objectionable on a diplomatic level given that the procedural rules of most of the EU's trading partners contain themselves exorbitant rules of jurisdiction. On the contrary, impact on third countries would be positive as Member States would not be entitled to maintain more generous conditions for access to justice in their national law. Should international negotiations on a worldwide judgments convention resume, the impact of the revision on the EU's negotiating position would equally depend on the substance of the harmonised rules. The alignment of national rules as such would be neutral in this respect and the introduction of a 'mildly exorbitant' forum in the Regulation could improve the EU's bargaining position in the negotiations.[27]

The outcome of the EU legislative process with regard to these proposals is of relevance even beyond the EU boundaries. As such, non-EU States (including Members of the Hague Conference) are closely monitoring the revision of EU rules to determine the impact on their own citizens as they engage in trade and commerce with the EU.[28] From a global perspective,

---

[26] Hague Conference on Private International Law, Conclusions and Recommendations adopted by the Council (Council on General Affairs and Policy of the Conference, 5–7 April 2011, <http://www.hcch.net/upload/wop/genaff_concl2011e.pdf>, para 15 and 17–20 April 2012, <http://www.hcch.net/upload/wop/genaff_concl2012e.pdf>, paras 16–19.

[27] Commission (n 17) 24.

[28] For example, the United States Department of State held a public meeting on 23 March 2011 to discuss the EC Proposal: see 'U.S. Department of State Advisory Committee on Private International Law (ACPIL): Public Meeting on Jurisdiction and the Recognition and Enforcement of Judgments' 76 Federal Register 32 of 16 February 2011, 9072.

developments in a region with a mix of legal traditions, like the EU, will no doubt be influential in plotting the course for possible future work in the area of international litigation at the Hague Conference.

2. Status quo *with regard to judgments rendered by courts outside the EU*

The Proposal does not alter the *ratione loci* application of the Regulation's Chapter III by extending it to judgments rendered by courts outside the EU. According to the Commission's Staff Working Paper, 'stakeholders seem to be more concerned that the issue in question risks overburdening the revision of the Regulation than with the protection of EU citizens and companies from third country judgments'.[29] Accordingly, it was decided not to propose any harmonised rules on the recognition and enforcement of non-EU judgments in the current recast proposal.

From an outside perspective, one could interpret this decision as a sign of support for multilateral action at a later stage or as a deliberate choice for diverse rules of recognition and enforcement at the national level. It is hoped that a future European Commission Paper on external policy in the area of cooperation in civil and commercial matters will provide further details on this matter.

B. *The revised section on choice of court agreements*

The ongoing review of the section of the Brussels I Regulation on prorogation of jurisdiction is of particular interest to the Hague Conference, in view of current efforts to secure widespread ratification of its global instrument in this area of law, the Choice of Court Convention. This Convention will enter into force when a second ratification or accession is completed and signals of support from interested States are most welcome, in particular from the United States of America and the EU, both signatories of the Convention since 2009.

Admittedly, the issue of the future *compatibility* of the European and international instrument on choice of court agreements will not be affected by the ongoing review. This issue – 'one of the most difficult'[30] to emerge during the Convention's negotiations – resulted in a *priority* rule (Article 26(6) of the Convention), which specifically deals with the intertwining of the Convention and the Brussels I Regulation. While the wording of Article 26(6) is not easy to grasp, the Explanatory Report, and the illustrations it contains, are extremely illuminating as to the envisaged operation of the so-called 'REIO give-way rule'. As helpfully paraphrased within the

---

[29] Commission (n 17) 25.
[30] T Hartley and M Dogauchi, *Explanatory Report on the 2005 Hague Choice of Court Agreements Convention* (2007), < http://www.hcch.net/upload/expl37e.pdf>, para 25.

Explanatory Report, the Brussels I Regulation prevails where both parties are resident in (an) EU Member State(s), or where one party is resident in an EU Member State and the other in a non-EU State which is not Party to the Convention. Where one party resides in an EU State and the other in a non-EU State that is a Party to the Convention, the latter prevails. Similarly, the relevant regime for the recognition and enforcement of foreign judgments depends on the origin of the rendered judgment (Article 26(6)(b) of the Convention). Accordingly, judgments originating in an EU court will always be subject to the recognition and enforcement rules of the Brussels I Regulation when recognition and enforcement is sought in another EU Member State.[31]

It follows from Article 26(6) of the Convention that the Regulation and the Convention can indeed operate side by side, avoiding conflict between the instruments both before and after the Regulation's revision.

However, the prospect of compatible, yet inconsistent, regimes is far from ideal for those involved in litigation with respect to choice of court agreements. Not only does the prospect of consistent regimes facilitate their application for courts and practitioners, but it also reinforces the increasing acceptance of the Convention as an internationally agreed standard at the global level. Enhancing the *consistency* between the Convention and the revised Regulation is therefore a commendable policy choice underpinning the Commission Proposal in respect of choice of court agreements.[32]

In the Green Paper, the European Commission identified a number of issues that could hamper the efficacy of choice of court agreements under the Brussels I Regulation. These were, above all, uncertainties surrounding the material validity of choice of court agreements, and concerns about the interaction between the provisions of the Brussels I Regulation on prorogation of jurisdiction and the *lis pendens* rule, as interpreted by the Court of Justice of the European Union ('CJEU').[33]

Following the consultation process, the Proposal has included a revised section on choice of court agreements that seeks to align the Brussels I Regulation with the mechanism established in the Convention.[34]

Firstly, the European Commission proposes to give priority to the chosen court of an EU Member State to decide on its jurisdiction, regardless of whether it is first or second seised. Accordingly, 'the courts of other Member States shall have no jurisdiction over the dispute until such time as

---

[31] ibid paras 292–301.

[32] This was the policy option favoured by the Permanent Bureau in its response to the Green Paper (n 20) 4.

[33] CJEU, Case C-116/02 *Erich Gasser GmbH v MISAT Srl* [2003] ECR I-14693. For a comparison between the operation of the current Brussels I Regulation and the Choice of Court Convention, see M Pertegás, 'The Brussels I Regulation and the Hague Convention on Choice of Court Agreements' (2010) 11 ERA Forum 19, in particular 24–25.

[34] See Commission (n 16) 6.

the court or courts designated in the agreement decline their jurisdiction'.[35] However, the Proposal in a new Article 32(2), does not specify how a court not chosen should proceed, while the chosen court decides on its jurisdiction. Some commentators have therefore suggested that further elaboration be made to the new article to clarify whether a court not chosen must stay or dismiss the proceedings before it, and if so, at which stage it must do so.[36] It will be interesting to see how the final text is worded and which lessons can possibly be drawn for the application, by analogy, of Article 6 of the Convention. [37]

Secondly, the proposed revised text of Article 23(1) introduces a harmonised conflict of law rule to determine whether the agreement is 'null and void as to its substance', referring to the law of the chosen court. The proposed introduction of a conflict of law rule may alleviate the uncertainty that had arisen from the lack of autonomous standards on material validity of choice of court agreements, in spite of several judgments of the CJEU on this matter.[38] From the perspective of the desired alignment with Article 5 of the Convention, a uniform choice of law clause is a welcome proposal. It would however be necessary to clarify that, in the spirit of consistency with the Convention, the reference to the law of the chosen court includes the conflict of law rules of the chosen Member State. While this issue is made clear for the Convention in the Explanatory Report,[39] the revised Brussels

---

[35] See Commission (n 16) Recital (19).

[36] C Heinze (n 19) 15 and A Dickinson (n 19) 42.

[37] For a discussion on the question of consent under the Convention, see for instance R Brand and P Herrup, *The 2005 Hague Convention on Choice of Court Agreements: Commentary and Documents* (Cambridge 2008) 79 and P Beaumont 'Hague Choice of Court Agreements Convention 2005: Background, Negotiations, Analysis and Current Status' (2009) 5 Journal of Private International Law 125, 137–140.

[38] U Magnus in U Magnus and P Mankowski (eds), *Brussels I Regulation: European Commentaries on Private International Law* (Sellier 2007) art 23, n 400 and A Layton, 'Prorogation and *Lis Pendens*' (Revision of the Brussels I Regulation: The Commission Proposal and the Way Forward, paper presented at an ERA Conference in Trier, 26–27 May 2011), paper on file with the author. However, criticisms have been voiced as to the appropriateness of the Commission's proposal of a uniform choice of law rule: C Kessedjian (n 19) 127 and A Dickinson (n 19) 46. On this issue, it should be noted that the European Parliament's *Rapporteur* (Mr Zwiefska MEP) has issued a draft report which proposes a different conflict of law rule to be introduced (a new art 23a). It is proposed that a choice of court agreement will be considered valid as to substance if it is regarded as being such not only by the law of the Member State of the designated court, but also by the law that is chosen by the parties to govern the agreement or, in the absence of a choice, the law applicable to the contract of which the agreement forms a part; or, in all other cases, the law applicable to the particular legal relationship from which the dispute between the parties arose. In addition, Mr Zwiefska's draft report specifically states that the reference to the law of the designated court (in the first limb of the new proposed art 23a) is to be understood as a reference to the internal law of the designated court, without reference to the private international law. See Draft Report submitted to the Committee on Legal Affairs on 28 June 2011, <http://www.europarl.europa.eu/oeil/file.jsp?id=5890332>.

[39] T Hartley and M Dogauchi (n 30) para 125.

I Regulation will not benefit from a similar commentary. The introduction of a uniform choice of law rule, which would nevertheless give rise to different interpretations of the phrase 'under the law of that Member State', therefore appears to be of limited value.

Most importantly, the Proposal does not extend the choice of court mechanism in the Brussels I Regulation to cases where the chosen court is outside the EU. On the one hand, this reflects the European Commission's intention to make way for the ratification of the Convention by the EU.[40] On the other hand, despite the best efforts of many interested States in ratifying the Choice of Court Convention as soon as possible, many choice of court agreements designating the court(s) of a non-EU State will not be subject to the mechanism in either the Convention or the Brussels I Regulation, by virtue of the fact that the chosen State is not (yet) Party to the Convention. To fill in this gap between the two mechanisms, a number of commentators have queried whether the EU Member States' courts may continue to decline jurisdiction on the basis of their respective national rules after the revised Brussels I Regulation enters into force.[41]

In line with the European Commission's policy, aiming to improve the efficacy of choice of court agreements, it appears indeed preferable for this gap to be filled in a way that supports party autonomy, whilst boosting the speedy ratification of the Choice of Court Convention. This could be achieved by making it clear that the national rules on declining jurisdiction in favour of a non-EU State will continue to apply insofar as that State does not become a Party to the Choice of Court Convention.

III. CONCLUDING REMARKS

The Permanent Bureau monitors national and regional developments relevant to the current work of the Hague Conference in the area of international litigation in civil and commercial matters.

In particular, as part of its ongoing efforts to promote the ratification of the Choice of Court Convention by the EU, the Permanent Bureau is aware that the Convention's anticipated ratification is linked to the recast of the Brussels I Regulation. The Permanent Bureau will therefore continue to

---

[40] Communication from the Commission to the European Parliament, the Council, the European Economic and Social Committee and the Committee of the Regions: Delivering an Area of Freedom, Security and Justice for Europe's Citizens, Action Plan Implementing the Stockholm Programme (COM(2010)171 final).

[41] R Fentiman, *International Commercial Litigation* (OUP 2010) 465 ff.; A Dickinson (n 19) 47; A Layton (n 38); J Harris, 'A Common Law Perspective on the Commission's Proposal for Reform of the Brussels I Regulation', (ERA Conference on the Revision of the Brussels I Regulation: The Commission Proposal and the Way Forward, Trier, 26 and 27 May 2011), paper on file with the author.

follow the decision-making process of this pivotal reform in EU private international law. At this interim stage, while the European Parliament and the Council are defining their positions, one could venture simply to say that the proposed alignment of the Regulation's rules on choice of court agreements with the Convention's mechanism is to be welcomed. In particular, it is noted with interest that the Commission Proposal does not extend the scope of these rules to cases where the chosen court is outside the EU, thereby leaving them to be addressed on the basis of the Convention, when the Convention enters into force and so far as the chosen court is in a Contracting State to the Convention. It is therefore important that the issue of the ratification of the Convention by the EU be addressed without delay, and that a solution be found for cases falling outside the Convention.

Another salient feature of the Proposal from a global perspective is the extension of jurisdiction rules in the Brussels I Regulation (except for those on choice of court agreements) to disputes involving non-EU defendants. It is highly likely that these and other related developments, in the broader European region and beyond, will influence the agenda of the Hague Conference in the field of international litigation.